O.W.C.

C.   mel

CW00547593

Improving Productivity for Competitive Advantage

Improving Productivity for Competitive Advantage

Lessons from the Best in the World

ERIK HÖRNELL

FINANCIAL TIMES

PITMAN PUBLISHING

Pitman Publishing
128 Long Acre, London, WC2E 9AN.

A Division of Longman Group UK Limited

First published in 1992

© Longman Group UK Ltd, 1992

A CIP catalogue record for this book can be obtained from the British Library.

ISBN 0 273 60040 0

All rights reserved; no part of this publication may be reproduced, stored in a retrieval system, or transmitted in any form or by any means, electronic, mechanical, photocopying, recording, or otherwise without either the prior written permission of the Publishers or a licence permitting restricted copying issued by the Copyright Licensing Agency, 90 Tottenham Court Road, London W1P 9HE. This book may not be lent, resold, hired out or otherwise disposed of by way of trade in any form of binding or cover other than that in which it is published, without the prior consent of the Publishers.

Typeset by PanTek Arts, Maidstone, Kent
Printed and bound in Great Britain by
Biddles Ltd, Guildford and King's Lynn

CONTENTS

FOREWORD

The Swedish government is aware of the advantages of a study reflecting corporate productivity worldwide. In this book, some 150 corporations have been evaluated, with 18 companies exclusively selected for thorough analysis.

The Swedish government provided the necessary resources needed to enlist the most professional experts for the study, and the companies selected cover most areas of the industrial world. The result is perhaps the most comprehensive volume ever provided in the area of corporate productivity principles and ability.

The Financial Times and Pitman Publishing are to be congratulated on a book that covers such an enormous span of material. The Royal Swedish Academy of Engineering Sciences (IVA), through Dr Erik Hörnell, has provided the global productivity profession with a reference work of outstanding calibre.

This book should be not only a reference for corporations worldwide, but also a textbook for engineering students, corporate planners, industrial managers and economists in general.

Productivity ability is clearly proven to be a continuous process, on which no corporation or individual will ever have the final say, but a study of the *Best in the World* will ensure ability and will be a vital tool for competitiveness.

Martin T. Tveit, PhD, MSc, DTC
Acting President: The World Academy of Productivity Science
Chairman: The World Confederation of Productivity Science

PREFACE

This book is based on a study entitled *Best in the World: What Can We Learn from Companies with High Productivity?* which the Royal Swedish Academy of Engineering Sciences (IVA) presented in the fall of 1991. In 1989, the Swedish government appointed a commission to investigate the slow growth of productivity, and to provide the government with the foundations of a policy for promoting growth. Comprised of experts from the corporate world, organizations, administration and research institutes, the commission was charged with answering four questions:

- How is productivity to be measured in an advanced, internationalized economy?
- What are the determinants of productivity development in Sweden?
- Does Sweden have productivity problems? If so, why?
- What can be done about them?

A summary in English of the panel's overall conclusions and recommendations was published in 1992. In reviewing the situation, the panel consulted a number of researchers. Their work resulted in a total of ten separate studies. A slightly longer version of this book was the sixth volume in that series.

The following chapters contain case studies of some of the world's high-productivity companies at work across eight industrial sectors. For each foreign company in the study, a corresponding Swedish firm in the same sector has been selected as a reference company. Where the leading company was Swedish, a foreign counterpart was selected.

The study was planned and conducted by the Office of Economic Studies at IVA. The work was superintended by a steering committee chaired by Dr Björn Svedberg. The different case studies were carried out by a team of researchers. On the basis of their extensive reports, I wrote the shorter case studies published here. (The members of the steering committee and the research team are to be found in Appendices III and IV.)

This study would have been impossible without the help of many individuals. First, there were the Swedish and foreign members of IVA and others who generously contributed their suggestions for companies to study. Second, invaluable help came from the companies under study, and particularly from our contact persons at each company, all of whom made immense efforts to assist with our work and to read and comment on our reports. Finally, I would like to thank the steering committee and all others who have read the manuscript and given valuable comments. Particularly deserving of mention are Enrico Deiaco, Klas Eklund, Mats Engwall, Ingemund Hägg, Per Stenson, Bengt Stymne and Daniel von Sydow. Special thanks go to Victor Kayfetz who translated the Swedish report and to Peter Kirwan who edited this book.

Erik Hörnell
Stockholm, July 1992

INTRODUCTION

This book for managers interested in comparative productivity originated
in a survey commissioned by the Swedish government. Both the Swedish
government and Swedish industrialists were anxious to preserve the
country's record for manufacturing success and recognised that without
comparisons, isolated sets of data produced by practical case studies are
often difficult to interpret. It was therefore decided that selected companies should be compared with reference companies from the same industry, but in another country.

Exhaustive inquiries led to an initial listing of some 150 companies
world-wide that seemed to offer good prospects for successful study. The
following chapters contain studies of ten of those companies. This group
of companies should not be regarded as some kind of corporate elite, but
instead as a representative selection from a larger group of companies
equipped with good earnings and excellent reputations. From instigation,
the selection of companies, the research, writing and editing of the following case studies occupied three years in the lives of a large team of
experts. Between ten and 45 individuals were interviewed for simultaneous case studies: technical directors, research directors, marketing managers, personnel managers and trade union representatives. Going into
those interviews, research associates were equipped with insights culled
from thousands of pages of official statistics, reports and press clippings
gleaned during the course of preliminary research. Inevitably, additional
written questions followed. The case studies presented here are distilla-
tions of original reports which, individually, ran to between 100 and 250
pages.

In our comparisons of world-beating and reference companies the
study of differences of management, organizational structure and institutional circumstances outweighed any narrowly nationalistic concerns.
Hence – the universal appeal of the following case studies. Was there
room, we asked frequently, for more than one successful solution in the

same industry? Our intention was thus not to compare good and bad companies: indeed, in some cases, the companies chosen for comparative purposes were so good that the differences between them and the acknowledged world class companies in the same fields were small or even open to discussion.

In the mobile telephone market, for example, Sweden's Ericsson and America's Motorola are similarly regarded as best-practice companies. Likewise, in machine tool manufacturing, Japan's Yamazaki Mazak leads in the production of machines; while Italian company Mandelli is fore-most in the separate machine tool systems market.

One case study provides a cross-border productivity comparison within the same corporate group. The topic is a factory in Fontenay, France, owned by the Swedish-based manufacturer SKF. Because there is only one manufacturer of industrial bearings in Sweden, it was natural to use SKF's closest equivalent factory in Sweden as the reference "company". Incidentally, this comparison points to the difficulties involved in making international comparisons of productivity – even within the same corpo-rate group. When it came to airlines, the natural choice as a reference company for the highly-successful Singapore Airlines was SAS, admit-tedly a Scandinavian rather than purely Swedish company. In the machine tool industry, Sweden has no counterpart to Yamazaki Mazak, the company under study. So from a closely-related industry, we chose ABB Robotics, Sweden's closest comparable company.

There were strong time constraints on our assignment. This meant that we had to base our study of intra-company conditions on information that was mainly provided through interviews. This information was eval-uated by the research associates, and where possible, information from different people and sources was compared. The material we present is thus essentially a reflection of the companies' own perceptions of the important factors behind their improvement in productivity. It should be emphasized that interviewees are responsible neither for the facts nor the conclusions in the following chapters.

Our primary purpose has been to study the conditions that enable companies to improve their productivity. We wanted to identify both internal and external factors. It is, of course, always possible to object that we could never know for sure which factors were important, since we could not conduct any quantitative analysis of causal connections. To double-check our conclusions on these connections, we subsequently dis-cussed the reports with individuals including labour union representa-tives who were familiar with each respective industry we studied.

The methodology of the research that underpins this survey has there-fore determined its structure and its boundaries. Its time perspective is largely the 1980s and a further refinement might have been to go back even further in time to determine what role such factors as the education-al system play in determining productivity. We are also aware that the factors that were important to productivity improvements during the 1980s will not necessarily be important a decade later, but in the short term, this survey provides insight into how comparative success can be achieved in the latter part of the twentieth century.

1 DEFINING PRODUCTIVITY

Productivity indicates how resources are being managed. In this study productivity is defined as the ratio of the value of a given output to a corresponding input. A simple and easily understood definition, you might think. The concept is obviously relevant; most people have an implicit understanding of its meaning. But the difficulties begin as soon as we attempt to measure and use the concept for practical purposes. In fact, very few systems of measuring productivity are alike – a reality that leads to obvious difficulties when one attempts to make comparisons such as we attempt to make in this book. Why is the idea of productivity so slippery? Why can't it be used as a simple yardstick?

The values of outputs and inputs are a function of quantities and prices. As a result, productivity will be determined by whether a company can improve the ratio between its quantity of output and quantity of input, not to mention the ratio between prices of outputs and inputs. Ideally, a company will consume the least possible resources in relation to its given output; further, it will achieve an output that is highly valued by the market.

The ratio between the quantity of outputs and inputs is often expressed as internal efficiency. The corresponding ratio between the prices of outputs and inputs is frequently described as external efficiency. Unfortunately, these labels are somewhat misleading. Looked at independently, they assume that a company cannot influence its internal efficiency by selecting cheaper input goods. So, instead, the following case studies use the idea of cost-effectiveness to express the efficiency of internal resource consumption.

This book also refers to a company's ability to improve its output in such a way that it is assigned a higher value by the market as innovative ability.[1] This concept encompasses product development and product innovations, together with improvements in such fields as distribution and sales. Innovative ability is synonymous with a company's ability to design products and production processes that are a cut above the rest. Thus, in this study, productivity becomes an expression of both effective use of resources and the capacity for innovation and self-renewal.

Why do companies with low productivity still exist when there are so many corporate cook books that promise a failsafe recipe for exactly the opposite? Clearly, what works well for one company might not work so well for other companies. A number of factors are responsible for this: differences in technology, size, industrial sector and institutional conditions are among them. Stumbling blocks are frequent. For whatever reasons, companies are sometimes prevented from discovering their own solutions: often, easily approved measures suddenly become hard-fought in the act of implementation. As always, the devil is in the details. Additionally, of course, it shouldn't be forgotten that only specific kinds of management talent and corporate cultures can transform advice into practical reality.

Given these provisos, can we learn anything from companies whose productivity levels are regarded as the best in the world? We felt that our study would be of greatest value if it could reveal the mechanisms that contribute to continuous productivity improvements at successful companies. In what kind of internal and external environments do these companies find themselves? How have they taken advantage of their opportunities? How have they avoided difficulties?

By external environment, we mean the forces that shape a given industry, as well as institutional factors such as systems of taxation. Here, at the furthest edge of our inquiry, in the form of certain institutional conditions, we reach the territory occupied by politics. At this point, we turn back to our central concern. By internal environment we mean a company's organizational structure, its technological and human resource practices, plus its methods for communicating the goals and expectations that are largely defined by the market. These factors palpably influence the tasks and responsibilities of managers and employees. In our judgement, productivity varies according to both internal and external environments. At the intersection of public and private sectors, industrial productivity depends on the efforts of both governments and companies.

A MACROECONOMIC PERSPECTIVE

National economies tend to function in such a way as to maximise ratios between overall production and overall input. Ideally, these ratios should be as high as possible and should also be growing rapidly. The result is an increase in the total amount of goods available for distribution.

Gross domestic product (GDP) consists of the sum of the value-added produced by any one nation's companies and public services. Defined as the value of the company's sales minus the cost of purchased goods and services, value-added expresses the degree to which a company has increased the value of products or services that pass through its hands. If overall value-added in the economy – in other words, GDP – is divided by total work input as measured by the size of the labour force or the number of hours worked, the result is an overall yardstick of labour productivity.

Productivity is a measurement that indicates how much a company can accomplish through certain sacrifices. Implicit within this is a notion of industrial efficiency. However, if there is nothing with which to compare it, the absolute size of the observed ratio between output and input may be difficult to evaluate. By studying productivity in a number of countries or companies, we gain a better idea of how good are our given outcomes. At this point, unfortunately, we come full circle. Fair comparison between the productivity of companies and countries is a task fraught with difficulties, not least because of the presence of almost as many methods of measurement as there are objects to be measured. Faced with such statistical variations between entities, many researchers instead content themselves with comparing the variations over time within a single entity – a nation or company.

GDP growth indicates increases in national value-added. Fluctuations in the level of a nation's economic prosperity are a thing apart. At this point, we must make additional allowances for the changes over time in a nation's population or, arguably, changes in the size of its work-force. In general, such changes are relatively small compared with rates of increase in GDP: annual population growth in industrialized countries amounts to one per cent, or a few tenths of a per cent. Clearly, most changes in GDP are thus attributable to higher productivity. But as Figure 1.1 indicates, at different times and in different places, average annual increases in GDP show major variations.

Viewed from a long-term perspective, even small annual differences in GDP growth are significant. If for one decade the annual GDP growth rate is one percentage point higher than it would otherwise have been, GDP obviously ends up a little more than 10 per cent larger at the end of the decade. Typically, the figures involved in such a decade-long expansion in a western democracy can equal annual health care expenditures.

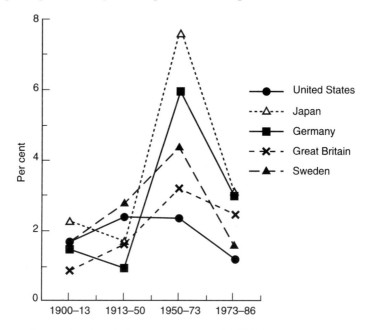

Figure 1.1   International variations, average annual GDP increases.
Source: OECD

Alternatively, they might dwarf industry's total annual bills for research and development. Slow productivity growth results in lower consumption; more seriously, it can indicate the start of a gradual national shift toward simpler manufacturing and less sophisticated working tasks. This is so because companies characterized by low increases in productivity are soon overtaken by international competitors. Typically, the companies that survive operate in industries where low productivity can be offset by low labour costs.

Productivity beneficial to most people

If a market's price formation mechanisms work, the concept of productivity reflects the market's valuation of increases in the ratio between the value of a company's output and input. In a free enterprise economy, companies constantly try to raise productivity, either in the name of higher profits or in response to competition from other companies that have improved their productivity already. Under such conditions, it is in the general interest of the greatest number for companies to increase productivity, since this leads to higher overall output from production.

Although improved productivity is a desirable goal, measures that raise productivity often have negative short-term consequences for individuals and companies. History offers many examples of new technology rendering obsolete existing skills and technology, triggering protests from adherents of old technologies along the way. Restructuring costs incurred when a company shuts down and its employees relocate can be another negative effect. More controversial, perhaps, is the question of whether there is any correlation between increased productivity and the more equitable distribution of income. If so, is this correlation is positive or negative? In other words: in whose interests does restructuring take place?

MEASURING PRODUCTIVITY

For two good reasons, value-added is often divided by the number of employees or the number of hours worked in the cause of its production. First, such measurements give some indication of the room available for employee wages and salaries and for consumption in the national economy. Second – and not to be underestimated – is the simple fact that this is a relatively easy ratio to obtain. Figure 1.2 offers a schematic presentation of relationships among factors used to calculate labour productivity and profitability. At the very least, value-added must suffice to cover three different types of expenditure. The first comprises wages, salaries and other employee costs. The second is depreciation, the equivalent of wear-and-tear inflicted on fixed capital. The third and final category is composed of earnings before interest expenses, an amount that is distributed among lenders (interest payments), the government (taxes) and shareholders (net profit).

In theory, productivity defined as value-added per hour worked can be increased in three ways. First, a company can sell more units, perhaps, though not always, by more efficient utilization of production equipment. Value-added per employee also increases when employees are furnished with better machines or when human labour is partly replaced by machine. In such cases, labour productivity increases because the volume of capital applied to a given task increases. Given an unchanged number of hours worked, if the number of units manufactured and purchased in Figure 1.2 increases by 10 per cent to 110,000, value-added will increase correspondingly to £11 per hour, or by 10 per cent. However, if we

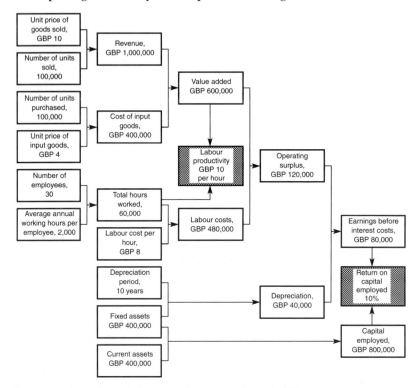

Figure 1.2 Calculating labour productivity and profitability.

instead assume that production volume remains constant while the number of hours worked falls by 10 per cent, value-added will climb to more than £11.10 per hour.

Second, labour productivity can also increase when the market assigns a higher price to better-made products. (The assumption here is zero inflation; price increases instead reflect higher quality and increased willingness to pay on the part of consumers). If, for example, the quality of our notional product improves so much that the price in Figure 1.2 can be raised by 10 per cent to £11, labour productivity thus increases by nearly 17 per cent (£11.67).

The third way to improve labour involves a reduction in the cost of input goods. A manufacturing company might simply find cheaper inputs. It might end up paying lower prices for its purchases because suppliers, in turn, have improved their productivity. In our model, a 10 per cent reduction in the price of input goods raises value-added per hour worked by nearly 7 per cent to £10.67.

These highly simplified numerical examples illustrate that product improvements leading to higher sales prices have the most important impact on the productivity yardstick chosen in this case. However, our example does not make any provision for the cost of development work. In reality, companies bear additional labour costs for personnel in research and development departments. To further complicate this line of reasoning, we can point out that while development work entails initial costs, its fruits – and the resulting revenues – only materialize at a later date. The problem of productivity-raising initiatives that do not immediately yield measurable results also applies to capital expenditure, training and other outlays.

Perhaps the biggest problem in measuring productivity comes with price changes attributable to inflation rather than to better quality. A general inflationary trend automatically causes a company's value-added to increase, as measured in current prices. (If inflation causes the prices of both sold goods and input goods in Figure 2 to rise by 10 per cent, value-added per hour worked will also rise by 10 per cent.) In order not to report misleadingly high increases in productivity, figures must be adjusted for inflation; in other words, for price increases unaccompanied by improvements in the quality of goods or services sold.

When compiling statistics on the productivity of industrial sectors and countries, researchers try to estimate the size of price changes. More problematically, they try to estimate what part of these price changes represents improved quality and what part represents the effect of inflation. Such corrections are difficult to make with precision, and statistics compiled in this way must be regarded as estimates.

Can adjustments for price changes on input items and goods sold lead to a fair measurement of a company's productivity and its return on investment? If all products and components follow separate price trends, as they so often do, even a company that manufactures different versions of a product that requires ten purchased components would find it hard to arrive at an accurate evaluation. The difficulties involved in such calculations are one good reason why companies fail to adjust their financial statements for inflation. Quite simply, the difficulties involved are so great that adjusted accounts probably would not provide a basis for decision-making of sufficiently higher quality to justify the extra expense. Thankfully, there are other ways of tackling the problem. One way of dealing with the impact of inflation in measuring productivity involves calculating the ratio between variables that are similarly affected by inflation. A comparison of value-added and labour costs, for example, can cancel out the effects of inflation, yielding over time and under certain conditions, a decent indication of productivity trends.

The relationship between profit and productivity

The overall financial objective of an individual company is profitability, otherwise expressed as return on shareholders' equity. In an economy closed to the outside world, in which free competition functions perfectly, the goals of companies and their countries will coincide. Under such conditions, companies could improve profitability in two ways: by lowering the cost of production or by improving their goods and services. (Here the assumption is that given free competition, there's no free lunch. In other words, one cannot raise a price without offering something – namely higher quality – in exchange). Theoretically, then, where a company works in free competition within a closed, inflation-free economy, a direct correlation will exist between productivity and profit. The corollary is clear: in industrial sectors characterized by unfree competition, incentives to improve productivity will be less powerful. In the absence of free competition, companies can achieve higher profits by merely raising prices. Admittedly, this is an attractive prospect, so attractive, in fact, that companies constantly strive to create a position of monopoly that facilitates increased profits regardless of productivity levels. Elsewhere, companies striving simply to increase productivity may find their operations hemmed in by regulatory pressures. Still others may find it more profitable to abandon efforts at boosting productivity and to seek shelter instead within a labyrinth of regulation and subsidy.

Clearly, if we expand our analysis to an open economy characterized by foreign trade and convertible currencies, it is by no means certain that the demands of profit and productivity coincide. Furthermore, all productivity improvements must be judged on the basis of international markets. Here, to some extent, shifts in currency exchange rates will correct the gaps between the average productivity growth of companies in different countries.

[1]Another term for this is ability to differentiate, which indicates that a company's product is sufficiently different from those of its competitors that the market should be willing to pay a higher price.

2 THE METHODOLOGY FOR THE CASE STUDIES

THE PRODUCTIVITY CONCEPT

This chapter presents an outline of the model on which the following case studies were based. Our model provides a basis for interpreting the information yielded by interviews, observation and responses to extensive questionnaires. The choice of model has been influenced by the intention of learning from good examples. This has been interpreted to mean that a long-term perspective is of greater interest than a short-term one, that it is more valuable to examine mechanisms and prerequisites than specific methods and that the topics of the study should be whole companies, not just their manufacturing departments.

We have already described our definition of productivity as an indication of cost-effectiveness and of innovation in products and processes. The relationship between cost-effectiveness and innovation is far from straightforward, however. Synonymous with change, innovation affects routines and established working methods. This, in turn, may disrupt efficiency. High cost-effectiveness is often achieved only some time after the advent of innovation, typically only after a new product has gone into production.

Cost-effectiveness

Greater cost-effectiveness means that a company manufactures and distributes at gradually declining cost. Such an improvement may be the result of using fewer inputs in the form of materials, labour or energy. Ordinarily, this is achieved when a company learns to use more efficient manufacturing methods and an improved organizational structure. Increased production volume also ordinarily enables a company to lower unit costs by increasing the capacity utilization of existing machinery or by obtaining larger, more efficient machines. In improving the ratio between the performance and price of input goods, large production volumes can have other beneficial effects. Typically, large-scale purchasers possess a strong position in price negotiations; alternatively, they can more easily influence their suppliers' product development work.

Innovation

Like greater cost-effectiveness, innovation leads to better utilization of resources. The effect is similar; the mechanism is different. For our purposes, innovation typically involves the development of new products – sometimes by means of new processes – to which markets assign a higher value than previously. Notably, however, innovation in the form of product development does not necessarily lead to higher prices. Competitors may carry out equivalent improvements at the same time. And if a product's price cannot be raised in such cases, innovation has not boosted productivity, at least not as measured by the ratios between value-added, on the one hand, and capital and labour on the other. Clearly, however, the effects of such a situation need not be negative: if the company had not innovated, quite probably it would have faced the greater evil of being forced to lower the price charged for its product.

Innovations that improve a product are generally considered more beneficial than price reductions in terms of a company's competitiveness.[1] Being first with product enhancement may help to strengthen brand name or reputation in such a way as to sharpen a company's competitive edge even after competitors have made equivalent improvements. Far-reaching innovations in manufacturing technologies may also prove very difficult to imitate and may thus give a company long-term competitive advantages. Price-cutting is easier to imitate than innovation: a company may lose its advantage relatively quickly once competitors have implemented a similar price-cutting strategy.

Incremental improvements in productivity

Measures aimed at improving productivity can be of two types. One-time efforts typically arise in connection with reorganizations or mergers, points in time at which fundamental changes in organizational structure and focus of operations can foster marked improvements in productivity. Overhead expenses can be reduced by shedding staff and spinning off departments as profit centres. Reduced product ranges and the reassignment of production facilities can lead to larger economies of scale. Indeed, the opportunity to raise productivity with such measures can act as an inducement to the buyer of a company.

A second type of productivity enhancement occurs within the framework of ongoing operations. If ongoing improvements are neglected, eventually the need for a far-reaching, one-time effort emerges. Because this study examines some of the world's most productive companies, we have concentrated on improvements that occur within the framework of ongoing operations. Consequently, we do not discuss one-time efforts at improving productivity, even though such measures have played an important role at many major industrial companies during the past decade.

Productivity-raising measures normally have no permanent value. New machinery, however, may lead to additional improvements and effects based on learning, thus enhancing the initial gain in productivity. Other measures lose their value with time because of changing circumstances.

A functioning market selects the best solutions and assigns them a higher value. Closer to ground level, established positions are constantly questioned and challenged by:

- New demands and market prices
- Changes in the performance of competitors
- New technology and new institutional conditions

Such changes lead to a continuous reassessment of productivity. An understanding of how companies achieve change is consequently the key to understanding why some companies can remain highly productive over a long period.

FROM MACROECONOMICS TO MICROECONOMICS

Following the approach of Professor Michael Porter's *Competitive Advantage of Nations*, we have assumed that continuous improvement in a company's level of productivity is dependent on both external and internal factors. External and macroeconomic factors operate outside companies. Thus, the following case studies typically begin by studying influences that are more or less specific to companies in a given nation, industrial sector or particular product area. From there, the case studies shift gear, adopting a microeconomic perspective to explore three cate-

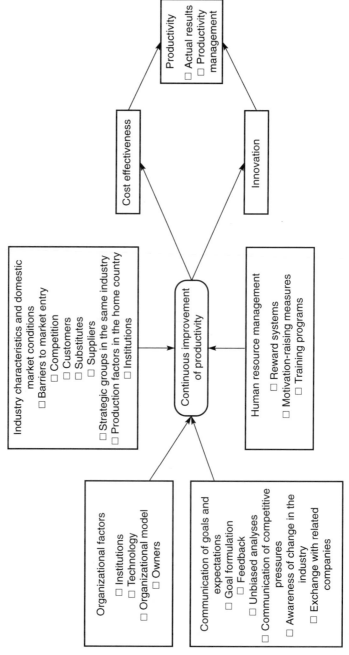

Figure 2.1 The path to productivity.

gories of internal influences on productivity: organizational structure and technology; internal communication of goals and expectations; development and management of human resources. The information presented in these chapters has been based on answers to a research questionnaire reproduced in the appendix. In addition to the questionnaire, our researchers also used an interview guide containing comments and instructions on the various questions. The companies examined are not ranked on any basis.

Productivity management

These case studies examine how the companies measure or estimate their own productivity. Companies measure productivity in different ways and with varying levels of ambition. The differences reflect variations in technology and organizational structure but depend on what internal control mechanisms a company chooses to apply. Cost accounting systems, for instance, rarely provide a good basis for decisions related to productivity management. Other criteria and rules of thumb, not necessarily expressed in dollar amounts, are needed for productivity management. We began with the hypotheses that highly productive companies have internal productivity criteria that are:

- Clearly formulated
- Understood and accepted as valid by employees
- Related to employee reward systems
- Resistant to manipulation[2]

THEORETICAL FRAME OF REFERENCE

Resource scarcity and efficiency

Following the methodology charted by Paul Lawrence and Davis Dyer in *Renewing American Industry*, we have adopted the concepts of resource scarcity and information complexity.[3] Relative levels of resource scarcity give some indication of a company's difficulty in ensuring sufficient resources for its survival. The most important factors here are customer demand for the company's products and the behaviour of competitors in obtaining the same resources. Other factors include government actions and the state of markets for input goods, and credit and labour markets. If its resources are not scarce or are not perceived as scarce, a company has no especially strong incentives to improve efficiency. If, on the other hand, its supply of resources is scarce, the company must allocate internal resources to co-ordinate and streamline its operations and thereby safe-guard its continued existence. If the resource situation becomes too scarce, the company may find itself in a situation where it can no longer allocate enough internal resources to improve its efficiency. On the curve that describes the correlation between resource scarcity and efficiency, the prerequisites for efficiency are optimal at intermediate points between extremely high and low levels of resource scarcity (see Figure 2.2).

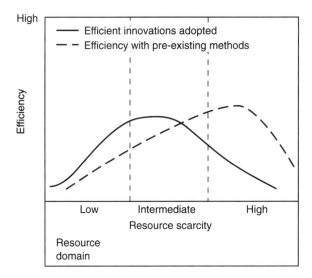

Figure 2.2   Relationship between resource scarcity and efficiency.

Reprinted with the permission of The Free Press, a Division of Macmillan, Inc. from *Renewing American Industry, Organizing for Efficiency and Innovation*, by Paul R. Lawrence and Davis Dyer, Copyright © 1983 by the Free Press.

Information complexity and innovation

The information complexity of a company's external environment influences its need to adapt and to pre-empt expected changes. Information complexity becomes the impetus behind adaptation and innovation and can be calculated on the basis of variables including the wishes of customers, the actions of competitors and the speed of technological developments. Conditions that act as a brake on change include monopolies, single technologies and single customers. The correlation between information complexity and innovation is shown at Figure 3.

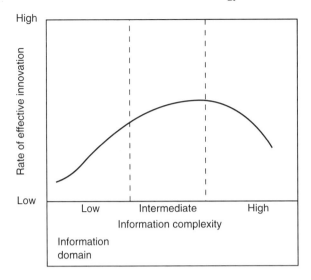

Figure 2.3 Relationship between information complexity and innovations.

Reprinted with the permission of The Free Press, a Division of Macmillan, Inc. from *Renewing American Industry, Organizing for Efficiency and Innovation*, by Paul R. Lawrence and Davis Dyer, Copyright © 1983 by the Free Press.

The information complexity of an industry such as truck manufacturing affects all manufacturers in a fairly similar fashion. On the other hand, the resource situation may vary substantially from one company to another. This is because the resource situation is influenced to a greater extent than information complexity by a company's own actions. As Lawrence and Dyer point out, companies will try to improve their resource situation and reduce information complexity by dominating their environment. In other words, companies will try to create a monopoly position by means of product development, vertical integration and alliances.

At the same time, forces around the company generate constant insecurity. The interesting question then becomes: how much, in the long term, can a company confine itself within the favourable "comfort" zone defined by a favourable resource situation and satisfactory levels of information complexity that promote efficiency and innovation?

Connections exist between external and internal factors that determine levels of productivity. Ideally, internal company tools such as reward systems should be tailored to the external factors that determine the company's resource situation and the information complexity around the company. For a more detailed discussion of the connection between macro-economic and microeconomic factors, we refer the reader to Lawrence and Dyer.

INTERNAL FACTORS

Organizational structure and technology

Earlier empirical studies of productivity in individual companies have examined the efficiency of the manufacturing process. Such studies have used explanatory variables including economies of scale, learning curves, production complexity, inventory reduction and wages. During the 1980s a number of studies examined the features that distinguish highly productive Japanese manufacturing operations: low-resource, lean production,[4] simultaneous or concurrent engineering, and just-in-time production.[5] These studies demonstrate that a number of traditional assumptions are no longer valid. Among these:

- Long production runs mean lower manufacturing costs, which amply justify larger inventories
- Higher quality and fewer defects in a product can only be accomplished at higher cost
- Shorter product development time is more expensive and leads to poorer results

Several of the recipes for success advanced in such studies bear little or no connection to theories of economic or behavioural science. This may be one reason why it is difficult to apply these methods in practical reality.[6] These recommendations would benefit from stronger theoretical underpinnings that would ease the task of specifying the conditions under which the recommended methods can be applied.

Company organization either emphasizes integration or differentiation. Integration gives top priority to co-ordination and stability. Differentiation cedes a leading role to specialization and decentralization. The choice of organizational model should be guided by a company's resource situation and the information complexity that surrounds it.

A rapid pace of change and a fairly good resource situation – as found in industries characterized by fast-growing demand – requires an informal, flat, decentralized organization. Typically, this model offers good innovative ability combined with some loss in efficiency.

More static environments require higher standards of efficiency. A mature engineering company, for example, might be better served by an integrated organization marked by rules and strong leadership. Because we assume that the most productive companies occupy a middle position in terms of their information complexity and resource scarcity, it follows that these companies should have an organizational model that is neither purely integrated nor purely differentiated, but has elements of both.

Our case studies also raise questions concerning labour union activity, workplace norms, attitudes toward work and social roles. These conditions conceivably influence a company's ability to achieve high productivity – in two ways. First, they may lead to a situation where, at best, the desire for efficiency springs from such feelings as duty and dedication. Second, strong norms and organizations ordinarily can act as obstacles to change.

Finally, we have also addressed the ownership situation of a company as an organizational factor. Mainly in the United States, but also in other countries, there has been a debate on whether short-term-oriented institutional ownership causes corporate managements to give higher priority to short-term profits than long-term ones. Fund managers aren't the only culprits: paradoxically, short-terminism can also emerge in large decentralized corporations characterized by numerous independent profit centres that are managed on the basis of profitability yardsticks. To ensure that their divisions do not neglect long-term innovation, group managers must have the requisite skills and resources to penetrate to the reality behind the profit figures that are reported to them.

Communication of goals and expectations

The demands of the market stimulate companies to innovate and increase their cost-effectiveness. But in order for external pressure to influence a company's operations, mechanisms must convey relevant external information into the company. One important task of corporate management is to communicate goals and expectations clearly and systematically to employees. There should be as little ambiguity as possible about the company's fundamental strategy, structure and working methods. Another method of disseminating an awareness of the outside world relies on forging business relationships with customers and suppliers noted for superior quality and levels of technological development. Quite frequently, innovations are created by combining technologies or approaches from different places into one potent solution. But knowledge is central to the enterprise. One would therefore expect highly productive companies to seek out new customers in markets that demand high standards and provide incentives for change.

In the *Competitive Advantages of Nations*, Professor Porter argues that companies can only preserve their advantages by constantly searching for other and better ways of making things. Yet the need for constant change conflicts with the organizational norms of most companies. Especially in successful companies, behaviour patterns become institutionalized. Company strategy becomes a religion: difficult to challenge and addicted to stability. Typically, it takes outside threats to force the pace of change. The difficulty of creating change from within teaches one lesson in particular: outsiders are innovators.

Human Resource Management

A company's personnel is generally regarded as its central productive resource. Employees must be motivated to strive for greater efficiency. We define a company's reward system as wages, salaries and other forms of direct compensation, plus the gamut of indirect rewards that includes promotion, travel and scholarships. We examine the type of pay system: bonuses, piecework, differentials and the use of individual or collective bargaining. What is the connection between performance and compensation? How large a percentage of pay is dependent on performance? The scarcer the resource situation and the greater the information complexity surrounding a company, the more financial rewards can be expected to impact on efficiency.

Although many companies pay employees for proposing major improvements, the relationship between financial rewards and innovation is less direct. Here, social incentives play a more important role. These incentives may range from the intrinsic status granted by a job at, say, a development laboratory, to feelings of community engendered by team spirit. Management plays an important part as a creator of such incentives and as a role model.

Employees must also possess the competence to innovate that is instilled through training. In our study, we asked questions about the size of company training programs on an annual and per-employee basis. What training, we asked, was available to newly hired employees? What was available for employees who wanted to advance in their company?

SUMMARY

The model for the study includes those factors in the world outside a company and inside the company that are important prerequisites for high productivity. If a company is to achieve long-term high productivity, both efficiency and innovation are required. It may be difficult to achieve both at the same time, however.

A company's need to innovate and adapt is influenced by changes in competition, customer demand, technology, institutions. A slow pace of change requires little innovation and therefore does not encourage such activity. A very fast pace of change, somewhere in the middle of the scale, is the best prerequisite for innovation.

The pressure to improve efficiency is influenced by a company's resource situation, whether it has enough resources to survive. If it has ample resources, a company has few strong reasons to make an effort to increase efficiency. If, on the other hand, its resources are very scarce, there is no room for efficiency-raising; resources must instead be used to keep its operations going. Our hypothesis it that to achieve greater efficiently, too, a resource situation somewhere in the middle of the scale is the most favourable.

In terms of resource scarcity and information complexity, a company can influence its own situation for the better by anticipating and actively attempting to be smarter than its competitors when it comes to efficiency and innovation. At the same time, constant changes outside the company have the opposite effect. Our hypothesis is that highly productive companies manage to maintain a favourable balance in this interplay with the driving forces surrounding them.

If a company is to succeed in achieving high productivity under favourable external conditions, it is necessary for certain intra-company mechanisms to function. Employees must be motivated to strive for greater efficiency and must have enough competence to carry out innovations in company operations. This, in turn, is influenced by three groups of factors: first, the way in which goals and expectations are communicated to employees; second, the company's prerequisites in terms of organizational structure and technology; and third, how the company handles personnel administration and training programs.

There is a connection between external and intra-company factors in the model. Intra-company factors, such as the design of reward systems should be adapted to external factors that determine the company's resource situation and the information complexity surrounding the company. Because we assume that the prerequisites for continuous improvement in productivity are best in a middle position in terms of resource scarcity and information complexity, it follows that we expect highly productive companies to have internal prerequisites that match this middle position.

[1]Porter (1990), p. 581 f.

[2]Armitage and Atkinson (1990).

[3]Lawrence, P.R. and Dyer, D., *Renewing American Industry*, The Free Press, Macmillan, New York, 1983.

[4]'Lean Production' was described in the study 'The Machine that Changed the World' as a description of Japanese automotive manufacturing.

[5]'Just-in-time production means producing required parts, at the required time, in the required amount, at each step of the production process in the most economical manner.' Suzaki (1987), p. 146.

[6]'Describing the concepts of superior manufacturing is not very difficult, nor is reporting case studies of the specific changes to achieve it. But explaining how to design and implement superior factory and systems improvements step by step, however, appears to be virtually impossible, based on available methodology.' Harmon, R.L. and Peterson, L.D., *Reinventing the Factory: Productivity Breakthroughs in Manufacturing Today*, Arthur Andersen & Co., 1989, p. 237.

3 MOTOROLA AND ERICSSON

INTRODUCTION

Since its beginnings in the late 1970s, the mobile telephone market has grown rapidly. Demand has grown almost exponentially; the pace of technological change has been frantic. During the 1990s, the introduction of digital technology confronts mobile telephone equipment manufacturers with their biggest evolutionary challenge so far. The industry's two leading companies are Ericsson and Motorola, manufacturers of both mobile telephones and related cellular telephone system equipment. Mobile telecommunications form only one segment of both companies' overall output.

Ericsson's strong suit is the design of radio base stations and mobile telephone exchange systems – also known as mobile telephone switching offices, centres or stations. Motorola, by contrast, is a leader in the production of mobile terminals. Both are outstanding companies in their fields. In 1988, for example, Motorola received the Malcolm Baldrige National Quality Award, the highest distinction a U.S. company can earn.

When a mobile telephone user or subscriber dials a number, the terminal calls a radio base station (see Figure 1). The nearest radio base station assigns to the subscriber an unoccupied radio frequency. If the subscriber is in motion during the call, at certain points, he may be able to make a better connection with another, adjacent, radio base station. At that point, his call is automatically transferred to the second, closer, radio base station.

The radio base station relays the call by cable to a mobile telephone switching office. At this point, the call enters the regular telephone system, or public network. From there, the call is routed in the usual fashion to its recipient. If the number dialled is another mobile telephone terminal, the call is connected to the exchange closest to the receiving party's radio base station.

There is no single, uniformly-specified international mobile telephone system. Instead, most countries have devised their own technological standard.[1] World-wide, there are roughly ten different standards, with several operating in Europe alone. As a result, mobile telephone termi-nals cannot normally be used in more than one country. However, work has now started on a joint European mobile telephone system – the GSM

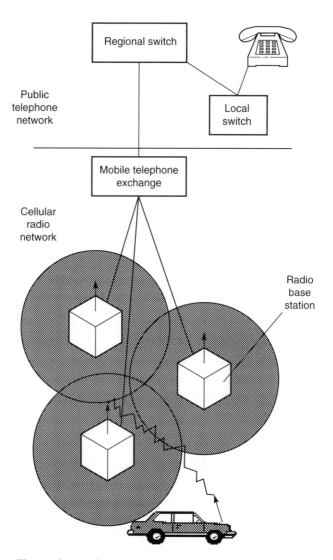

Figure 3.1 The workings of a mobile telephone system.

system.[2] In this model, information on the carrier waves between the terminal and the radio base station will be digitally, rather than analogue coded. At first, the new system will be one of at least three mutually incompatible system standards: one each for Japan, North America and Europe. Nevertheless the new all-European GSM network should allow subscribers to use the same terminal in at least 18 countries.

STRUCTURE OF THE INDUSTRY

Although it had been operative in Japan since 1979, the world's first commercial mobile telephone network really got off the ground only in 1986. The Japanese network was soon followed by systems in the Nordic countries (1981), the United States (1984) and Britain (1985). Mobile telephone systems made rapid breakthroughs: world-wide, subscribers numbered more than 7 million by the late 1980s (see Figure 3.2). By the end of 1990, there were 2,800,000 mobile telephone subscribers in Europe, 3,500,000 in the United States and 650,000 in Japan.

So far, it has been customary for the agencies or companies that run national hardwired public telephone networks to operate national mobile telephone systems as well. Yet in a number of countries, competition now exists between system operators assigned to different portions of the frequency band. System operators collect subscription charges and call-based charges from the subscribers to the system. The licensing authorities –

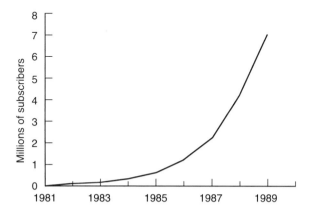

Figure 3.2 Mobile telephone network users, 1981–1989.

Source: EMC World Cellular Report, No. 10, April 1990.

government agencies such as the Federal Communications Commission (FCC) in the United States and the Department of Trade and Industry in Britain – issue licences entitling system operators to run mobile telephone networks. As with regular public telephone networks, the subscribers connected to these systems include companies and private individuals.

The overall market for mobile telephone system equipment consists of a system market and a terminal market. System suppliers assume responsibility for the entire system, ensuring the smooth operation of connections between radio base stations, exchanges and the public telephone network. With world market shares of 39 and 28 per cent respectively in 1989 (see Figure 3.4), Ericsson and Motorola are the world's dominant system suppliers.

In terms of sales, the mobile telephone terminal market is about twice as large as the market for systems. There are numerous terminal manufacturers. Of these, Motorola has a world market share of about 30 per cent; Ericsson's share is about 7 per cent (see Table 3.1). Terminal manufacturers include different types of companies. There are companies with strong traditions in land mobile radio,[3] such as Motorola and Ericsson. For these companies, mobile telephone terminal manufacture is a natural

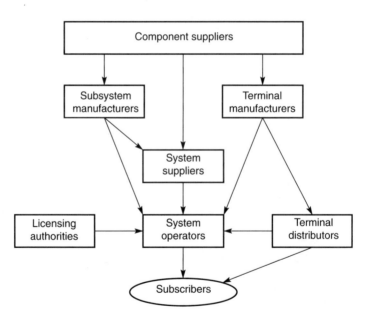

Figure 3.3 The mobile telephone industry: from supplier to subscriber.

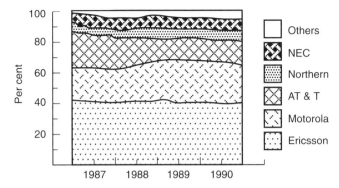

Figure 3.4 World market shares: Mobile telephone system suppliers.
Source: Ericsson

progression from earlier product lines. By contrast, other terminal manu-facturers such as Panasonic (a branch of Matsushita), NEC and Mit-subishi trace their roots to the consumer electronics sector. In turn, the terminal distributors who sell to subscribers exert great influence at the point of purchase. Notably, customers in most countries still generally have little product knowledge.

	1987	*1991*
Motorola	12.8	30
Ericsson/GE	3.9	7
Mitsubishi	6.7	9
Mobira	13.5	n.a.
NEC	11.2	12
Panasonic	8.0	9
Toshiba	9.5	9
Philips	3.6	n.a.
Siemens	3.1	n.a.

Table 3.1 World market shares for manufacturers of mobile telephone sets, as a percentage of terminals connected to systems.

n.a. not available.
Sources: Mobira, Ericsson and Langham.

The mobile telephone terminal market is turning into an oligopoly. Around ten major players – of which Motorola is the leader – are now competing for market share. The main competitors are multinational companies with access to an array of technologies. In addition, there are numerous small and often exclusively national or regionally-active players, including companies such as Siemens, Technophone and Fujitsu, each with world market shares below 5 per cent.

Motorola has continuously boosted its world market share with the periodic introduction of new high-performance products. In the mobile telecommunications market, a clear connection between product performance and market share became evident in the American market at an early stage. Motorola has worked systematically to establish a presence in major new geographic markets including Scandinavia, the United States, Britain and Japan.

To greatly varying degrees, suppliers of mobile telephone terminals and systems rely on outside component suppliers. Companies like Motorola and NEC manufacture a very large proportion of components in-house. Others such as Nokia (Mobira) and Novatel outsource practically all components.

PRODUCTIVITY AT ERICSSON AND MOTOROLA

The mobile telephone industry is marked by its dynamism. The products are complex. Markets demand rapid upgrading of product performance and frequent introductions of new products or functions. Given such conditions, the casual observer could be forgiven for thinking that innovation through product development takes precedence over cost-effective processes. But stiff competition among several similarly-sized competitors in fact results in high standards of cost-effectiveness and lead-time reduction, both in research and development and production.

Terminals

Terminal performance largely determines the customer's choice of brand. Brand loyalty hardly exists, though Ericsson's market share is much higher in Scandinavia than elsewhere. Many customers are making their first terminal purchase. In this context, the customer seeks more for less: enlarged market share goes to the company that can rapidly introduce new models that offer better performance – in terms of weight, size and

		ERICSSON	MOTOROLA	ERICSSON	MOTOROLA
		Mobile telephone systems		*Terminals*	
Revenue per	1989	100	100	100	100
R & D engineer,	1990	74	57	108	73
Index	1991	53		132	
Profit per	1989	100	100	100	100
R & D engineer,	1990	77	63	120	64
Index	1991	57		140	
Revenue per	1989	100	100	100	100
R & D expenditure	1990	67	58	100	73
Index	1991	41		100	
Profit per	1989	100	100	100	100
R & D expenditure	1990	70	61	125	65
Index	1991	46		100	
Lead time in product development				18 months	12 months
		Radio base stations		*Hand-portables*	
Lead time in	1988	100	100		
production	1989	75	63	100	100
	1991	25	13	67	50
		Mobile telephone systems			
Engineer	1988	100	100		
productivity	1991	125	580		
-software per year					

Table 3.2 Some yardsticks of productivity at Ericsson and Motorola related to mobile telephone systems and terminals.

Indexed numbers show the development for each company. Productivity is higher at Motorola for terminals and at Ericsson for systems.

Sources: Compiled from statistical material and interviews at Ericsson and Motorola.

operating life (i.e. operating time and stand-by time) – at a price not dissimilar from the market standard. These constraints set high standards in terms of reducing costs and lead times in both production and research and development.

Thus far, from design to production start-up, Motorola has been able to develop new products faster than its competitors. The MicroTac, Motorola's current best-seller, was developed in less than 15 months. By contrast, Ericsson's product development time for terminals currently stands at around 18 months. In recent years, Motorola has launched new hand-portable terminals on an annual basis. The company now aims to reduce development time to six months or less.

Notably, development costs for Motorola's MicroTac were substantially higher than for Ericsson's corresponding mobile telephone terminal. In terms of the customer's essential performance criterion, the MicroTac boasts a weight advantage over competing terminals of 100 grams – a subtle advantage that has undoubtedly contributed to the product's sales success. With the launch of the MicroTac, Motorola increased its world market share from 20 to 30 per cent.

Systems

Most mobile telephone systems begin their search for a specific subscriber when a call is placed. Typically, a system will begin by searching his home base; next, the exchange will run its search through all cells. If a subscriber happens to be located far from his home base, the unit can take some time to search and access his number. By contrast, Ericsson's AXE 10 digital telephone exchange continuously monitors subscriber locations, offering highly efficient call connections. At the heart of the system, a powerful central unit continuously stores and processes data on the functioning of large mobile telephone systems.[4] Flexible and designed for expansion, this exchange offers superior capabilities for the construction of mobile telephone systems in demanding environments such as major cities. For subscribers on the move, the Ericsson system offers rapid transfer between radio base stations, resulting in less disruption and higher voice quality than rival systems. Importantly, the Ericsson system does not have to be shut down for maintenance.

Between 1982 and 1984, Ericsson set to work on its first mobile telephone systems for the U.S. market. Development took 18 months. Within similar parameters, another European company proved unable to develop a functioning system over a period of five years. Overall, Ericsson's product development and production time for entirely new analogue systems has been slashed in half between 1986 and 1991.

How do Motorola and Ericsson measure up in terms of productivity? Both companies' research and development expenditure doubled between 1989 and 1991 – an effect of the imminent change-over from analogue to digital mobile telephone technology (see Table 3.2). Substantially higher productivity returns on research and development productivity can be expected during 1992 and 1993, as sales of new digital products and systems start to climb. Notably, however, productivity at Motorola is higher for terminals. At Ericsson, productivity peaks with systems.

WHAT EXPLAINS HIGH PRODUCTIVITY AT ERICSSON AND MOTOROLA?

In keeping with the model for this study, we will seek explanations for the high productivity of these two companies at three levels.

- Industrial. What factors affect productivity in the industry? Why have these two companies outstripped their competitors?
- National. Which conditions in each company's home country have been particularly favourable to growth?
- Corporate. Which internal mechanisms explain continuous improvements in productivity?

Industry

Technological base
The size of company market shares in the terminal sector is largely determined by how rapidly new and better performing products reach consumers. Clearly, research and development lead times are vital to this equation. With the proviso that the timescale and quality of product development have a major impact on cost effectiveness, shorter research and development lead times result generally in a longer shelf-life for products on the market. The ultimate goals are higher volume sales and lower per unit manufacturing costs. Productivity is therefore closely tied to a company's ability to harness and develop its technological competence. For the mobile telephone industry the following conditions are vital in this context:

- The industry draws its vitality from a wide range of technologies
- Although some technological items are available to all-comers, others are controlled by one or a few companies
- Nothing lasts forever: technical progress, and in particular, the shift from analogue to digital systems, will transform the industry's technological base

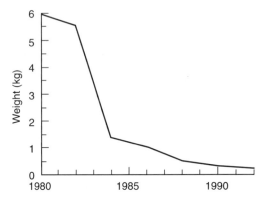

Figure 3.5 Average weight of mobile telephone terminals, 1980–1990.
Source: Falk-Sjöberg (1989).

THE TERMINAL MARKET

Given standardized interfaces with radio base stations, manufacturers in the terminal sector possess only limited opportunities to differentiate their terminals from one another. Features essential to the customer include weight, size and operating life. During the decade-long existence of the mobile telephone industry, remarkable advances have been made in all three areas. The average weight of a terminal has been reduced dramatically in the context of maintained or improved operating life (see Figure 5).

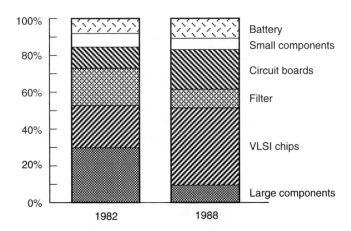

Figure 3.6 Component shares of material costs: 1982 and 1988.
Source: Falk-Sjöberg (1989).

Manufacturing costs have fallen substantially since the early 1980s. There have been shifts in the proportions of total manufacturing cost occupied by various cost items. Increased automation and reduced numbers of components have seen assembly costs, for example, decline by 14 per cent between 1982 and 1988. As part of this process, as Figure 3.6 demonstrates, very large-scale integrated (VLSI) chips now account for a much larger share of material costs. Overall, a larger percentage of value-added is attributable to a small number of key components. Ten years hence, a terminal may consist exclusively of a few circuits and chips, filters and other small components.

Development and manufacture of terminals requires competence in a number of technological areas. *Performance-driving* technologies determine a terminal's features, and thus, indirectly, the level of demand on the market. *Cost-driving* technologies primarily affect manufacturing

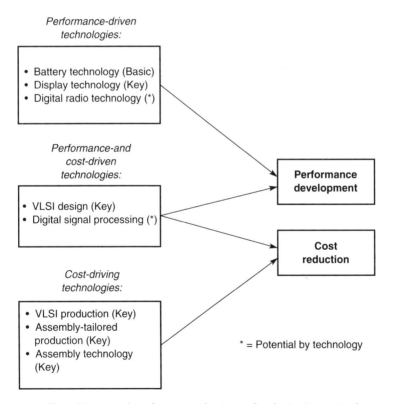

Figure 3.7 Cost-driving and performance-driving technologies in terminal manufacture.

costs (see Figure 3.7). Some technologies have a bearing on both a terminal's features and its manufacturing cost.

In Figure 3.7, widely-known technologies are referred to as basic technologies. Less widely available are key technologies, controlled by a small number of companies that have developed these technologies in-house. As knowledge spreads, key technologies are usually transformed into basic technologies. In a separate category, technologies such as digital signal processing and digital radio appear likely to become key technologies in the future. Figure 3.8 shows how these various categories of technology affect the different features of a terminal.

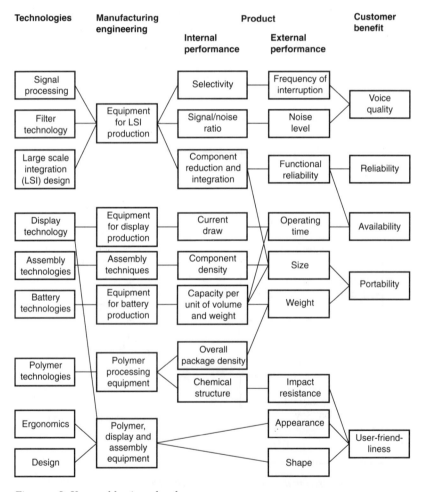

Figure 3.8　Key and basic technology.

In terms of reducing manufacturing costs, VLSI chips (driving both performance and cost) and the design of manufacturing and assembly facilities (driving cost) are most important of the key technologies. Motorola is a world leader in both areas: correspondingly, in 1986 and 1989, the company introduced low-priced terminals that offered performance at least as good as that available from competing models.

VLSI chips employ the kind of expensive, complex technology that permits major economies of scale. In VLSI design, special development tools are used to create semiconductor chips, such as cellular and functional libraries in databases. Incorporation of more and more functions within VLSI chips reduces a terminal's total number of components, cutting down on weight, bulk, purchasing and assembly costs, while improving reliability and operating time. Development work takes place in partnership with a suitable chip manufacturer, with the latter's production process in mind.

THE SYSTEMS MARKET

Development and production of mobile telephone systems requires a rather different form of technological competence (see Figure 3.9). First, a system vendor must deal with a larger number of key technologies. Second, by contrast with the terminal market, key systems technologies relate more to performance than to manufacturing costs. For clients, the most-valued features of a mobile telephone system are as follows:

- Reliability and dependable operation
- Availability (how long does it takes to restart radio base after a shutdown)[5]
- Capacity
- Flexibility (how easily connected are system components from different vendors?)
- Voice quality
- Ease of operation and maintenance
- User-friendliness.

The relatively small number of system buyers possess a very high level of technological and commercial competence – and thus, higher levels of bargaining power – than buyers in the mobile telephone terminal market. Consequently, profit margins on systems tend to be relatively narrow. Radio base stations account for about half of the overall cost of mobile telephone systems. Skillful cell planning across a specific geographical

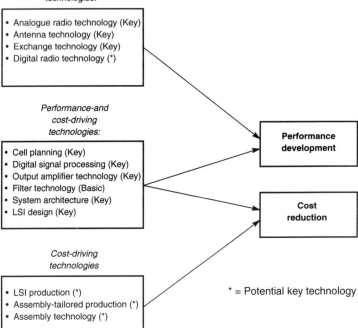

Figure 3.9 Pivotal production skill in terminal and systems markets.

region – reducing the number of base stations to an effective minimum – can help to cut costs. But cell-planning has finite limits: too many, and the system risks mutual interference from stations placed cheek-by-jowl; too few, and the system may suffer from inadequate capacity. Advanced antenna technology can be harnessed to overcome some of these problems; lowering the manufacturing cost of components offers another route to reduced manufacturing costs.

Access to key technologies

When it comes to performance-driving technologies, Motorola, Ericsson and some of their major competitors possess very high levels of competence in disciplines that are pivotal in both systems and terminals markets (see Figures 3.7 and 3.9). Ericsson is a world leader in the digital switching technology that is crucial to mobile telephone system performance. The company's unique competence in digital switching and radio technology results in short product development lead times and high levels of research and development productivity in the mobile telephone system market.

Motorola, meanwhile, enjoys prominence in antenna, display and battery technologies, all vital to terminal performance. Any company with superiority in technologies that drive both cost and performance – digital signal processing, VLSI design, system architecture and cell planning – will most likely enjoy higher revenues and lower costs than its competitors. Both Motorola and Ericsson hold strong positions in these areas.

Economies of scale
With by far the largest share of the world market for terminals, Motorola has a substantially larger accumulated production volume than its competitors; roughly four times larger than Ericsson's, for example. Motorola consequently possesses far greater potential for economies of scale and experience. Motorola's target for in-house producers and external suppliers alike mandates cost reductions of 30 per cent for every doubling of manufactured volume. The targets are easily enforced: the company simply refuses to buy components – internally or externally – unless suppliers accept price reductions adjusted in line with volume levels.

In the system market the picture is not so clear-cut. Component performance and price are crucial with small mobile telephone systems. Hence Motorola, with its large component production volumes, achieves the better competitive position. When it comes to medium-sized and large systems, however, switchboard performance and system design are more essential. In these two areas Ericsson has the stronger position. Consequently Ericsson specializes in competing for medium- and large-sized telephone system contracts.

A special aspect of economies of scale is the modular strategy used by Ericsson in developing hardware as well as software components. The engineers at Ericsson have been able to use various modules from different parts of the group of companies knowing that they have already proved to have high performance and quality.

With each new generation of terminals and systems, research and development efforts increase; in general, product life cycles tend to decrease. Because progressively shorter periods are available for the purpose of recovering the costs of research and development, the successful company looks to spread the burden of such costs across ever longer production runs. For each mobile telephone terminal, revenue dollar and each point of market share, Motorola's research and development costs are substantially lower than Ericsson's, even though Motorola employs more engineers and incurs higher gross research and development costs overall. Clearly, economies of scale are vital, and increasingly so, in the struggle for cost effective production.

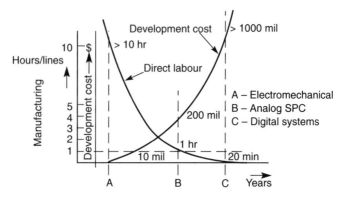

Figure 3.10 Development cost and direct labour costs for some technologies.
Source: Dr Toshiro Kunihiro, NEC

The transition from analogue to digital technology will increase development costs, and to some extent, the industry will be starting over in terms
of imposing new forms of economies of scale and experience. Conceivably, therefore, Ericsson might be suspected of wanting to speed up the
transition to digital technology, where it holds some advantages. For
Motorola, the situation is different. The company boasts large economies
of scale and superiority in cost-driving technologies – but within a technological context with a limited life cycle.

Economies of scope and experience
The technologies applied within the mobile telephone industry often trace
their origin to other product areas. Conversely, technologies developed or
improved by the mobile telephone industry can be applied anew in other
fields. Productivity in the mobile telephone industry is therefore partly a
function of a company's ability to spread research and development costs
across a number of product areas and thus achieve economies of scope, or
application of a new or improved technology to more than one category
of product. Ericsson, for example, consistently tries to exploit and combine its resources in the areas of radio and switching technology; hence
such ventures as cordless telephones and mobile data systems.[6]

Like NEC and Panasonic, Motorola achieves economies of scope by
diversifying outward from its core technological base of radio and semiconductor technology, thereby shortening research and development lead
times and trimming both development and manufacturing costs. Motoro-

la therefore specializes in terminals for all types of radio communications: pagers, cordless telephones, mobile telephones, land mobile radio telephones and military radio equipment.

Economies of experience that draw their impetus from accumulated production know-how are as vital for terminal manufacturers as they are for other consumer electronics manufacturers. Ericsson has many years of experience in the fields of telecommunications and radio communications. The company has been supplying telephone exchanges since the late 19th century and has worked with radio communications since the 1960s. History offers Ericsson some unique competitive advantages in relation to AT&T, Northern Telecom and Alcatel, competitors accustomed to operating as pure telecommunications companies. Ericsson also draws on this heritage in its competitive relationship with Motorola: although it may be the world's leading radio communications producer, the American company lacks extensive public switching experience.

Vertical integration in component production
Today Motorola generates in-house more than 90 per cent of its terminals' aggregate value-added. The company even carries out research and development work on components such as liquid crystal displays (LCDs) and certain types of batteries that are purchased externally. Motorola manufactures its own components and acts as a leading component supplier to other companies. Large-scale component production enables substantial cost and performance improvements. In-house production also offers access to protected key technology at an early stage, and reduces product development and production lead times. Shared methods can be used in product and process development. This kind of vertical integration yields cost advantages that enable the company to place pressure on outside suppliers to lower their prices.

Localization of purchasing and production
Industry specialists estimate that production costs in Asia are around 20 per cent cheaper than in the United States or Europe. Despite these advantages, many European and American companies choose not to manufacture in Asia because of the time and costs incurred by the transfer of necessary technological and management skills. Motorola has taken the plunge, moving entire product lines to Malaysia and Singapore and retaining American managers and Motorola methods in the process. The company's foreign-based units show quality and productivity levels at least as good as corresponding units in the United States.

Threats from substitutes and new companies

Threats from new entrants in the markets for analogue terminals or systems are unlikely. Producers of mobile telephone systems do, however, face challenges from cordless telephones and paging systems that offer steadily improving performance quality, range of applications and price levels. In the future, price-sensitive customers may well choose simpler radio communications formats. It is therefore in the interests of the mobile telephone industry to cut costs at least as rapidly as manufacturers of substitute systems.

The threat of new competition is more pronounced in the still young market for digital terminals. Depending on which technologies assume a pivotal role and whether the digital terminals will become standardized or differentiated products, three kinds of potential entrant loom on the horizon. The first group comprises the consumer electronics giants like Hitachi, Texas Instruments and Gold Star. From the information technology sector, a second group of computer companies includes IBM and Digital Equipment Corporation, already strongly positioned in the fields of digital communication and VLSI technology. A third group, mostly based among the newly industrialised economies of the Pacific Rim, is composed of producers that specialise in replicating products originated within the big companies.

At the same time, obstacles to entry are pitched high around the digital systems market. Given the tremendous research and development costs involved, the only serious new players in the digital market are likely to emerge from the ranks of those computer companies sufficiently large and liquid to attempt to establish themselves as manufacturers of telecommunications switches.

Factors that affect productivity at the national level in mobile telephone systems

Domestic market demand has been central to the development of mobile telephone systems. Early standardization and procurement of mobile telephone systems by Nordic telecommunications authorities offered Ericsson a vital advantage in the early and mid-1980s.[7] Almost a protected enclave by default, the Nordic market was sufficiently small to be passed over by large extra-regional telecommunications companies. By 1987, when rival terminal manufacturers began to enter the Nordic market, Ericsson had accumulated a valuable reservoir of knowledge and resources that was to prove useful in its next move into the big but highly competitive U.S. market.

By way of comparison, the Japanese mobile telephone network expanded relatively late, in 1986: one reason, perhaps, for the otherwise surprisingly indifferent performance of Japanese companies as system suppliers. In the early 1980s, Japanese companies like NEC were hamstrung by Nippon Telephone and Telegraph's largely self-sufficient development of a mobile telephone system. NEC's role became that of a sub-contractor denied access to the benefits of economies of scale or initial hands-on experience in a domestic market.

For Motorola and Ericsson, encounters with state-controlled agencies appear to have had more benign effects. The military connection has been particularly important. During the past three decades, the world's armed forces have been among the most significant consumers of advanced analogue and digital radio communications equipment. Motorola, for example, owes much of its accumulated competence in radio technology to the impetus derived from its status as America's largest supplier of land mobile and other radio equipment from the 1960s onward. For Ericsson and Motorola, the cutting-edge technologies called forth to fulfil complex defence contracts have proved valuable in the subsequent development of civilian mobile telephone systems.

Both companies have enjoyed access to cutting-edge technologies in their respective domestic markets. Ericsson has benefited from a tradition of academically-oriented research in the fields of digital radio and digital signal processing. Other national factors, such as the limits on the number of qualified engineers, may have hampered Ericsson's freedom of action in research and development projects. For Motorola, a cluster of U.S. companies and institutions with advanced competence in VLSI design and radio technologies has contributed primarily to product development. Domestic competition in these technologies also encourages in-house productivity improvement. Motorola has enjoyed access to a sufficiently large pool of qualified personnel: the company hires about one out of twenty applicants after a thorough screening process.

Obviously, competition at home has also proved vital to productivity improvements in mobile telephone terminal production. Since 1985, Motorola has faced the kind of stiff domestic competition that forces improvements in performance and fosters cost-cutting strategies. By comparison with Ericsson, Motorola also enjoys cost advantages. In the United States, numerous suppliers and competitors contribute both competence and components in the fields of computing and radio technology. Similar conditions exist in the tough Japanese terminal market.

Intra-company mechanisms behind productivity improvements

Productivity management

'Motorola's fundamental objective is total customer satisfaction,' runs one company motto. Another describes 'total customer satisfaction' as 'everyone's overriding responsibility'. The company spells out five company-wide key initiatives aimed at achieving this objective: six sigma quality, total cycle time reduction, product and process leadership, profit improvement and participative management.[8] Six sigma quality is a statistical measurement of quality that provides the theme of Motorola's programme to improve quality 'in everything we do'. In 1981, Motorola formulated a long-term quality target: quality should improve tenfold during the next five years, regardless of separate measurements of quality in different operating units. In 1987, Motorola established new quality targets that involved improving quality levels – reducing the proportion of defects – tenfold by 1989 and one hundredfold by 1991. The target of six sigma quality was set for 1992: a maximum allowance of 3.4 defects per million process steps. The company has been successful in reaching other targets related to shorter lead times, especially in purchasing, production and distribution.

Motorola uses a number of methods to achieve its fundamental objective. The company creates customer advisory groups that make suggestions on ways of improving products. In product development work, Motorola attempts to take into account the customer's views, which are continuously conveyed to the company by its sales force. Motorola also evaluates the quality of its marketing and distribution strategies. The yardsticks here are order quality, sales quality, billing routines, time elapsed from order to delivery, adjustment costs and the length of time, if any, over which customers possess a defective product.

To boost understanding of customers' needs and situations, all Motorola managers – up to and including the chairman of the board – make at least two visits to customers each month. By including top management in this effort, the company underscores the importance of satisfying each customer. Salesmen know that the head of the company conceivably could visit one of his customers.

Targets are imposed for delivery. Average elapsed time from order to production has improved from 20 days in 1988 to 3.85 days in 1990 and 1.85 days in 1991. For pagers, the time that elapses between the booking of an order and the hour when the product leaves Motorola has been reduced to between 55 minutes and a maximum of 1 hour and 40 minutes.

The salaries of all field personnel and line managers are dependent on the outcome of these measurements.

Motorola's philosophy is to use straightforward measurements common to all areas of the organization. Thus the same target can be formulated for almost all departments and functions. Motorola measures only variables that employees can directly influence: quality and lead time reduction. The thinking here is that with improvements in these two key areas, increased profitability and productivity follow as a direct consequence.

Motorola believes that employees are motivated by measurements to which they can relate and over which they can exercise some direct influence. By contrast, financial yardsticks are often abstract. Simple, understandable and exact yardsticks reduce an employee's uncertainty about how to behave in a complex working environment. Although Ericsson's use of targets that employees can influence directly has been confined mainly to production workers, the company is currently applying quantitative targets to its development departments.

Motorola's entire management philosophy rides on the back of the target system. The 'six sigma quality' yardstick, for example, focuses attention equally on all operations, including traditionally low-priority and peripheral activities. According to Motorola, the quality target lowers the number of defects per unit, which, in turn, reduces costs. When Motorola takes additional steps to shorten total lead times, this is done partly by reducing the number of operations. The effect, once again, is a further reduction in the number of defects.

Communication of goals and expectations
Monitoring objectives and providing feedback to all employees are essential elements of productivity management. At Ericsson, feedback occurs when employees present reports to supervisors and during discussions with colleagues. At Motorola, each value-adding stage in the company is regarded as a supplier to the next value-adding stage. Every Motorola employee has a 'customer' who will provide feedback within 72 hours. If internal customers are satisfied, runs the thinking, external customers will also be satisfied. The feedback process can be summarized as a system of simple quantitative measurements that provide quick follow-up and pay handsome dividends to those who prove successful – a philosophy similar to the Japanese concept of total quality control.

Long-term strategic objectives are formulated by top management at both Ericsson and Motorola. Although short-term targets, such as those for product development, are mainly controlled from above, discussions also take place between hierarchical levels. This ensures that employees support the objectives: high targets are thus presented as a challenge rather than a provocation. Product planning targets are established by product management teams consisting of senior managers from different departments. The teams that will develop each product must, however, approve the targets before a project can start. Approval is formalized by having the team sign contract books that contain extensive competitor information in the form of market shares, cost structure, product performance. This device helps to control the tendency among engineers to want to improve a product even further – thereby exceeding agreed specifications – by taking advantage of the very latest technology. Such deviations may prolong the development process, giving the end-user a superfluous level of performance or even unsuitable combinations of performance.

In industry, deviation from plans and targets has been the origin of many great inventions. At Motorola, a strong commitment to the contract book format during product development does not seem to hamper innovations. Quality targets even enforce a form of programmed creativity, if only because highly ambitious targets tend to demand fresh solutions. The company expects its engineers to come up with products that can be patented – on average, once a year. The patent department is expected to turn out finished blueprints in 18 hours. Overall, lead times for patent approval have been reduced from 18 months to 60 days.

The importance of getting top executives at Motorola and Ericsson involved and letting them serve as role models can hardly be overestimated. Executives play a major role in the implementation of company strategy and in the creation of corporate culture. Motorola's legendary former chairman Bob Galvin, a member of the company's founding family, drew attention to quality problems during the late 1970s. Galvin placed the issue at the top of the agenda at management meetings in which he was involved. After discussion of the quality issue, and *before* presentation of the latest financial results, Galvin would get up and leave. It was a dramatic device designed to define the company's top priority. Furthermore, Galvin's approach has become habitual: quality reports now always occupy the top of the agenda at line-organization employee meetings. After discussion of quality, managers get up and leave the meetings. This behaviour leads to a focus on quality and lead time reduction, objectives to which top management assigns top priority.

For more than a decade, Motorola has been running a participative management campaign designed to take better advantage of employee resources through more open dialogue between managers and employees at all levels. Meeting the standards of a specific management style is also a criterion in the selection of personnel for promotion. At Motorola, managers can lose out on promotion because of excessively self-centred behaviour, despite very good results in other respects.

For years, Ericsson Radio Systems President Åke Lundqvist,[9] with his tight-knit group of executives, was the driving force behind the development of mobile telephone systems at Ericsson. In its early days, this group operated as a team without any strict division of responsibility. This worked well, with members of the group substituting for each other as necessary. Lundqvist's commitment to the task of development became widely known among employees. Even today, management authority at Ericsson is more often exercised through examplary behaviour than through more formal means – a method that naturally requires a high standard of management competence and commitment.

The long-term visions and objectives of top managers at Ericsson and Motorola have played vital roles in the development of these companies. Both companies operate on the basis of a vision that foresees them becoming the world's leading company in personal communications. These visions have been turned into operational concepts and measurements, leading to shared values, language and approaches. The fact that Ericsson and Motorola have established lofty long-term goals has been of great importance to innovation in product development and cost-effectiveness. Employees have been forced to reassess their working methods and in many cases they have devised new methods in order to achieve the stated objectives.

Neither Ericsson nor Motorola has avoided stiff international competition by concentrating on markets where competition is not so vigorous. Instead, these companies have adapted their organizational structures when competition has escalated. Behind such behaviour lies the belief that a company ensures its long-term growth if it becomes a leading supplier in large and rapidly growing markets. Motorola maintains that it always seeks out markets and product areas with the largest growth potential, regardless of the level of competition that the company risks encountering in such areas.

Motorola has adopted an explicit strategy of beating the Japanese in Japan, mirroring the aggressive stance of Japanese companies in the U.S. market. Motorola has consequently carved out a 25-30 per cent market share for paging terminals in Japan – a larger proportion than that held by Japanese companies in the United States. Ericsson acted in similar fashion in 1982 when the company ventured into the United States, the world's toughest mobile telephone system market. Ericsson has pursued the same strategy with terminals, developing products for a growing number of markets and joining battle for market share with American, European and Japanese companies. This kind of strategy rules out the possibility of a company growing complacent, and instead provokes constant adaptation to the need for lower costs and higher performance.

As organizations, Ericsson and Motorola are characterized by a high level of awareness of their environment. At Ericsson, this awareness takes shape during product development work. The company looks for the latest and most advanced components, methods and technologies on the world market and then tries to utilize them in its own products. Motorola integrates an awareness of the overall competitive situation into all functions and thoroughly communicates hard external realities to all employees. Motorola also uses the performance of the best companies as a way of benchmarking its own activities in all customer-related functions, such as order procedures, delivery precision, invoicing and customer satisfaction.[10]   Benchmarking serves to ensure that an awareness of competition permeates all levels of the company. At the pinnacle of the organization, Bob Galvin himself believed in continuously evaluating his own performance against that of counterparts from rival companies.

Constant renewal of company objectives can lead to continuous improvement in productivity. The establishment of ambitious goals can also revitalize an organization through reassessment of existing ways of working. Ericsson establishes demanding objectives in terms of the time frames and costs of specific activities. It involves employees in the process of formulating goals, creating a sense of commitment on the part of those who are charged with performing specific tasks. In product development work, this means detailed performance goals, target times and cost objectives for products.

Motorola bases a large proportion of its corporate culture on objectives that apply to all employees and all tasks. The belief is that this creates the conditions for positive internal competition and direct comparisons. Over the past ten years, Motorola has continuously raised its quality targets. To meet its six sigma target by 1992, starting from quality levels current in 1987, the company needed to achieve an annual average improvement of around 68 per cent. During the same period, the target for total lead time reduction was 50 per cent annually. In a similar fashion, Ericsson raised production quality targets from the mid-1980s, calling for quality improvements of as much as 100 per cent a year.

Human Resource Management

REWARD SYSTEMS

Motorola has always used a pay structure clearly based on performance. Ericsson is moving in the direction of greater pay differentiation. Wage and salary differentials remain substantially wider at Motorola than at Ericsson. Figure 11 shows the span of salaries for newly hired engineers in the two companies. 'Lower category' refers to newly-hired engineers in the lowest salary class; 'higher category' refers to the best qualified of the newly-hired engineers. Ericsson's lowest salaries are higher than Motorola's lowest salaries, while Motorola's highest salaries are substantially higher than those at Ericsson.

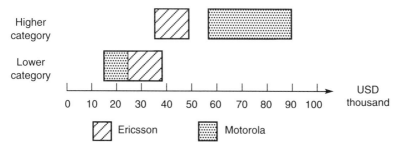

Figure 3.11 Salary comparisons: Ericsson and Motorola.

Motorola's philosophy is that if people's behaviour can be changed, their attitudes and values will follow and support their new behaviour. According to Motorola, this way of working often leads to far quicker results than use of the opposite tactic of attempting to achieve desired behaviour patterns by first changing people's attitudes and values. To obtain quick results, Motorola focuses on directly changing its employees' behaviour without taking a detour through their value systems.[11] To influence behaviour, ambitious goals are not enough. There must also be positive feedback mechanisms when goals are achieved. For this reason, the company has established reward systems linked to lead time reduction and quality improvement targets for all employees. There are bonuses for departments and individuals. Managers are part of the Motorola Executive Incentive Programme, where the average bonus runs to around 15-25 per cent of salaries with a ceiling of roughly 50 per cent. Managers' performance is normally reviewed every quarter according to quality and customer satisfaction criteria. The maximum bonus for employees below top management levels is 30 per cent. Calculated as an average for the whole company, bonus pay amounts to about 3.5 per cent.

TRAINING

Both Ericsson and Motorola assign high priority to training. Motorola employees receive an absolute minimum of 40 hours' training annually. Managers whose employees do not receive the minimum training requirement can count on a reduction in bonus pay. It is also incumbent on managers, in consultation with employees, to plan training programmes that genuinely improve the ability of individuals to reduce lead times and raise quality.

At Ericsson, training mostly involves the company's development engineers and technicians. Ericsson is also making a large-scale effort to introduce the ISO 9000 standards system, a set of rules detailing quality assurance implementation. Fulfilment of ISO 9000 standards is among the requirements for submitting public procurement tenders within the European Community.

JOB SECURITY

Job security is widely thought to reduce employee resistance to change, thereby enhancing prospects of improved productivity. But in the case of Motorola and Ericsson, the role of job security must also be seen in light of rapid industrial expansion over the past decade. The companies have faced the problem of recruiting a sufficient number of highly qualified employees.

Motorola offers virtual lifetime employment. In general, employees are reallocated within the company rather than fired. After ten years of employment, an employee becomes a member of the Motorola Service Club. The company chairman himself must approve the dismissal of a member of the club.

Swedish labour legislation gives employees at Ericsson similar or even greater formal job security. In terms of productivity, it may be significant that job security at Ericsson is based on legislation, rather than on explicit corporate priorities.

WORKING HOURS

Ericsson's employees work between 1,500 and 1,700 hours each year. To this total, we can add annual overtime of some 100-300 hours. Occasionally, Ericsson has been granted a waiver from Swedish regulations that impose an annual ceiling of 200 hours on the overtime worked by individual employees. In general, the company cannot count on receiving approval for extensive overtime on the part of large categories of employees.

At Motorola, a large percentage of employees work overtime. Individuals who wish to work 24 hours a day are allowed to do so. Nominal annual working time at Motorola is 2,000 hours: the average is closer to 2,500 hours.

Interestingly, Motorola has very low absenteeism levels: about 1.5 per cent for production employees and, according to estimates, less than 1 per cent for white collar employees. For production workers, bonus pay is heavily dependent on attendance levels. The company does not normally keep records of absenteeism among white collar employees who, in any case, put in so much unpaid overtime that two or three days away from work because of illness is regarded as completely legitimate when it occurs.

At Ericsson, absenteeism among white collar workers in production departments runs at around 3 per cent. Although a low figure in the context of Swedish industry, Ericsson's rates are around three times higher than comparative rates at Motorola. Indeed, on occasion, blue collar absenteeism at Ericsson runs as high as 20 per cent.[12] Such high levels of absenteeism adversely affect productivity figures. The hiring of supplementary employees clearly results in a good deal of higher costs and some reduced efficiency.

UNION ORGANIZATION

A large percentage of the employees at Ericsson belong to labour unions. By and large, top management and the unions work together smoothly. Exceptions to the rule have occurred, as when top management attempted to introduce productivity yardsticks for white collar employees. The union argued that measuring the productivity of white collar employees and development engineers would single out particular individuals as low-performing. At Motorola there are no labour unions, and no employees are affiliated with unions. The company adopts the simple expedient of not hiring employees who wish to join a union: employees, it is said, should not have double goals and loyalties. On this basis, the rationale is that what is good for Motorola also works to the benefit of employees, whose company assures them of a job and a future.

Organizational structure and technology

Both Ericsson and Motorola depend on corporate cultures and structures that foster creativity. Both companies strive to adopt a rather open, relaxed and informal, almost familial approach. Decision-making processes are correspondingly rapid. During the mobile telephone industry's decade-long existence, Ericsson's corporate culture has been characterized by a strong entrepreneurial spirit. Performance rather than position generally commands respect.

At Motorola, regardless of their rank, all employees walk around in shirt-sleeves. Colleagues up to and including such luminaries as former chairman Bob Galvin are referred to on a first-name basis. Like other employees, Galvin sports a photo ID card on his shirt-front. An open-door policy applies, with managers eating in the regular employee dining room unless subject to customer visits. High-level executives seem to be on first name terms with many employees. Clearly, an open corporate culture can be combined with strict management by objectives. In line with the ethos of management-by-example, the company refrains from punishing under-achievers, preferring instead to reward those who turn in good performances.

Delegation of decision-making and responsibility for earnings is considered a prerequisite for high cost-effectiveness in the mobile telephone industry. Ericsson has applied a very flat organizational structure, with close connections between hierarchical levels and parallel units. In the past four years, Motorola has also worked to flatten its organizational structure. The number of hierarchical levels within each business area has been reduced from nine in 1988 to four in 1991. In both companies, individual employees often have great freedom to make decisions regarding purchases, resources, costs and production functions. Both companies also enforce almost aggressive systems of management by objectives, including contractual procedures that establish definitive boundaries for employee actions. Employees thus assume heavy responsibilities, but are given the freedom of action necessary to achieve tough targets.

Both Ericsson and Motorola also apply a clear strategy for handling new products and business areas. This philosophy states that new product areas should be separated and turned into business areas of their own, so that new units are not consumed by the main operations around them. Interestingly, Ericsson and Motorola are the only companies that, almost from the outset, made the manufacture of mobile telephone systems a separate business area, divorced from overall telecommunications operations.

Efforts to modularize components and software are a contributing factor to high productivity levels at both companies. Advanced development methodologies and large investments in computer-aided systems for design engineers allow designers to work with databases that contain information about modules and with programmes that suggest combinations of modules. Modularization involves the reutilization of existing know-how but results in fewer quality problems and shorter development time. Systems become less expensive and work better from start-up if only a small proportion of their software is new.

One prerequisite for rapid product development and high cost-effectiveness in mobile telephone systems, as indicated earlier, is the reduction of lead time in research and development and production. Motorola and Ericsson have implemented this by means of:

- Concurrent engineering
- Reduction in the number of components and product functions necessary to satisfy customer requirements
- Reduction in the number of process steps

Simultaneous engineering means that, rather than being sequential, the various steps in the development process overlap in time as much as possible. Lead time reduction generally also means higher quality, through reductions in the potential sources of defects. It also generally implies cost savings, through reductions in direct materials, lower assembly costs and smaller inventories held on company premises.

High and uniform quality levels are promoted by reducing the number of product parts and process steps, but also by adapting products to the production process. To monitor the latter, Motorola has a company-wide yardstick for design engineering and manufacturing, known as a capability (CP) index. The CP index – a ratio between a component's tolerance and variations occurring in production – is calculated for each component and each process step. The larger the tolerance in relation to production variation, the smaller the risk of quality problems. Tolerance is determined by designers; variation is in the hands of production employees. The use of the CP index as a quality management tool means that two departments are measured by a common yardstick, which they can only improve by working together. In this way, a natural alliance is created across departmental boundaries. In general, the company does not evaluate the performance of employees from different departments with what might be called competing variables or yardsticks in which a high score for one department can leave another department at a disadvantage.

CONCLUSIONS

In the mobile telephone industry, technical development is pivotal to company productivity. Product performance, product development times and cost-effectiveness are dependent on how well companies exploit and improve their technological competence. Ericsson and Motorola have been successful in this respect; the former with its strengths in systems technologies, and the latter in technologies for terminals. From the early days of the industry, both companies possessed technological skills and resources from other closely related operations, ensuring that they had good prerequisites to succeed in an industry characterized by tough competition. The main reason for their success, however, is that the two companies have managed to organize their operations skillfully, enabling them to respond to the need for rapid product development and cost-effective production.

Both companies, but especially Motorola, approach productivity management issues in a systematic manner. The central targets in quality and lead times are evaluated with extreme thoroughness. Both firms are also very much aware of market requirements. At Ericsson, this awareness is created, among other things, by careful monitoring of relevant technological developments outside the company. For its part, Motorola has institutionalized follow-up visits to customers and rules requiring internal feedback within 72 hours on all activities. The dedication and example provided by top management have proved very vital factors in the corporate culture of both companies.

In organizational terms, both companies are characterized by few hierarchical levels and by far-reaching decentralization of responsibility. At the same time, they practice extremely firm management by objectives. Decentralization offers employees freedom to discover new solutions; target fulfilment requirements prevent this far-reaching freedom from being used in ways that do not benefit the company. The human resource practices of the two companies show a number of similarities. This is especially true in their emphasis on training programmes.

[1]AMPS (United States); TACS (Great Britain); C-Net (Germany); NMT 450, NMT 900 and Comvik (Nordic countries) etc.
[2]General System for Mobile Telephone Communication. Originally: Groupe Special Mobile.
[3]Radio nets with limited coverage and normally not connected to public networks. Examples of clients are taxi companies, the police, rescue services and trucking or other transporting companies.
[4]The systems being compared here have mainly been developed according to the American standard, Advanced Mobile Phone System (AMPS). This is a standard that is specified in less detail than the Swedish NMT standard, for instance. AMPS therefore allows greater room for

systems suppliers to devise their own technological solutions.

[5]Restarting an Ericsson system generally takes only a few minutes. In other systems, however, it may take several hours.

[6]Ericsson's mobile data communications system (Mobitex) is similar to land mobile radio but is specially tailored for data and text transmission, and to a lesser extent voice communications.

[7]In a recent advertisement marking the inauguration of GSM, Ericsson wrote that Sweden is the world's leading mobile telephone country. 'The Swedish National Telecommunications Administration (Televerket) deserves most of the credit for this. Televerket saw the potential of this new technology more clearly than others and eagerly committed itself to building up the new service.' *Svenska Dagbladet*, July 1, 1991.

[8]At Motorola all employees receive a plastic card the size of a business card, on which the company's goals are briefly and concisely formulated. The card is supposed to be carried at all times in the suit or shirt pocket by all employees.

[9]Now president of Ericsson GE Mobile Communications Holdings Inc.

[10]Some of the companies that Motorola uses as benchmarks are IBM, Digital Equipment, Hewlett-Packard, American Express, American Airlines, Federal Express, First Chicago Bank, Xerox, Seiko and Toshiba.

[11]According to Motorola vice president Bill Smith, this approach is one of the differences between Motorola's quality philosophy and that of Japanese companies, which prefer to teach their employees first how to think in quality terms, before implementing any changes.

[12]Absenteeism declined noticeably during 1991, as in other Swedish industrial companies after the rules of the social security (sick pay) system were tightened and after unemployment had increased.

4 NATIONALE-NEDERLANDEN AND SKANDIA

Together with Britain, the Netherlands has the lowest insurance premiums and the least regulated insurance market in Europe. The Netherlands is also home to one of the most profitable non-life insurance companies in Europe, Nationale-Nederlanden. In both 1986 and 1987, this company was honoured as the Dutch insurer that provided the best service to its customers. In 1989, Nationale-Nederlanden was also awarded a prize as the best public service company in the Netherlands.

Nationale-Nederlanden's Swedish counterpart is Skandia, Sweden's most profitable insurance company during the 1980s. In many respects, Skandia resembles Nationale-Nederlanden. The two companies are about the same size, offer a broad range of insurance policies and are the largest in most of their fields of operations in their respective home countries.

What does productivity mean in a service industry such as insurance? In insurance, cost-effectiveness is a function of administrative and sales expenses – and of claims costs, a difficult variable to influence. Although insurance companies find innovation difficult, national regulatory systems do have a palpable influence on levels of productivity. Given lighter regulation of insurance services in the Netherlands than in Sweden, the role of regulation in boosting productivity seems worthy of examination.

INSURANCE – A MAJOR SERVICE SECTOR

In the countries of the European Community, about 12 million people are employed by insurance companies. Their output is equivalent to 5.5 per cent of combined GDP. Although the insurance business is one of Europe's largest service industries, it still consists largely of companies that operate mainly in their home countries. Cross-border business was once the preserve of reinsurance and transportation insurance sectors, but

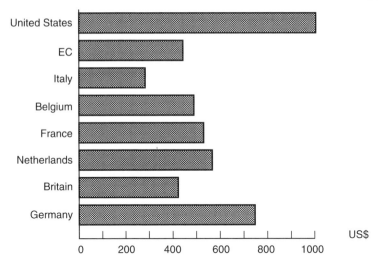

Figure 4.1 Per capita non-life insurance expenditures, 1987. Source: Sigma

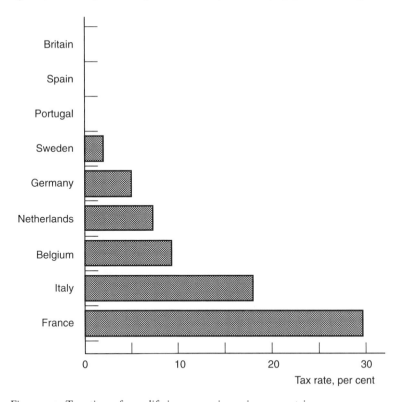

Figure 4.2 Taxation of non-life insurance in various countries.

Source: Swedish Private Insurance Supervisory Service (FI), 1988

the advent of a single market in Europe should see national boundaries losing their importance in the insurance business during years to come.

The major differences in the relative size of European national insurance markets are attributable to variations in economic living standards, value of insured items, willingness to take risks, the protection guaranteed by each respective government and other factors (Figure 4.1). For example: buildings in southern Europe are less expensive than in more northerly countries. Another example is Italy, where nearly half of all policies (including life policies) are for motor vehicles. More than Italian driving styles are at stake here: Italians are less inclined than other Europeans to buy personal insurance coverage in the form of life insurance policies or deferred annuities. Overall, in Europe, the size and distribution of non-life insurance policies on different items co-varies with economic growth, demography and income changes.

Non-life insurance – risk-taking and investment management

The insurance business can be divided into:

- Life insurance
- Reinsurance
- Non-life insurance

The latter area is the one under study here. In terms of total premiums paid, non-life insurance policies comprise about two-thirds of the insurance market in the EC. Non-life insurance is purchased by individuals in the form of homeowners', householders' and motor insurance policies. Corporate insurance policies provide against fire and other kinds of damage to buildings or business assets.

Insurers attempt to spread their risks across large numbers of policyholders. Premiums should be calculated to cover both expected claims and the insurance company's administration costs and profit margins. In the case of policies with very high coverage ceilings – for example, fire insurance for major corporations – an insurance company may share risk with one or more other companies by means of reinsurance.

Because premiums flow in before claims costs arise, insurance companies have funds at their disposal. In both the Netherlands and Sweden, insurance companies must allocate funds to contingency reserves designed to guard against claims costs that exceed total premiums. Known as consolidation funds, these reserves, at least in Sweden, should total approximately 50 per cent of premiums earned.[1] This generous risk buffer is tied to the size of premiums rather than to the size of risks. Another consequence of premium prepayment and the presence of consolidation funds is that large insurance companies, in particular, function as financial institutions, playing an essential role in capital markets.[2] The skill of insurance companies in financial investment management affects their competitiveness. High returns on financial assets may enable a company to charge lower premiums.

Besides general management, insurance companies specialize in the following operations:[3]

- Underwriting: risk evaluation, issuance of insurance policies and renewal of policies
- Claims adjustment: how quickly is damage or injury inspected? How is the compensation issue resolved, and how large a payment is disbursed?
- Investment management: ability to achieve high returns on financial assets
- Information technology: insurance companies process large quantities of information about customers and about factors that may affect the frequency of insurance claims
- Product economics: calculation of terms of insurance for existing and new policies and their premiums

Managers in the insurance industry are not accustomed to thinking in terms of economies of experience. In general, companies do not retain any information on the accumulated number of insurances sold. However, experience – of a kind – does accumulate in files containing data on sold policies and incurred claims. Skilled manipulation of this data increases a company's ability to differentiate prices charged to different policy holders depending on relative levels of risk. Use of such databases is more advanced in the Netherlands than in Sweden, partly because the Swedish Private Insurance Supervisory Service has in the past discouraged discretionary pricing.

Major profitability differences among countries

The fact that insurance markets in Europe are still mainly national partly explains the major differences that exist in terms of premium levels and profitability among insurance companies in various countries. Comparisons are further complicated because of the use of different accounting principles in different countries. Figure 4.3 shows the average profitability

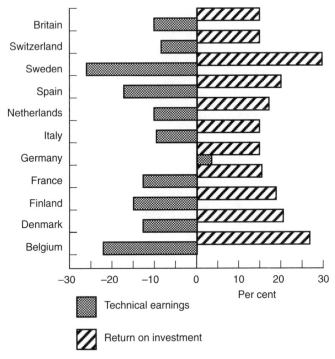

Figure 4.3 Average profitability of non-life insurance sectors in Europe.
Source: Swedish Private Insurance Supervisory Service (FI), 1988

of at least two-thirds of the non-life insurance sector in each respective country. Profitability is divided into two components: return on financial investment and technical earnings (premiums earned minus operating expenses and payments on claims incurred). As Figure 4.3 indicates, with their stable competitive context and slow rate of claims costs rises, only German companies report a small surplus in technical earnings. The Netherlands and Britain, with their deregulated markets and stiff competition, show relatively good technical earnings. In general, however, it is difficult to see any correlation between the degree of regulation in a market and the size of technical earnings.

Although Swedish, Belgian and Danish insurance companies turned in large negative technical earnings during 1983–87, very good returns on financial investment offered compensation. Indeed, there seems to be a reverse correlation between return on investment and technical earnings. To put this another way: a high return on investment is employed as a way of lowering premiums. The fact that companies hold down premiums in this way indicates that price is a competitive tool in national markets.

EC studies have indicated that if insurance policies could be sold throughout Europe at the same premiums as in the four countries where insurance companies report the lowest operating expenses, prices could be reduced by 51 per cent in Italy, 32 per cent in Spain and 31 per cent in Belgium. By contrast, prices would remain roughly constant in the Netherlands and Britain. It is difficult to say how much such calculations can be relied upon, not least because there are genuine differences in claims costs from one country to another. As an example of this, Figure 4.4 shows the relative occurrence of traffic deaths.[4] An international comparison of premiums is not entirely misleading, however, and the economic integration of Europe will certainly expose companies with high prices and low efficiency to some degree of price competition from more efficient companies.

A large proportion of insurance company expenses is devoted to sales activities. Opportunities for utilizing different forms of distribution such as insurance agents and brokers vary from country to country. There are differences both in legislation and business practices. Selling without intermediaries, French insurance companies have rapidly increased their market share, mainly by identifying occupational categories – taxi drivers, for example – and designing inexpensive insurance packages for

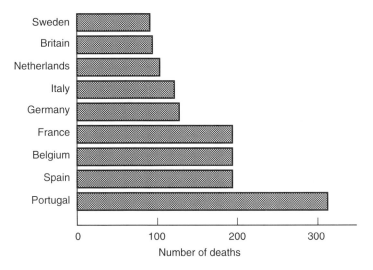

Figure 4.4 Mortality rates: Europe.

Source: Foisàkungstidunigen, I, 1990.

them. In the Netherlands and Britain, independent agents and brokers have always played a major role, pushing up commission levels. In Britain, commissions are around 30 per cent. Commissions earned by brokers in Netherlands are 20–30 per cent. In Sweden rates run in the range of 12–15 per cent for corporate insurance, the main speciality of brokers.

The line separating banks and insurance companies has been eroded further in France, Spain, Britain and the Netherlands than elsewhere.[5] Banks have started to sell life insurance, including deferred annuities, as part of full-service personal finance packages. Banks also have lower sales expenses (estimated in France at 2–3 per cent of premium with customary commissions running at 20–30 per cent).

The Netherlands

Long tradition

The Netherlands has a long insurance tradition, and a number of institutional arrangements indicate that the insurance industry enjoys a strong position within the national economy. Besides the strong educational and training infrastructure behind the Dutch insurance business, Amsterdam and Rotterdam both boast insurance exchanges that have dealt with major industrial risks for more than a century. Indeed, prices for this type of insurance have been so low that, unlike their counterparts in the U.S., Dutch corporations have little incentive to assume their own insurance risks in the form of so-called captives, subsidiaries that arrange insurance deals for diversified parent companies.

Many companies; few dominant

The Netherlands contains nearly 500 insurance companies. Some major Dutch insurance companies are internationally active and earn up to 50 per cent of their premiums from operations abroad, where their biggest foreign market is the United States.

Support to sales channels is the most important means of competition. Nationale-Nederlanden offers the same type of insurance policies as its major competitors and is the largest company in all categories except health and 'other' forms of insurance, where it is second-largest. The company's most vital competitive tool is not terms or even prices, but the levels of service provided through sales channels. While it pays the same commission rates, Nationale-Nederlanden provides more sales support and training than its competitors.

Company MGBP	Premiums	Market Share: %	Type of Company
Nationale-Nederlanden General*		7.1	Listed
AVCB		6.4	Mutual
Aegon		5.6	Listed
Interpolis		5.6	Mutual
Zilveren Kruis		5.0	Mutual
Total market	5,600		

Table 4.1 Market sales of the five largest non-life insurance companies in the Netherlands, 1989.

*Nationale Nederlanden Group 11.9 per cent.

Source: Assurantir Magazine, 1990.

Independent insurance agents and brokers are the most common sales conduit in the Netherlands. In the Dutch market there are more than 30,000 registered insurance intermediaries. (Sweden, by contrast, boasts just over 300 brokers and 3,000 field sales personnel). In the Netherlands, consumers appreciate home sales visits. This might explain why such a large percentage of insurance is sold via field salespeople or intermediaries. Dutch banks also play a larger than usual role as sales conduits (see Table 4.2). In the Netherlands, the market share of companies with direct writers who sell policies via mail and telephone increased from 23 per cent to 29 per cent during the 1980s.

Sales channel	Market Share %	Trend
Independent intermediaries	46	–
Insurance company sales forces	5	=
Banks	13	+
Direct writers	29	+
Other channels	7	=
Total	100	

Table 4.2 Market shares and trends, insurance distribution channels in the Netherlands.

Source: de Wit & Vrancken, 1990.

Regulatory system

The Netherlands has a comparatively liberal regulatory system. Before 1990 banks and insurance companies were not allowed to develop cross-holdings exceeding 15 per cent – an obstacle to merger scrapped only recently. The tax rules governing technical reserves are favourable, and insurance companies consequently have a very solid capital base.

Dutch insurance companies are not protected from foreign competition; Swedish companies, by contrast, are accustomed to competing only on the basis of prices and terms and still enjoy protected status. Pressure on Dutch insurers is mainly generated by competition from direct writers and independent insurance intermediaries. The latter are professionals who force the insurance companies into competition on prices, terms and service.

Sweden

Corporate structure

In Sweden, the four largest companies enjoy roughly a 80 per cent share of the non-life insurance market – a much higher concentration ratio than applies in the Netherlands. The market's maturity is demonstrated by the five largest companies' virtually unchanged share of the market during the 1980s (see Figure 4.5).

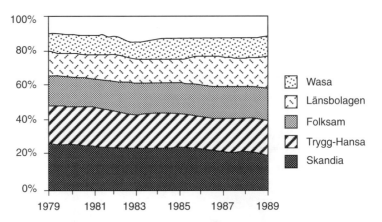

Figure 4.5 Market share in Sweden's non-life insurance market.

Sources: Trygg-Hansa company comparisons and Swedish Private Insurance Supervisory Service (Swedish direct insurance market excluding discharge, employers' no-fault, aviation, animal and credit insurance).

Company	Premium Volume MGBP	Market Share %	Ownership Type
Skandia		20	Listed
Folksam		20	Mutual
Trygg-Hansa		18	Listed
Länsförsäkringar		17	Corporation, association
WASA		10	Corporation, mutual
Foreign companies		1	
Total	2,500		

Table 4.3 Market shares, direct non-life insurance, Sweden, 1989.

Source: Swedish Private Insurance Supervisory Service (FI), 1990.

Loss in actual insurance operations

Slow growth makes for stiff competition. The market is cyclical and oligopolic, leading to price competition during economic downturns. As Table 4.4 indicates, technical earnings in the Swedish non-life insurance business were negative during 1984-88; return on investment was so high that overall earnings were nevertheless positive.

	1989	1988	1987	1986	1985	1984
Operating expenses	29.9	29.2	29.5	30.5	32.6	31.2
Claim costs	89.9	90.0	88.7	87.0	95.9	92.0
Technical earnings	−19.7	−19.2	−18.2	−17.5	−28.5	−23.3
Return on investment	29.7	32.8	29.6	35.4	29.1	26.4
Gross earnings	10.5	13.4	11.1	17.7	0.5	3.0
Pre-tax profit	2.0	1.8	2.7	1.2	0.7	1.3

Table 4.4 Profitability in Swedish insurance companies, non-life policies.* Percent of premiums earned.

*Including reinsurance received.

Source: Swedish Private Insurance Supervisory Service, 1986–1990, Table 5 and Table 2.

Cartels and government regulation
The major Swedish insurance companies resemble one another in terms of operations and product range. Until 1968, non-life companies belonged to a price cartel later dissolved after Skandia's withdrawal. Free pricing, then, can hardly be called traditional. Indeed, a cartel to set insurance policy terms remained in place until the early 1980s.[6]

Trygg-Hansa was previously a mutual insurance company owned by its policyholders. Reorganized into a joint-stock company, the company was floated on the Stockholm Stock Exchange in 1989, a move said to have resulted in increased competition at a national level.

The Swedish insurance market has traditionally been hemmed in by regulatory pressures. Before 1985, when the burden of proof was shifted to insurance industry regulators, new market entrants had to prove that their participation would have a positive effect on the market. New companies have joined the market since this loosening of restrictions, but rules remain in place on the formulation of insurance policy terms. In the field of motor third party insurance, regulations on risk and vehicle categories, geographical zones and driving distances are utilized to determine premiums.

Economies of scale in certain functions
The Dutch and Swedish insurance markets have both very large and very small insurance companies. Company performance figures on the Swedish insurance market indicate no obvious economies of scale: quite simply, operating expenses as a percentage of premiums earned seem similar in large and small companies alike. Return on investment and claims incurred as a percentage of premiums earned also appear to operate independently of a company's size. Either major economies of scale do not apply in the insurance business or there are both economies of large and small scale. Economies of small scale are conceivable in cases where a company specializes in one type of insurance, developing to a high level the skills required for good risk evaluation and premium setting. In addition, claims against smaller companies whose policyholders comprise a discrete group may be lower than for larger corporations.

Indisputable economies of scale are enjoyed by companies large enough to spurn reinsurance, thus avoiding the need to share premium income with rivals. Large companies also enjoy certain economies of scale in terms of computer systems. Notably, Skandia and Finnish insurance company Pohjola co-operate for the purpose of reducing outlays on computer systems.

There are standardized insurance policies that are sold through mass distribution channels, and there are complex insurance policies that are sold through qualified experts. As Figure 4.6 indicates, insurance companies may bear widely-divergent expense burdens for the sale of different types of insurance policies. Statistics on the Swedish insurance market do not indicate that offering a broad range of policies entails particular advantages in this respect.

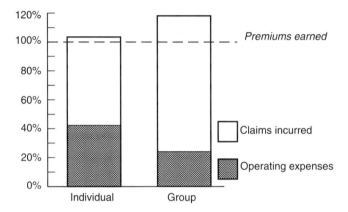

Figure 4.6 Cost burdens on individual and group insurance policies.
Source: Swedish Private Insurance Supervisory Service, 1988.

Service and brand names important means of competition
The updating of insurance industry products is a thankless task. Innovation is easily emulated. Insurance companies therefore compete primarily on the basis of service, price and brand name. Good service can mean a friendly telephone switchboard operator or a knowledgeable, reassuring salesman to quick claims adjustment. With corporate image-based advertising, companies attempt to inspire customer confidence. Statistically, customers tend to buy new policies from the company that contacts them first. With more expensive insurance policies, customers may shop around. When policies run out, most private individuals renew without any survey of alternatives on the market. A customer may want to change company if he is dissatisfied with a claim adjustment or if premiums rise sharply, or if another company lowers its premiums. Customer loyalty varies from one segment of the insurance market to another.

New sales techniques gain major role

Sales channels are an important element of the insurance business. It is very costly for a company to have its own sales offices and retail sales outlets. A sales organization therefore functions as an obstacle to entry into the industry. Only six out of Sweden's 500 insurance companies have their own sales force. The lowest barriers to entry are found in reinsurance.

There are a number of indications that the role of traditional sales organizations may decline in the future. Clearly, it is now possible to enter the industry by using other channels. Volvia, for example, sells insurance through nearly 150 Volvo sales outlets in Sweden. Direct mail and other new information media such as videotex are already being used in the United States, the Netherlands and elsewhere. Indeed, United States data indicates that direct writing costs 10–12 per cent of premium totals. Equivalent costs within a company sales force range between 12.5–17.5 per cent. For independent intermediaries, the figures are closer to 25–30 per cent.[7]

In the Swedish market, two major changes in the sales area may prove crucial to the industry. One is the emergence of independent insurance brokers who help customers to choose advantageous combinations of insurance terms and premiums. This has increased price competition, particularly in corporate insurance markets. Concentrating primarily on medium-sized corporate policies with premiums of about £10,000 to £30,000, brokers tend to request three to five quotations and then subsequently help the customer to compare premiums and terms. After damage or injury, brokers also help policyholders to deal with the claims adjustment process.

One could almost say that these brokers have found their niche because insurers are unaccustomed to competing on the basis of both prices and terms. Insurance companies have devoted insufficient energy to describing their services so that policyholders can make rational choices. In the future, competition in the Swedish market will probably become just as stiff as it is in the Netherlands. In fact, Swedish insurance companies may encounter stronger competitive pressures than their Dutch equivalents, if only because Swedish brokers appear more closely allied with their customers.

A second challenge to the Swedish insurance industry comes in the form of the risk management departments and captive insurance subsidiaries increasingly being established by major industrial corporations. Unlike the Netherlands, industrial insurance policies in Sweden have accounted for a large proportion of the non-life market.

If brokers are successful in the middle segment of the Swedish market and major industrial corporations become their own insurers via captive companies, small policyholders would seem to be all that remains for the sales organizations of traditional insurance companies. On their own, small policies will become too costly to sell on a person-to-person basis. Direct writers – telemarketing, direct mail or videotex – and group policies may well become the norm.

More competition, but also more countervailing forces in the Netherlands

The non-life insurance industry has been fairly stable until relatively recently. In the Netherlands, deregulation and technical progress have changed that. With its late start in terms of deregulation, the Swedish market remains less dynamic.

The insurance business, like many other service-producing industries, is based on core skills deployed in a few areas. Such skills can, above all, be utilized to increase cost-effectiveness and to a lesser extent, to further development of products. Cost-effectiveness is influenced by more efficient sales and claims adjustment procedures. Prices can be influenced by giving better service to insurance intermediaries and customers. Better service may indirectly raise prices by 5-10 per cent, but without it new products to which the market can assign higher prices are hard to develop.

Changes in the structure of the Dutch insurance industry have been hampered by the dominant role of independent intermediaries. Major reductions in sales costs cannot be achieved so long as the typical Dutch policy holder wants to sit at his kitchen table and buy insurance. There is probably a greater openness to new sales mechanisms in Sweden: in the longer term, the Swedish insurance market may end up being the more dynamic of the two.

On the whole, Nationale-Nederlanden is in a favourable position in terms of its potential to generate improved productivity by means of both cost-effectiveness and innovation. The Dutch market is characterized by competitive pressure and dynamism. Skandia's prerequisites are somewhat less favourable, mainly because of less liberalization. Notably, Sweden does not really offer an equivalent climate in terms of the availability of skilled personnel and favourable financial conditions.

NATIONALE-NEDERLANDEN

Nationale-Nederlanden began business 140 years ago. The company has traded under its present name since a 1963 merger between the Nationale-Levensverzekering-Bank of Rotterdam and the Netherlands est. 1845 of The Hague. During the past decade, Nationale-Nederlanden has grown rapidly as a result of various acquisitions. The group now includes nine different Dutch-based companies. This study focuses on Nationale-Nederlanden General Insurance Company, the largest company in the group outside of its life insurance operations.[8]

About 50 per cent of Nationale-Nederlanden sales come from domestic markets. The group aims for roughly equal sales volumes in three sectors: domestic markets, the United States and the rest of the world. Tight cost controls and high productivity plus well-trained and motivated personnel also figure among the company's priorities.

Cost-effectiveness

Nationale-Nederlanden describes its operating expenses as low. The company's premiums are also among the lowest in Europe.[9] In the Netherlands, however, they are 5–10 per cent above domestic market averages. Competitors set their premiums on the basis of Nationale-Nederlanden's price list.[10] In exchange for higher prices, Nationale-Neder-

	Per cent
Underwriting*	29
Claims administration**	15
Fixed expenses	2
Commissions	54
Total	100

*Risk evaluation, issuance and renewal of poilcies.
**Claims administration does not include claims incurred.

Operating expenses and claims incurred in relation to premiums are as follows:

	Per cent
Operating expenses, including commissions	35.4
Claims incurred	56.5
Total	91.9

Table 4.5 Operating expenses of Nationale-Nederlanden, 1989.

landen pays reasonable terms for claims handling, generates higher sales expenses and assumes higher costs in training both its own sales force and independent insurance intermediaries.

Independent intermediaries account for about 80 per cent of premium income. As Table 4.5 indicates, commissions to intermediaries comprise more than half of operating expenses at Nationale–Nederlanden. Competition in the non-life market mainly takes place between different forms of distribution channels, including direct writers.

The above data on expenses are summarized in Figure 4.7. These figures are for 1989, a favourable year for insurers. In 1988, claims incurred stood at 60–63 percent of premiums.

In order to lower sales expenses, Nationale-Nederlanden has merged with NMB Postbank, which will operate as a direct writer. Nationale Nederlanden General will continue as before, but on the NMB Postbank side of the arrangement, the disappearance of commissions will result in less costly levels of service and support on relatively simple policies such as fire and homeowners' insurance. Nevertheless, the merger has provoked protests from independent insurance intermediaries, a few of whom have justified blacklisting Nationale-Nederlanden with the claim that the company has betrayed them.

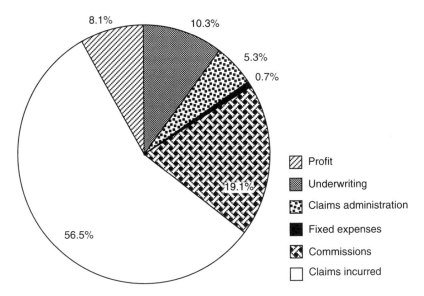

Figure 4.7 Profit and costs: Dutch insurance industry, 1989.

Source: Nationale-Nederlanden.

Innovation

Nationale-Nederlanden regards its insurance intermediaries as customers and works to provide them with such good service that they choose to sell Nationale-Nederlanden's insurance policies instead of those of its competitors. Within a 1,700-strong work-force, Nationale-Nederlanden General Insurance's 200 sales managers provide back-up for insurance intermediaries. Each sales manager is in contact with some 80 intermediaries. By offering free training and better service, Nationale-Nederlanden can maintain a level of premiums higher than elsewhere in the industry.

Nationale-Nederlanden's strategy assigns potential policyholders to a premium category after intensive examination. If this works smoothly, the company can be more reasonable when it incurs a claim. Nearly 10 per cent of Nationale-Nederlanden General Insurance employees work in the technical department with responsibility for investigating claims. This relatively high percentage of labour cost enables the company to process claims quickly.

Advanced actuarial skills are required to differentiate premiums, and Nationale-Nederlanden certainly gathers more information about its customers than Skandia. This information can also be put to use for future premium-setting. A few years ago, the Dutch insurance regulatory agency attempted to control pricing in the name of narrowing differentials between different companies' premiums – regulatory practice that has been discontinued in the face of ever closer European union.

Controlling productivity

Productivity seems to be discussed at all levels of Nationale-Nederlanden. Operating expenses as a percentage of premiums earned are the dominant yardstick for measuring internal efficiency (see Table 4.6). This yardstick is the basis for comparisons between departments and types of insurance and, not least, for comparisons over time. Return on financial assets is not calculated in the same way in Sweden.

Quarterly financial statements for the units that make up Nationale-Nederlanden include written comments on strengths, weaknesses, threats and opportunities, plus forecasts for a period three years hence. The group has no overall profitability target. Instead, each unit in the company possesses an individual target, which is set after consideration of that unit's prerequisites. If a unit has low productivity, company headquarters attempts to pinpoint an explanation by requesting supplementary figures

	1989	1989	1987	1986	1985
Operating expenses	35.4	37.4	38.2	38.3	38.2
Operating expenses, excluding commissions[a]	16.3	17.9	19.0	18.8	18.9
Claims costs	56.5	60.5	63.6	63.3	63.0
Technical earnings[b]	6.3	0.5	−3.8	−3.5	−1.6
Return on investment[c]	7.0	7.5	7.6	8.1	8.3
Gross earnings	13.1	6.0	2.7	3.4	6.3
Pre-tax profit	13.6	8.4	4.6	5.4	8.2

Table 4.6 Profitability, Nationale-Nederlanden General Insurance. Percentage of premiums earned.

[a]Before transfer of claims processing reserve.
[b]Including change in premium reserve.
[c]Does not include change in value of assess, but only interest income and dividends.

on numbers of policies sold, numbers of sales conversations per week, sales-force strength, salaries, commissions and fixed costs.

The lead times between sales conversations and the post-mark date on a mailed policy is another valuable yardstick. Victoria-Vesta, a company within the Nationale-Nederlanden group, has adopted far-reaching productivity controls, based, in part, on number of sales conversations per day, per employee and on sales volume per salesperson. A few years ago the company even attempted to measure all use of time on its premises. Employees were asked to report on how they used their time. The practice was dropped when the company discovered that it had no use for such figures.

Claims costs as a percentage of premiums earned are another common internal yardstick. Because claims costs are hard to influence in the short term, this yardstick is used mostly by executives more interested in risk management strategy. Notably, however, this yardstick gives a good indication of how efficiently claims are adjusted and processed.

The bosses of Nationale-Nederlanden General Insurance's five biggest divisions are evaluated with figures that take operating expenses as a percentage of sales. This yardstick is not unproblematical: there are differing opinions within the group as to its validity. Divisional executives maintain that only 5-10 per cent of operating expenses can be influenced. The rest, they say, are more or less fixed: computer costs and salaries, for example. At group headquarters the view is different: payments for central services, it is said, are influenced by how the divisional heads organize their operations.

Productivity in the insurance business is also influenced by whether companies seek out profitable segments of the market. Nationale-Nederlanden analyses the household market with the aid of indices produced by market research company A.C. Nielsen. The indices classify customers from A to D. At the top of this ranking are households with the highest standard of living; D represents those existing at or below the poverty line. In the A category, life insurance policies predominate. Nationale-Nederlanden General Insurance concentrates mainly on the A and B categories, where non-life insurance policies account for most business. Other companies in the group focus on other segments: Nationale-Nederlanden Life tackles A and B categories, with Victoria-Vesta concentrating on C and D.

Internal sources of motivation

Organization and technology
Nationale-Nederlanden has the ambition of leading its competitors in information technology use. Indeed, the Dutch company is a few years ahead of Skandia in this respect. Victoria-Vesta is probably even further ahead. This company gave personal computers to its tied intermediaries as administrative and sales aids. Nationale-Nederlanden General Insurance chose to wait for an industry-wide solution in this area, so as not to hand any indirect advantages to its competitors. Information technology fulfils an essential function in premium setting. Competitors employ similar procedures, but because of its size Nationale-Nederlanden can perform better analyses based on more extensive data.

Despite its size, Nationale-Nederlanden has only five or six levels within its organizational hierarchy. Group management insists that a further level could be removed. Elsewhere, Nationale-Nederlanden's product-based organizational structure poses problems for intermediaries who would prefer to offer a broad range of insurance policies with only one or a few contact persons at Nationale-Nederlanden.

Communication of goals and expectations

Nationale–Nederlanden's independent intermediaries are sophisticated and demanding purchasers. They know exactly what the competition is offering and can easily switch companies when they find the terms unfavourable. Because of this intensive and exacting contact with its sales channel, Nationale-Nederlanden is subjected to constant pressure to come up with better solutions than its competitors. This pressure does not result in pure price competition. One explanation for this may be that all insurance companies offer approximately the same commission rates based on premiums.[11]

The boards of the various companies in the group draw up three year plans which contain a discussion of strengths and weaknesses, threats and opportunities. The plans are distributed to managers at lower levels. Employees then receive a one-year plan based on the three-year plan. Group management hopes to go further by formulating individual goals based on quarterly personal development discussions. At present such sessions only take place once or twice each year.

The United States is the world's toughest insurance market. Given its U.S. operations, management at Nationale-Nederlanden is notably well-informed on important industry trends. In the crucial area of distribution costs, for example, company officials are well-placed to learn from developments in the United States, where new direct distribution strategies have captured large portions of the market.

Trade unions are generally weak in the Netherlands; Nationale-Nederlanden has an employee council that combines representatives of both union and non-union employees. According to law, employee representatives must be informed of major issues. Managers are recruited entirely on an internal basis. The boards of the various companies are also largely composed of managers from other group companies. Nationale-Nederlanden boardrooms thus contain no managers with experience of other forms of business.

Human Resource Management

Nationale-Nederlanden is proud of its training programme. Employees receive an average of 3.5 days of training each year. Specialized training programmes exist for different groups of employees. When a new computer system or a new insurance product is introduced, the company arranges special training for all personnel concerned. After giving personal computers and electronic mail capability to a group of independent intermediaries, the company arranged a free five-day training programme. Nationale Nederlanden also has a one-year programme design-ed to groom future managers. The programme includes courses and shorter periods of work in different departments.

Salaries at Nationale-Nederlanden are about 10 per cent above the industry average, with regional variations. In recent years, salaries have increased by four to six per cent annually, resulting in higher real earn-ings against a background of inflation constant at less than 1 per cent. In the 1970s, inflation index-linking of salaries provoked a price-wage spi-ral. During the 1980s, salaries in the insurance industry were influenced by agreements between trade unions, employers and the government.

Except for top management, salaries range from £11,000 to £54,000 per year (1990). The lowest salary is based on £750 per month for 14 months plus £450 in profit-sharing, which is distributed on the basis of age and basic salary.

Excluding illness and retirement, personnel turnover at Nationale-Nederlanden runs to four to five per cent annually; average periods of employment are thus relatively long. This is especially true of the inter-nally-recruited management class. The company has a slogan: 'No Secrets – No Surprises'. Management tries to live up to the promise. There are fairly extensive contacts between different parts of the group in the form of joint meetings of the companies' boards. All executives of the European-based companies meet once a year, as do all actuaries.

SKANDIA

Like Nationale-Nederlanden, Skandia boasts a long history. Today's com-pany is the product of numerous mergers. Sweden's most profitable insur-ance company for the five years 1984–1989 scored average net earnings compared with premium volume of 14.0 per cent. Trygg-Hansa, Skandia's closest competitor, averaged 8.0 per cent.

Cost-effectiveness

In the past decade, Skandia has started to broaden its operations across Scandinavia. Although formally two separate companies, Skandia bases its non-life and life insurance operations within the same organization. Overhead costs are divided between the two operations by means of a standard rule. As Table 4.7 indicates, Skandia managed to lower its oper-ating expenses substantially during in the run-up to 1988. In addition, it enjoyed a remarkable return on financial assets, including capital gains. By comparison with Nationale-Nederlanden, however, during the same period, claim expenses ran at a much higher level, and with more variability.

	1989	1988	1987	1986	1985	1984
Operating expenses	25.8	24.3	26.1	27.3	32.5	31.4
Claims costs	90.5	89.0	80.0	77.0	100.0	90.8
Technical earnings	−16.3	−13.3	−6.1	−4.3	−32.5	−22.2
Return on investment	37.0	36.8	41.5	35.5	−24.0	24.0
Gross earnings	20.4	20.8	34.9	30.5	−8.6	1.4
Pre-tax profit	6.9	5.2	3.0	2.2	2.2	1.6

Table 4.7 **Profitability of Skandia's non-life insurance business, 1984–89. Percentage of premiums earned.**

Source: Enskilda försäkringsbolag (Individual Insurance Companies), Swedish Private Insurance Supervisory Service.

High return on financial assets have made it possible for Skandia and other Swedish insurance companies to hold down premiums. By 1989, automobile liability insurance cost half as much in real terms as it had in 1977 (see Figure 4.8).

Innovation

Insurance companies lack powerful incentives to introduce new services. Innovations are easily copied by competitors. Some new products are introduced, however, and in this respect, the Swedish insurers have been at least as innovative as their Dutch colleagues. Examples worth mentioning are group policies and motor insurance policies sold through car dealerships. Swedish insurance companies were also early entrants into the market for packages such as homeowners' insurance policies that cover fire, theft, travel expenses and legal costs. Combined policies benefit customers with lower premiums and simpler processing.

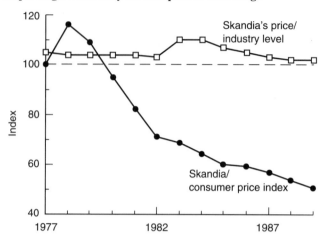

Figure 4.8

Skandia early on noticed changes in corporate insurance and established Sinser, a management company for 'captives' and one of the European leaders in its field. In the Netherlands, large industrial insurance policies are generally arranged through insurance exchanges, ruling out development of a similar captive management strategy.

Insurance companies compete in terms of the time it takes to arrange policies for customers. Skandia's fastest processing time ranges between three days and a week. The slowest occurs with insurance on major risks, where a policy may take three months to arrange. According to statistics maintained by the Swedish Private Insurance Supervisory Service, Skandia has the fewest customer complaints. The company also promises to inspect industry damage covered by its policies within three hours. It is the only company in Sweden to make such a guarantee.

Like Nationale-Nederlanden, Skandia has worked actively to find better criteria for determining premium charges. The company tries to determine the causes of damage and to apply this knowledge to future pricing. Premiums for aircraft insurance policies, for example, are typically based on the number of flying hours. Skandia discovered that the number of take-offs and landings functioned as a better criterion. Elsewhere, while Skandia takes into account a building's number of water taps when it sets premiums for homeowners' insurance, many companies are content merely to note whether or not the property has a water supply.

Productivity controls

Skandia monitors productivity by analyzing operating expenses and claims costs. All divisions report these figures. Regional organization allows productivity comparisons. Some jobs are assigned to the regions once competing centres have presented bids.

Other yardsticks are quality-based. The various divisions study each other's claims adjustment procedures. In an exercise called closed file review, four highly-skilled claims adjusters go through a thousand claims and discuss their handling with individuals who have been responsible for the actual cases. Experts give cautious estimates of viable compensation levels.

A few years ago, Skandia started a project to develop new yardsticks of productivity. Among other things, it was suggested that the company should measure the number of times that terminals were logged on and the number of transactions per terminal, but a pilot study demonstrated little use for such figures.

Internal factors

Organization and technology
In the 1960s, Skandia and other Swedish insurance companies were among early users of information technology. Skandia built separate data systems for premium calculations on different products. These systems had two limitations. First, it was difficult to use them for follow-up of actual outcomes. Second, it was not possible to combine data on one customer, for example, from several systems. These days, data from the product systems is fed into the accounting system, but very little comes back in the form of usable information such as earnings calculated for certain customers, insurance categories or distribution channels.

Skandia carries out systems development almost entirely under its own auspices. In certain cases, it has moved slowly, with some systems costing much more than would similar products bought in the open market. Skandia has decided to continue using mainframe computers and recently made a major investment in terminals. The company is studying the possibility of outfitting field sales people with portable personal computers – a technological leap that probably will be delayed until recently purchased equipment is first written off. Some members of the field sales-force appear somewhat reluctant to work with computers. Even with their own terminals at the district offices, some hand over their day's work to office staff for premium calculations and letter typing. Two factors prevent Skandia from realizing the full potential of information technology: the traditional division of labour between field salesmen and support staff; and lack of intensive training with new systems.

One successful foray into the realm of information technology has been on-line contact with Sweden's national motor vehicle registration system. Motor liability insurance matters are now handled much more effectively. In another efficiency-raising system known as *Skandia-konto*, the company reaches an agreement with the customer to automatically withdraw premium payments from the customer's bank account on the due date or once a month. In information systems for corporate management, Skandia is ahead of the competition. The system takes information from the various product systems and the accounting system, offering data on every customer, product, insurance category and claim.

Communication of goals and expectations
Until very recently Skandia was the only Swedish insurance company operating as a joint stock company. It was the first Swedish insurance company to secure a stock exchange listing, and its articles of association state that no shareholder may vote with more than 30 shares at meetings. Unlike many other listed companies, the company therefore lacks a dominant stockholder. Yet Skandia remains highly profit-oriented. Although the company has the express ambition of being an industry leader, this overall goal is not broken down into objectives for lower level employees.

In 1989 an internal study indicated that employees wanted more information from their superiors. Middle managers themselves appeared not to have been given sufficient information about the repeated reorganizations that had taken place since 1983. In addition, there is a tendency among the company's middle managers to concentrate on internal efficiency at the cost of external concerns or any vision of the manner in which the company's parts form a whole. The inherent risk is that managers do not sufficiently inform and motivate their personnel.

Skandia carefully monitors its competitors' operations, in part by analysis of statistics compiled by the Swedish Private Insurance Supervisory Service. There seems to be less emphasis on monitoring new, small insurance companies. Through its subsidiary company Skandia International, the company obtains information on product development abroad. A number of the company's corporate customers also operate internationally, making international competition a reality for Skandia.

Human Resource Management

Salaries are set individually on the basis of schedules agreed with employee unions. Skandia's salaries are below the industry average, according to the union. Management thinks of them as about average. During most of the 1980s, Stockholm's overheated labour market made it difficult to recruit new personnel. Salary differentials are mainly attributable to age differences. The gap between top and the bottom among the key group of insurance underwriting specialists is only 25 per cent. In the field organization, pay is based 100 per cent on commissions. Otherwise, only top management has any element of a bonus system in its compensation package.

Skandia's profit-sharing system covers all employees. But the rules for calculating amounts to be set aside for profit-sharing are so complicated that no one seems to understand them. Consequently, motivational impetus is somewhat blunted. There are also benefits in the form of loans on favourable terms and the use of summer cottages. Notably, Skandia paid its employees child allowances before the Swedish government introduced universal public child allowances several decades ago.

CONCLUSIONS

Productivity in both of the insurance companies studied here is affected by efficiency-raising measures on the cost side. On the revenue side, premiums need to be set correctly, product ranges must be adapted and the right kind of customer has to be selected. Figure 4.9 provides an overview of differences in cost structure at Nationale-Nederlanden and Skandia. Disbursements on claims incurred, commissions and operating expenses are shown in relation to premiums earned. According to this method of calculation, Skandia has the lower share of operating expenses. In absolute terms, it remains difficult to say which company has the lower operating expenses, because we cannot compare two identical ranges of insurances.

Skandia's low share of operating expenses is attributable to a concentrated sales organization and certain economies of scale in terms of sales support. Skandia also has a large proportion of direct writers. On the whole, Swedes are more inclined to buy via direct writers. It is interesting to note that this transformation appears not to have been imposed so much as taken shape in response to customers' wishes. The Dutch, by contrast, traditionally buy their insurance from visiting representatives.

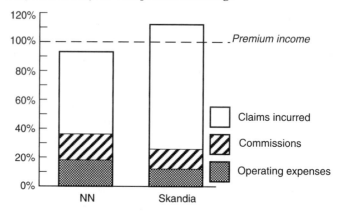

Figure 4.9 Cost structure differences at Nationale-Nederlanden and Skandia.
Sources: Nationale-Nederlanden and Skandia.

In Sweden, transactions are eased by use of national identification numbers consisting of birth date plus personal code. In addition, insurance companies are on-line with the national motor vehicle registry. Thus, automotive insurance is easily arranged by telephone. The prevalence of group policies sold to trade union members, for example, offers a third explanation for lower Swedish operating costs.

The share of commissions is also lower at Skandia. While Skandia sells through its own channels, Nationale-Nederlanden must pay fairly high commissions to independent insurance intermediaries. Claims incurred comprise the other major element of cost structure. Nationale-Nederlanden has a far lower share of expenses for claims incurred. Nationale-Nederlanden simply may be better than Skandia at estimating risks. Its detailed calculation system tends to support such a conclusion, but the effects of risk assessment capability on claim payments remains difficult to judge with certainty.

Although Nationale-Nederlanden and Skandia are similar-sized companies that sell similar product ranges, accurate comparisons of productivity remain difficult. Nationale-Nederlanden works in a less protected market, but is the more profitable company. Nationale-Nederlanden appears to benefit from a higher professional skills level, a greater degree of internationalization and a lead in development work.

Both companies work under roughly similar institutional conditions. Ties to independent intermediaries affects Nationale-Nederlanden's freedom of action. In terms of organization and technology, two facts are worth noting. First, it is Nationale-Nederlanden's clear ambition to take advantage of the latest in information technology. Besides the advantages that accrue in terms of sales work, such aims have probably contributed favourably to the company's cost-effectiveness. Second, Nationale-Nederlanden's relatively flat organizational pyramid undoubtedly yields a number of advantages. However, the company's product-based structural cast remains problematic. In overall terms, however, it is hard to argue that another organizational set-up would perform better.

Skandia has good, if weaker, organizational mechanisms. Its organizational pyramid is taller, courtesy of at least two more hierarchical levels than Nationale-Nederlanden. The company's public listing probably explains why Skandia has beaten its domestic competitors in the race to improve cost-effectiveness.

One obvious advantage possessed by Nationale-Nederlanden lies in the area of communication of goals and expectations. Top management actually controls operations, and employees know that their performance is noticed. Skandia's new organizational forms have not strengthened management roles. On the contrary, they have perhaps helped to blur the outlines of management responsibility.

Turning to human resource management, Nationale-Nederlanden's mix of pay and reward encourages innovation and cost-effectiveness. Skandia is good at 'clan mechanisms', systems that help generate a sense of solidarity.[12] On the other hand, pay is very little affected by employee performance.

Nationale-Nederlanden appears to have achieved steady improvements in productivity through a combination of market pressure and internal mechanisms. Lack of regulation and the existence of independent insurance intermediaries clearly have forced the pace at Nationale-Nederlanden, but such pressures are counterbalanced by the availability of skilled personnel and the Netherlands' deeply rooted insurance industry traditions. Among the internal mechanisms underlying the Dutch company's success are an emphasis on productivity management, high professional skills levels and a commitment to leading in the use of information technology.

[1] Less premiums paid for reinsurance.
[2] Most of this capital however, is invested by life insurance companies.
[3] Goodman (1990).
[4] In addition, the level of claims incurred for injuries varies between countries.
[5] In Sweden, a law went into effect in the summer of 1991 allowing certain types of mergers between banks and insurance companies.

[6]For life insurance, a cartel remained in existence until the late 1980s.

[7]*The Economist* February 24, 1990.

[8]Nationale-Nederlanden Life Insurance, Victoria-Vesta and Vola.

[9]The Netherlands and Britain have the lowest prices in the EC.

Source: *The Trauma of the Single Market*, EC Commission, 1988.

[10]In some cases, competitors have even copied typographical errors from Nationale-Nederlanden's insurance policies.

[11]Insurance companies have reached agreement on a recommended list of commissions.

[12]Skandia's personnel magazine used to be very comprehensive and won a competition among Swedish companies some years ago. Skandia also has many social activities like retiree and sports clubs.

5 NIPPONDENSO AND LUXOR

In the automotive industry, pressures to raise productivity increasingly are manifested at the supplier stage. Automotive manufacturers buy a growing proportion of components from outside sources, placing pressure on suppliers to manufacture cost-effectively and to assume responsibility for a larger share of technological development. These more onerous demands and new roles have prompted restructuring among automotive component manufacturers.

Originally part of Toyota Motor Company, Nippondenso has a reputation as the world's most productive supplier of components to the automotive industry. In the late 1940s, Toyota decided to spin off its cooler and electrical component departments into a separate company. Twelve years later, Nippondenso received the Deming Prize, Japan's most prestigious industrial quality award. By the late 1980s Nippondenso had received several other prizes for quality and productivity. The company's main customer is Toyota, but the company also supplies Japan's other automotive manufacturers – with the sole exception of Nissan.

Of great importance to Nippondenso's development was its technical alliance with the German automotive component company Robert Bosch, which began in 1953. Under this agreement, Nippondenso received product licensing rights. With this commercial alliance as a foundation, Nippondenso grew rapidly. The company learned from Bosch, improved its own products and gradually began to vie with its German partner firm in what could be described as friendly competition. Today Bosch is still the larger company, but Nippondenso has become the world's biggest supplier of vehicle components.

Nippondenso's initial goal was to learn how to be as good as its competitors. Now its ambition is to become a global corporation. Nippondenso's international expansion is based partly on commercial alliances. Cost superiority over its competitors is based primarily on economies of scale within Nippondenso's production system. The company also boasts an impressive research and development programme. The company can be regarded as a good example of the current trend toward a larger role for suppliers of entire automotive systems, rather than individual components.

The Swedish company Luxor Electronics employs 400 and manufactures 1.5 million automotive loudspeakers each year. About 90 per cent of its sales go to the car industry, with Volvo and Saab as its largest customers.

AUTOMOTIVE COMPONENT SUPPLIERS –
A MAJOR INDUSTRY OVERSHADOWED BY
VEHICLE MANUFACTURERS

A modern automobile contain tens of thousands of parts. Development and production involve a complex process of collaboration between numerous companies. The final vehicle manufacturer takes primary responsibility for development work and the assembly process. American manufacturers, for example, produce about half of their components in-house and buy about the same proportion from component suppliers. Notably, Japanese car companies purchase as much as 70-80 per cent of their components. The proportion of outside purchases made by Saab and Volvo lies somewhere between the equivalent levels in the United States and Japan.

There are different types of component suppliers. Some simply manufacture components using blueprints, materials and even financing provided by the customer. Others develop and market standard ranges of components. A third type, of which Nippondenso is an example, develops proprietary components that satisfy the specific requirements of automotive manufacturers. Nippondenso also supplies component systems. An automatic air conditioner, for example, typically contains such components as a computer, compressor, condenser, evaporator, receiver, exterior air sensor, interior air sensor and solar sensor. Delivery of this kind of system is expected to grow in importance.

The vehicle component industry in Japan

There are nine car manufacturers in Japan (see Table 5.1). These companies manufacture about 9 million cars a year, about a quarter of total world production. Domestically, Japan's auto manufacturers employ 200,000 people, with some 550,000 additional employees retained by component suppliers. An estimated 500,000 more work within industries that produce materials for these automotive companies and their component suppliers.

	Production	*Sales in Japan*	*Exports*
Toyota	33.7	40.0	30.0
Nissan	21.8	22.6	20.4
Mitsubushi	7.8	5.3	9.3
Mazda	10.7	6.7	14.5
Isuzu	2.1	1.0	3.3
Honda	12.8	10.4	15.5
Suzuki	4.8	3.2	5.9
Fuji (Subaru)	3.4	3.1	3.2
Daihatsu	2.9	3.6	1.8
Other		4.1 (Imports)	

Table 5.1 The Japanese automobile industry, 1989. Percentages of overall Japanese production, sales in Japan and exports of cars.

Source: Nippondenso.

Only 0.5 per cent of the components used by Japanese auto manufacturers are imported: clearly, Japanese component manufacturers have a very large domestic market. At the same time, these auto makers purchase a larger proportion of their components from outside companies than either their American or Swedish counterparts. Japanese car companies also make their purchases from a relatively small number of suppliers. Table 5.2 below summarizes some important differences between the relationship of the auto industry and its component suppliers in Japan and the United States.

	Japan	*USA*
Ratio of parts produced in-house by auto makers	Low (30%)	High (50%)
Structure of auto parts industry	Pyramid style	Nonpyramid style In-house made ratio of auto parts makers is high
Number of component assemblers	200–300	3,500 (GM)
Contract for supply	Long term and stable Basically 4-year contract	Open tender system
Relationship with auto makers	Co-operative	Confrontational

Table 5.2 The auto industry and component supplies in Japan and the United States.

Source: Nippondenso.

The vehicle component industry in Sweden

Within the Swedish car market, the vehicle component industry is less important in relative terms. Volvo and Saab, the two Swedish-based auto manufacturers, buy only one-third of their components domestically. According to Volvo and Saab, Sweden simply lacks the kind of companies that produce the necessary components. A glance at the figures for the component industry confirms the assertion: of the 80 largest European component suppliers, only one, SKF, has its headquarters in Sweden (see Chapter 9).

After General Motors bought a 50 per cent stake in Saab Automobile from the Saab-Scania Group and assumed management responsibility for the car company in 1989, Saab Automobile aimed for a sharp reduction in purchasing costs by subjecting component suppliers to international competition. In the case of a new model designed to replace its aging Saab 900 series, the company has drawn up tender lists for component procurement. For each component, a schedule selects around ten conceivable suppliers, mostly multinational companies which are rated in terms of pricing, quality and delivery performance. Saab Automobile also asks employees from its own production department to present their views of the potential suppliers' ability to deliver on a just-in-time basis. According to Saab Automobile's purchasing manager, the company that guarantees the biggest long-term price reduction usually gets the order: 'Prices used to be raised automatically by 3-4 per cent (yearly). Now they must be lowered by 4-6 per cent.' [1]

Industry trends

There are probably few industries where customers have greater negotiating power than in the automotive component industry. Vehicle manufacturers have become fewer and larger, while the component supply business is still dominated by small firms.[2] It is not unusual for an automotive company to be a supplier's principal customer and to specify in detail the design of its products, how and when component shipments are to be delivered, and perhaps even the price of components.

During the past decade, manufacturing strategies at automotive companies have been transformed – with important repercussions for component suppliers. Vehicle manufacturers increasingly require suppliers to assume responsibility for their own development work. A larger proportion of components are purchased in the form of systems that can be directly installed during vehicle assembly. In a third change, automotive companies now tend to spread their manufacturing operations over a number of countries. In response, a number of component suppliers have started to internationalize their operations in similar fashion.

Once oriented toward domestic markets, automotive component suppliers have become more international in outlook. Many have become genuinely global companies which operate internationally, and often aim at being 'multi-domestic' by attempting to gain local acceptance in specific markets by behaving like a domestic company. Such international groups operate independently of fluctuations in the relative competitiveness of individual nations.

The new production strategies of automotive groups mean that their manufacturing operations increasingly assume the form of final assembly of components and component systems. Production has become more flexible in an attempt to respond to customer specifications. These days, few cars in a model series are exactly alike; production can quickly be adapted to shifting demands. Functions such as inventory maintenance and quality assurance are increasingly delegated to suppliers. Furthermore, vehicle manufacturers assign higher priority to the flow orientation of production, which in turn affects their purchasing strategies and the requirements they impose on suppliers.

The ability to manufacture at low cost is still of great strategic importance to the competitiveness of component suppliers, but some companies enjoy other advantages that offset the low production costs of their competitors. Among the demands that the automotive industry is imposing on its component suppliers are:

- Increased development efforts
- Delivery of systems rather than components
- Quality assurance
- High reliability of deliveries and short delivery times
- Computer skills
- Business ties with other automotive manufacturers, which raise the supplier company's level of skills, making it less financially vulnerable to market fluctuations
- Management skills and administrative procedures on a par with those of the customer company

The automotive component industry used to be divided between primary and secondary suppliers. A battle is underway in the automotive industry for positions as system suppliers. A number of primary suppliers have moved up to this level. Others have found a place in the hierarchy as secondary or tertiary suppliers (see Figure 5.1). Generally speaking, secondary suppliers have little negotiating power vis-a-vis their customers. Competition is stiff: at this level it is common for several suppliers to provide the same component. Pricing becomes vital as a means of competition. Thus Swedish automotive manufacturers and systems suppliers are purchasing more and more components from abroad.

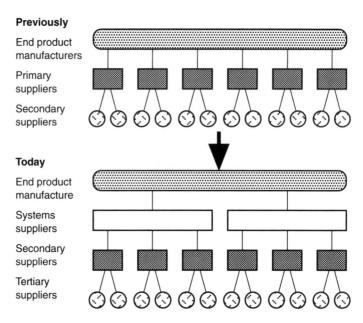

Figure 5.1 The changing structure of relationships between suppliers and auto industry manufacturers.

NIPPONDENSO

In terms of size, Nippondenso alone is nearly comparable with Volvo, one of Sweden's biggest industrial groups. The company's largest stockholders are Toyota Motor (23 per cent), Toyoda Automatic Loom Works (8 per cent), Robert Bosch (6 per cent) and Tokai Bank and Mitsui Taiyo Bank with 5 per cent apiece.

Rank	Company	Country of Head-quarters	Sales of (1) Automotive Components	(2) Total Sales	Ratio (1)/(2) (percent)	Major Products
1	Nippon-denso	Japan	9,000	9,288	97	Air conditioners, EFI-systems, starters alternators
2	Robert Bosch	West Germany	8,210	15,758	52	EFI systems, ABS starters, alternators
3	Aisin Seiki	Japan	4,324	4,600	94	Transmissions, clutches, power steering systems
4	Dana	USA	3,853	4,940	78	Chasis components, piston rings, clutches
5	Allied-Signal	USA	3,808	11,900	32	Seat belts, brakes, filters, spark plugs, clutches
6	TRW	USA	3,069	6,982	44	Air bags, seat belts, stearing gears, valves
7	Magneti-Marelli	Italy	2,900	2,900	100	Starters, alternators, radiators, air condi-tioners
8	Valeo	France	2,766	2,766	100	Starters, alternators, air conditioners, radiators
9	Lucas	UK	2,161	3,513	62	Starters, alternators, meters, brakes
10	Rockwell	USA	2,154	11,946	18	Brakes, steering components, sun-roof systems

Table 5.3 Auto component suppliers: the top ten world-wide.

Source: Annual reports and Nippondenso.

More than 90 per cent of Nippondenso's sales consists of automotive components: air conditioning equipment, controls, interior fittings, engine components and fuel injection systems. In 11 of its product areas, Nippondenso is the largest manufacturer in the world. The company's aims to expand this number to 15 by 1995.

Organizational structure and technology

Purchasing operations

Nippondenso has relationships with about 200 raw materials suppliers and 500 component suppliers. It has direct computer links with 100 of these companies. During the past decade, the requirements that Nippondenso imposes on its suppliers have changed. Previously, the company looked for special equipment, low costs and flexibility. Today, Nippondenso searches for companies with particular technologies, advanced and sophisticated equipment, new product development potential and, not least of all, good management. A demonstrated ability to keep abreast of technological developments forms the most important criterion.

Research and development

Nippondenso believes that its research and development programme is one of the most important factors in accounting for the company's success. Since 1986, research and development expenditures have run to at least 6.5 per cent of net sales. Out of a total 40,200 employees, 6,700 – or one sixth – are engineers.[3] Nippondenso's research and development strategy is as follows:

1. Basic and applied research

Nippondenso's research laboratories work with a range of diverse technologies, including artificial intelligence, superconductors, bioelectronics and advanced materials. Among other things the company develops theories for control of components and optoelectronics.

2. Emphasis on systems

Nippondenso studies individual component quality, but the company also tests the systems and vehicles of which individual components are a part. Thus the company has its own road course, a skid-testing track, a crash-testing unit and a weather simulation laboratory. To the casual observer, the company looks more like a car manufacturer than a mere systems supplier. Because Nippondenso tests entire systems, the company provides its customers with data that can shorten manufacturing time at a later stage. Occasionally, test results lead Nippondenso to propose alternative solutions to the customer, which may result in improvements in design and performance.

3. Joint development with the customer

Nippondenso builds close ties with vehicle manufacturers during the planning of new models. In consultation with the customer, the company performs initial tests before making modifications or additions, performing further development work and testing yet again before systems are made ready for delivery.

4. Concurrent engineering
Personnel from Nippondenso's production department participate in new product development from the outset. In this way, the development department benefits from input that enables products to be designed in ways that ease manufacture. The production department can begin to plan the manufacturing process before the new component is developed. Figure 5.2 shows the principle of overlapping developmental stages.

5. Market-adapted development work
Depending on which part of its life cycle a product has reached, Nippondenso thinks in terms of three types of product development: minor changes in existing products; entirely new products; and major changes in existing products. The latter category may include: weight reduction, new materials or increased efficiency. In a working method known as *jikigata-ken*, product and process are developed by different teams working in parallel.

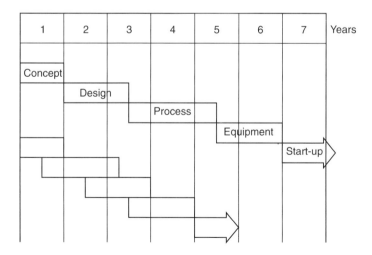

Figure 5.2 Nippondenso's principle of overlapping development.
Source: Nippondenso.

Production

Manufacturing is a central function at Nippondenso: the company has ten production plants in Japan and 21 in other countries. Of Nippondenso's employees, 46-47 per cent are blue collar, a low percentage that is gradually declining in the face of an ever more automated production apparatus. Most of the company's Japanese plants are located close to one another in an area just south of Nagoya. Instead of expanding its existing factories, Nippondenso has generally opted to build new units, avoiding bureaucratization and operational overload. Each plant specializes in particular types of production.

• *Continuous development of production systems*   Nippondenso's production system has changed over the years (see Figure 5.3). During the 1950s and 1960s, the company used imported technologies. Before the late 1960s, Nippondenso had caught up with technological developments in other countries. The company then focused on improving its production lines. It began to introduce Flexible Manufacturing Systems (FMS)[4] that involved the mass production of components. During the 1970s, Nippondenso conducted its own technology development work and

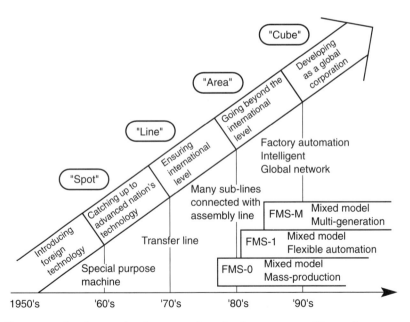

Figure 5.3 Continuous development of production systems at Nippondenso.
Source: Nippondenso.

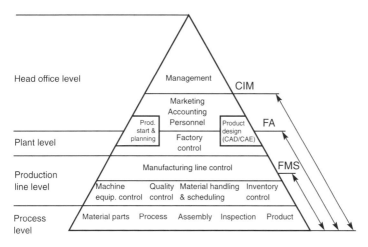

Figure 5.4 Evolutionary methods of production organization.

Source: Nippondenso.

increasingly automated its lines. Toward the end of the 1980s, the company began to integrate entire plants into Factory Automation (FA) systems. During the 1990s, Nippondenso adopted the advanced Computer Integrated Manufacturing (CIM) systems through which the whole company is now integrated. Figure 5.4 shows how Nippondenso describes its gradual evolution of methods for organizing production.

Nippondenso originally operated one line for each of its cooler models. Now production is built up around a single flexible automated line based on self-adjusting robots. Thus it is now possible to manufacture more than one model in the same production line. The robots have been developed by Nippondenso itself. After introducing flexible automated lines, floor space requirements associated with these operations have fallen to less than half their former amount; working time has been slashed by four-fifths, and the cost of production line changes has been more than halved.

● *Quality assurance*   Nippondenso's quality assurance programme encompasses all stages of operations.[5]   Close co-operation with Toyota contributes to high levels of quality. Toyota's just-in-time production system requires that component suppliers guarantee both deliveries and product quality.

● *Broad product range*   Nippondenso offers a broad array of products, each in many versions. The company offers seven major versions of its vehicle air conditioning units, 21 styles of alternator and 29 types of starter.

• *High manufacturing throughput in both mass and mixed production* In its mixed model change production system, Nippondenso can now manufacture all models of a product on any one of several production lines without needing to halt production for changes

• *Just-in-time system*   Just-in-time manufacturing demands that all materials should be deployed in active operation, as part of an on-going production process that rules out inactive inventory costs

• *Original Equipment Manufacturing (OEM)*   Many system suppliers to the automotive industry manufacture components using blueprints from the purchasing company. A large percentage of Nippondenso's products are developed within the company and sold in different models to a number of automotive manufacturers

• *In-house manufacturing of production equipment*   Nippondenso does not purchase finished production robots from outside companies, because it believes that in-house manufacture of production equipment promotes competitiveness and strengthens team spirit. Nippondenso believes that close co-operation with robot manufacturers would offer outside access to the company's manufacturing secrets; in any case, adaptation of generic equipment to Nippondenso's special requirements would be both time-consuming and expensive. The company devotes great energy to developing its own lines and tooling. On the other hand, Nippondenso does not sell robots externally, partly because the company wants to avoid giving competitors access to its unique advantages. With its own robot production capacity, Nippondenso has achieved long-term competitive advantages through product innovation and increased cost-effectiveness

Human Resource Management

Nippondenso assigns great importance to its research and development programmes. The company expends much effort on the recruitment of capable engineers and assumes responsibility for their continuing education. More generally, all employees are constantly encouraged to develop their skills. By Japanese standards, Nippondenso also has good contacts with nearby universities and engineering schools.

Nippondenso's production system thrives on the group mentality. Team members employed in different parts of the company wear distinctive uniforms. Including vacations, absenteeism stands at 5 per cent. Working hours are longer than the Japanese average.

Communication of goals and expectations

Nippondenso maintains extensive outside lines of communication with component suppliers and customers. In some cases, this assumes the form of joint development task forces. Market monitoring includes careful, long-term planning. To ensure that the company meets customer requirements and wishes, internal communications are also important. For this reason, people from several departments are appointed to the various planning groups. Top managers at Nippondenso say that they often visit the factory floor.

Productivity management

Nippondenso admits that the company is especially good at measuring and managing factors that influence direct work costs. In other areas the company believes it still has a lot to learn. In administration departments, key information networks cover such fields as sales, accounting, personnel and purchasing. In engineering departments, Nippondenso utilizes a technology information control system and CAD to support activities of engineers. During the past four years value-added as a percentage of sales has remained relatively constant (see Figure 5.5). The same applies to wage and salary costs as a percentage of value-added and manufacturing costs, (see Figures 5.6 and 5.7).

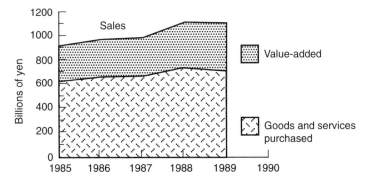

Figure 5.5 Value-added in relation to Nippondenso inputs.
Source: Nippondenso.

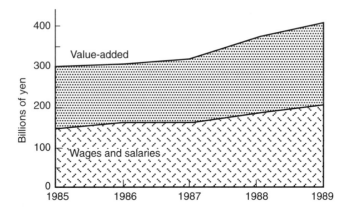

Figure 5.6 Value-added in relation to Nippondenso labour costs.
Source: Nippondenso.

Nippondenso's productivity management efforts focus on rationaliza-
tion of labour input, measures to increase employee motivation and other
production-oriented activities.

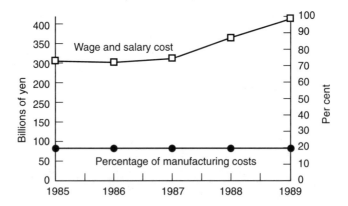

Figure 5.7 Labour costs as a percentage of Nippondenso manufacturing costs.
Source: Nippondenso.

a) Rationalization of labour input
Highly automated production processes lead to high levels of labour productivity. One of the company's goals is to reduce the number of employ-

ees directly linked to production. The company therefore aims at reducing the quantity of man-hours per product to levels that are set on a monthly basis. Automation, time-and-motion studies, improvements in physical production flow and design changes all contribute to this aim. The company has been able to reduce the number of man-hours required in cooler production, for example, to one fifth of their original levels.

Nippondenso attempts to keep numbers of indirect employees, or employees not working directly in production, constant in absolute numbers. If production volume then raises, the productivity of the same number of indirect employees can be assumed to go up. The company also monitors its competitors' efforts to increase labour productivity. Figure 5.8 shows figures that Nippondenso uses when it compares itself with two companies in terms of the number of man-hours expended on the production of particular products.

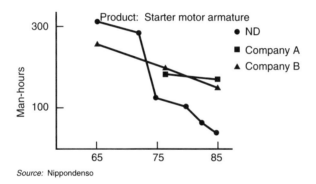

Source: Nippondenso

Figure 5.8 Nippondenso's comparisons with competitors: man-hours per product.

b) Measures to increase employee motivation

● *Level up programme* Nippondenso has a number of education centres in which employees are trained in specialized fields on paid working time. Evening courses are also arranged on a voluntary basis. A suggestion system is encouraged as a tool for improvement of daily work routines.

● *Management attitudes* In what is known as 'management by walking around', top managers frequently visit the company's various units. It is hoped that this and other means will increase levels of contact between employees and top management, leading to a commonality of views in the face of problems.

• *Wage-setting* Japanese industry does not have a reputation for large salary differentials between different groups of employees. Nippondenso considers the wage and salary differentials between top managers and employees relatively small: these spreads, says the company, do not have the effect of widening the distance between hierarchical levels.

c) Production-oriented activities

Various activities are underway in the attempt to promote improvements in manufacturing productivity. In design, modifications including Value Analysis (VA) and Value Engineering (VE) are aimed at simplifying the production process. In assembly, evaluation systems are being utilized in the name of reducing the number of component parts and unifying the direction of flow of assembly. In production, the company has adopted continuous improvements (*kaizen*) to component flow.

Figure 5.9 below summarizes Nippondenso's strategy for continuous increases in productivity.

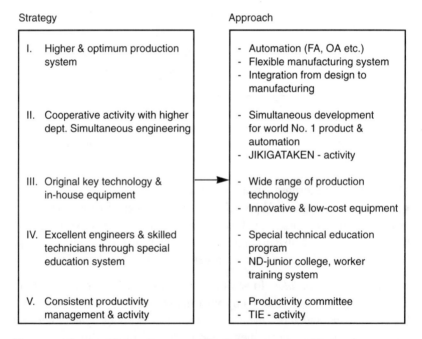

Strategy

I.	Higher & optimum production system
II.	Cooperative activity with higher dept. Simultaneous engineering
III.	Original key technology & in-house equipment
IV.	Excellent engineers & skilled technicians through special education system
V.	Consistent productivity management & activity

Approach

- Automation (FA, OA etc.)
- Flexible manufacturing system
- Integration from design to manufacturing

- Simultaneous development for world No. 1 product & automation
- JIKIGATAKEN - activity

- Wide range of production technology
- Innovative & low-cost equipment

- Special technical education program
- ND-junior college, worker training system

- Productivity committee
- TIE - activity

Figure 5.9 Strategy for continuous productivity increases at Nippondenso.

Source: Nippondenso.

LUXOR ELECTRONICS

Aside from in-house production at Saab and Volvo, Luxor Electronics is one of Sweden's two major manufacturers of vehicle electronic systems. The company's main products are automotive loudspeakers. Luxor reports annual sales of £40 million and has 400 employees. With its German sister company, Luxor is part of the Nokia Group, a Finnish-based industrial conglomerate. Nokia estimates that it accounts for about one third of the European OEM[6] market for automotive loudspeakers.

Luxor manufactures seven other types of product. Some are standardized and sold to customers in different industries. Most, however, are tailored to customer requirements. In attempting to avoid the manufacture of simple components, such as printed circuit boards, the company hopes to avoid becoming a mere sub-contractor that competes on the basis of price. Because of its high levels of expertise in assembly work, the company concentrates on manufacturing differentiated products that require assembly. Around 90 per cent of Luxor's sales go to the automotive industry. Between them, Volvo and Saab account for two-thirds of all sales.

In terms of employees, Nippondenso is almost exactly one hundred times larger than Luxor. On this basis, it is obviously worth investigating to what extent Luxor can achieve economies of scale. In the context of the components industry battle for status as systems suppliers, it is also worth assessing whether the company has been relegated to a role as a secondary supplier.

In the automotive electronics industry, economies of scale and levels of automation are high. Luxor believes that its relatively small size puts it at a disadvantage. Only larger production volumes would justify increased automation. Management also believes that the company makes too many products. Here lies the problem: product lines are eliminated only at the company's peril since increased depth of focus on remaining lines is unlikely to be crowned with better sales performance. Increasing sales volume outside Sweden has thus become an important strategic task.

Aside from the problem of insufficient production volume, Luxor does not believe that the company's prerequisites for good productivity differ greatly from those of its international competitors. Luxor can certainly purchase components as cheaply as other companies. Its manufacturing processes are not particularly labour-intensive, leaving wage costs with little overall relative impact on competitiveness.

Indeed, the merger between Saab and GM has enabled comparisons between prices charged by suppliers to the American and Swedish companies. Given Luxor's belief that its prices are competitive, there seems to be some chance that the company will become part of GM's Global Purchasing network.

Officials at Nippondenso emphasize the importance of the company's research and development programme. Research and development costs at Luxor total about 7 per cent of sales, about the same as at Nippondenso. About 15 per cent of Luxor's employees are engaged in development work; half of them have doctoral degrees. By way of comparison, just under 17 per cent of Nippondenso's employees have university-level engineering degrees, leading to the conclusion that there is a rough equivalence between the two companies in terms of the relative level of financial and human resources devoted to development work.

At Luxor, production consists of component manufacturing and assembly work. The company has a mixture of wholly automated lines and manual assembly operations. For several years, Luxor has been working hard to devise a quality control system based on the 'zero-defect concept' and ISO-9000.[7] All employees have completed a 40-hour quality training programme. As a result of these efforts, Luxor received the 1987 Saab quality award. Because levels of quality control are so highly developed, Luxor says that its customers do not need to perform inspections on receipt of products.

Luxor purchases components direct from a number of the leading international manufacturers, leading to close co-operation in research and development and offering the opportunity to test incoming products at an early stage. Luxor uses CAD systems, a computer simulation station and an environment testing lab. Customers take high quality and reliable delivery for granted, instead paying more attention to research and development, financing and management.

Luxor's general manager, Mr Lindy Yngvesson, has worked at the company for 20 years, previously serving as development and production manager. He believes that productivity and quality are largely a problem of management, a question of time, tooling and training. Results are dependent on delegation, communication and, not least, the provision of sufficient tools and time. Not entirely successfully, the company has attempted to apply Japanese styles of production management to its production operations. 'We work too much according to the principle of 'one defect – one person responsible', says Mr Yngvesson. 'If things grind to a halt at a Japanese company, several people immediately pounce on the problem. In Sweden, first you have to go to the boss.'

Luxor uses some 20 yardsticks of productivity including efficiency, quality, number of defects and capital management. Hoping to avoid an excessive focus on production, the company has also begun to measure performance in areas such as the ratio of orders to tenders. Elsewhere, a close watch is kept on the progress of products to manufacture within projected time periods.

High wage costs and high levels of absenteeism are often highlighted as causes of low productivity in Sweden. Managers at Luxor believe that there are other explanations. Despite shorter working hours and longer vacations than Sweden, German industry reports higher levels of productivity. The solution, Luxor executives insist, lies in better work systems devised and communicated by managers. 'Management bear the heaviest responsibility for productivity,' Luxor's general manager says of management's role at the company.

Luxor believes that Swedish companies have a lot to learn from Japan in terms of productivity. Among other things, Luxor's management sees the boundaries between departments of Swedish companies as too rigid. Design and production departments, for example, should co-operate more intimately. By comparison with their Japanese counterparts, Swedish companies tend to be poor at winning employee support for decisions. High levels of turnover in top management positions can be a problem: executives can be replaced by others with different views before a new strategy has been implemented.

CONCLUSIONS

Component supply companies often operate under strong competitive pressures. Few industries operate in the context of such heavy demands to achieve annual improvements in productivity. For manufacturers of simple components, this is primarily a matter of the kind of improvements in cost-effectiveness that are frequently achieved with increased production volumes and increased automation. By contrast, Nippondenso and other systems suppliers also assume responsibility for the development of new products and the improvement of existing components. The relationship between systems suppliers and the automotive industry is more co-operative in nature and involves a more constructive form of competitive pressure than pure price competition.

Nippondenso works especially closely with Toyota. Co-operation between the two companies in terms of research and development co-operation is sufficiently long-term for Nippondenso to become involved at an early stage in development of Toyota's new models. Toyota's equity stake (23 per cent) seems well-balanced: large enough for an open relationship, yet sufficiently small to give Nippondenso the freedom to sell to Toyota's competitors. With its geographic proximity to customers, Nippondenso can exploit production and distribution systems that offer just-in-time deliveries.

Nippondenso co-operates closely with its suppliers. These relationships, too, are based on a long-term perspective and a sense of trust. In Sweden, neither primary nor secondary suppliers enjoy such close links with their customers. Nippondenso's method of choosing suppliers – the most important selection factors are technical competence and good finances – also helps to increase the prerequisites for high productivity.

Nippondenso's scarcest resource seems to be labour. With automation of its production apparatus, the company has turned this situation to its advantage. In the areas of capital supply, union organization and government industrial policy there are few obstacles to expansion. The company's product range is undergoing fairly rapid technical development. The pace of change is definitely not slow; neither is it as rapid as, for example, in the mobile telephone industry.

With a stable balance of power vis-a-vis its customers and a controllable pace of technological development in terms of its products, Nippondenso enjoys a favourable degree of the kind of external pressure that prompts productivity improvements.

Working under such favourable external circumstances, Nippondenso possesses internal mechanisms to promote increased productivity. Internal mechanisms contribute to good cost-effectiveness and high levels of innovation at Nippondenso. Communication between various departments is very good. Nippondenso also has a very highly developed system of productivity management. The company creates constant incentives for improvement with its frequent updating of goals – as often as once a month in the case of use of working time.

Employee skill levels play an important role in productivity at Nippondenso. The company spends large sums on internal education programme and boasts a well-functioning suggestion system. Most top managers have worked at Nippondenso for their entire careers. On the way to their current positions, they have worked in each of the company's most important departments. Their management style presupposes a clearly-defined hierarchy and a sense of discipline, yet relies on consensus and on the winning of employee support in the name of common goals.

Luxor operates under somewhat tougher competitive pressures because of its poorer negotiating position in relation to its customers. Luxor is a small company; its products, automotive loudspeakers, do not play a part in the primary functions of motor vehicles. In any comparison of internal conditions, Nippondenso's advantages act as benchmarks:

- More in-house product development
- Closer co-operation with customers
- More automated manufacturing
- Better communication and co-operation between departments

[1]*Dagens Industrial*, May 2, 1991, p. 16.

[2]In Sweden alone, there are about 200 small or medium companies (with less than 200 employees) that are suppliers to the vehicle industry. Swedish National Industrial Board, SIND (1990).

[3]About half of them worked with research, development and design, the others with production and quality.

[4]FMS is elaborated in chapter 11.

[5]It is said that Saab became aware of Nippondenso's zero defect quality when Saab sent its first order to Nippondenso. Saab prescribed among other things 'Quality standard: 5 defects per thousand'. When Saab then received the first shipment it contained 1,000 items – and a separate box with 5 defective items.

[6]Original Equipment Manufacturing.

[7]A system for quality assessment.

6 SCANIA AND IVECO

During the 1940s the management of Swedish automotive manufacturer Scania-Vabis – forerunner of Scania – established a new corporate strategy. Until that point, production had been based on the craftsmanship of highly skilled workers who had enjoyed considerable freedom in devising technical solutions to satisfy consumer demand. The company's new guiding principles aimed to combine technological supremacy with fewer versions and fewer components. Nearly 50 years on, this clear and far-sighted philosophy continues to permeate Scania's attitudes to the production process. The company has a solid reputation for quality, and for many years it has been the world's most profitable heavy truck manufacturer. Although it accounts for under 7 per cent of the world truck market, Scania accounts for almost half of the industry's profit. In 1989, Scania's new Series 3 was named 'Truck of the Year' by an international jury of motor journalists.

The case of Scania – now a division of Saab-Scania AB – shows how a company can turn negative prospects into positive realities. Fifty years ago, Sweden's combination of thinly populated countryside, long distances, severe climate and poor roads seemed to promise little to the prospective truck manufacturer. At the very least, this hostile environment would test product quality to the extreme: if Swedish trucks could survive on the domestic market, other markets were unlikely to prove more demanding. High standards of occupational safety regulations and environmental protection posed another challenge, forcing manufacturers to develop advanced designs that have periodically enjoyed competitive advantage in foreign markets.[1]

As Figure 6.1 indicates, manufacturers generally specialize either in heavier or lighter trucks. Scania, for example, specializes in vehicles with a total loaded weight (gross vehicle weight or GVW) in excess of 16 metric tons. Established through mergers of several manufacturers, each with different product ranges, Iveco produces trucks on both sides of the weight divide. A pan-European company with far-flung production

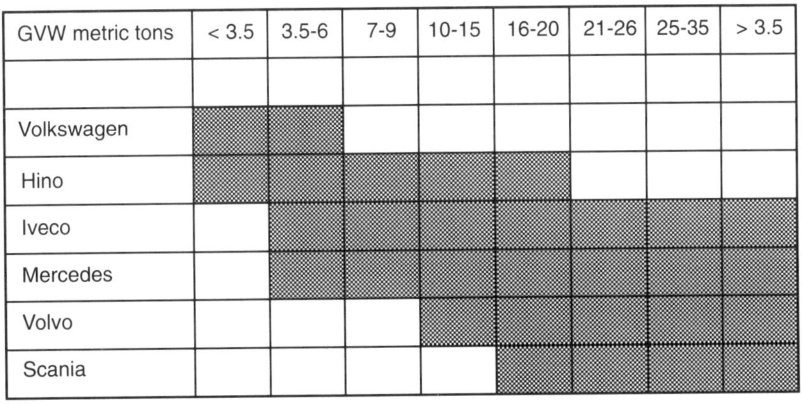

GVW metric tons	< 3.5	3.5-6	7-9	10-15	16-20	21-26	25-35	> 3.5
Volkswagen	▓	▓						
Hino	▓	▓	▓	▓	▓			
Iveco		▓	▓	▓	▓	▓	▓	▓
Mercedes		▓	▓	▓	▓	▓	▓	▓
Volvo				▓	▓	▓	▓	▓
Scania					▓	▓	▓	▓

Figure 6.1 Truck manufacturers' specializations, by vehicle weight.

Sources: The Saab-Scania Griffin, 1990/1991. IVECO – Magirus AG Koncerngeschäftsbericht IVECO BV, 1989.

facilities, Iveco has set ambitious goals for quality improvement, making it a suitable case for comparison with Scania.

THE TRUCK INDUSTRY

A truck consists of a number of main components:

● *The frame*: a torsionally elastic and load-resistant framework upon which other components are mounted. Consisting of a varying number of joined sections, whose thickness and shape is determined by the vehicle's intended tasks, the truck's frame is not an especially technically complex component.

● *The cab*: In designing the driver's workplace, the suspension system and the mode of connection to the frame are important: among other things the choices made in this area affect convenience of servicing. Depending on vehicle use, interior fittings range from Spartan to sumptuous: long distance drivers, in particular, need to combine space for sleep and work.

● *The power train*: engine, gearbox and transmission, all connected by a universal drive joint assembly. Technologically very highly advanced, these components are continually improved and modified.[2]

Smaller sub-systems include the brake system, and the front axle with its steering system. Truck bodies generally are designed, built and assembled by specialist body fabrication firms.[3] Attached to the frame, bodies may consist of a flat bed or a flat bed with walls and a roof. More complex bodies are fabricated for vehicles such as cement mixers or petrol tankers. In general, body fabricators also manufacture trailers for attachment at the rear of truck tractors.

A heavy truck with a body costs about (£100,000) and is generally replaced after five to seven years, although replacement intervals can be longer. Customers' vehicle depreciation costs generally comprise only around 10 per cent of total operating costs. Total life cycle cost is therefore more important for the customer than simple purchase price. Availability of service is a major competitive tool. In Europe, more than 80 per cent of trucking companies have five or fewer vehicles in their fleet. In Japan the haulage industry likewise consists mainly of small companies. In the United States, by contrast, large trucking companies predominate.

So long as they do not maintain their own stockpiles of spare parts, the cost to customers of a switch from one maker to another is not especially large. For manufacturers attempting to break into new markets, the need for servicing facilities presents a crucial obstacle. Scania, for example, has found it just as hard to establish operations in South East Asia as Japanese truck manufacturers have found it to move into Europe. Quite

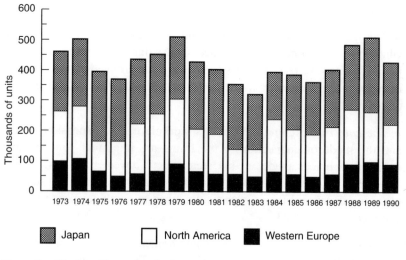

Figure 6.2 World-wide truck sales by region.
Source: Scania.

often, if it exists, an automotive manufacturer's existing passenger car servicing network cannot be relied for the very different tasks involved in the servicing of trucks.

Markets

A wildly fluctuating business cycle is the primary scourge of the truck manufacturing industry. Sales may fluctuate by more than 20 per cent from one year to the next (see Figure 6.2). Between 1979 and 1983 the overall market for heavy trucks fell by 37 per cent. These violent swings in demand are one of the primary reasons behind the industry's far-reaching and continuing transformation. Typically, manufacturers that lag in expanding their production capacity go on to lose market share during periods of economic expansion. Yet during recessions, excessive fixed costs can endanger a company's very existence.

There are clear differences between markets in Europe, the Far East and the United States, each of which account for almost one third of the world market. National peculiarities are more pronounced in truck markets than in car markets. Customer requirements in the United States are particularly variable: American trucking companies are accustomed to specifying engines, gearboxes and drive shafts for their trucks, a tendency that readily explains the modest export successes enjoyed by American truck manufacturers. Japanese truck manufacturers, likewise, export a percentage of their product far below the volumes sold abroad by their car-making counterparts. World-wide sales volumes from 1979 and 1989 are shown in Figure 6.3.

The truck manufacturing market divides into three segments: light (3.5-4.9 metric tons), medium (5.0-15.9 tons) and heavy (16 tons and above). Over the past two decades, trends in world demand have seen light truck sales increase by an annual average of 3.2 per cent. Heavy truck sales have shown a more modest 1.7 per cent increase over the same period. Medium-sized truck sales, by contrast, have declined by an average of 1.5 per cent year-on-year. The figures show an overall polarization toward light and heavy trucks. Observers predict that the trend toward concentration of production will continue. In the context of weak overall market growth, the number of heavy truck manufacturers has already declined from about 40 in 1970 to about 15 in 1990. Obstacles to market entry are so high that new manufacturers are unlikely to emerge. Japanese expansion poses the only conceivable threat to the existing companies in Europe and the United States.

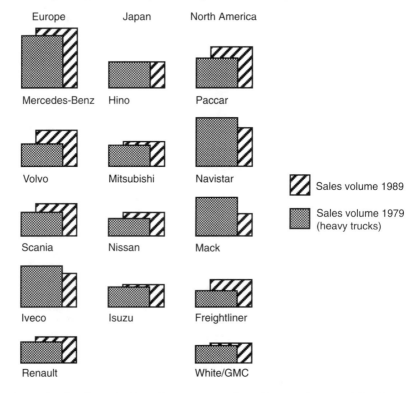

Figure 6.3 Producers' sales volumes 1979–1989 in Europe, Japan and North America.

Sources: Annual reports of companies.

Notably, Japanese heavy truck manufacturers are not nearly so well-positioned as their counterparts in the auto industry. As Figure 6.1 indicates, Japanese manufacturers Hino, Mitsubishi and Nissan only compete with Scania in the 16-20 tonne segment of the market. Once again, the ebb and flow of international competition can be traced to domestic prerequisites: in this instance, the banning of trucks weighing over 20 tonnes from Japanese roads (see Table 6.1). As a result, Japanese truck manufacturers have been unable to replicate the strategy of their national car industry, which gained vital initial impetus from domestic competition that produced a small number of large, efficient companies that proved successful in export markets. By contrast, under Sweden's relatively liberal road regulations, vehicle manufacturers like Scania are restricted only by a maximum vehicle length of 24 metres and a grand total weight (GTW) of 51.4 tonnes.[4]

	United States	Europe	Japan
Length	18–28 m	16,5–24 m	12 m
GTW	33–49 t	26–54 t	20 t
Axle weight	8/10 t	10/12 t	10 t
	14/20 t	16/20 t	

Table 6.1 Maximum lengths and weights allowed for trucks in different parts of the world.

Source: Östling (1990).

Development costs are high for components such as engines and gearboxes. Corporate mergers have enabled manufacturers to spread these costs over larger production volumes. Additionally, manufacturers make constant attempts to reduce the number of versions of single components. Many companies concentrate on developing diversified ranges of products that can operate with the same basic high-cost components: a truck manufacturer might therefore move into the market for buses. With minor modifications, engines can be sold on a stand-alone basis to industrial or marine end-users. Used to similar extents by all vehicle manufacturers, other technically complex components like compressors and generators are purchased from large-scale European, American and Japanese manufacturers.

In terms both of product differentiation and corporate reputations for quality, analysts typically think of European truck manufacturers as belonging to one of two groups. The first group usually includes Scania, Mercedes and Volvo; a little lower on the scale, a second group includes companies such as Iveco, MAN and DAF. As the perceived gap between these two groups of manufacturers has narrowed over time, major breakthroughs in terms of technology and quality have become increasingly rare. Notwithstanding recent generalized increases in quality standards, technological development remains vital, with new developments in diesel engine and power train technology, in ceramic engine components and turbocompound engines, all promising to deliver a source of future competitive advantage. Participation in the development of new technology is thus crucial for companies that wish to maintain a leading position within the industry.

Competition

In 1989, world-wide heavy truck production totalled about 500,000 units. The ten largest manufacturers accounted for more than 60 per cent of the world market (see Figure 6.4).

In general, truck manufacturers participate in extensive networks of mutual relationships in the form of joint ventures and looser alliances that amount to co-operation agreements. Scania is an exception to the rule: the company has no ownership ties with competitors and is accustomed to developing components under its own auspices. Scania is unusual in another regard: it is one of only two companies world-wide – the other is the American firm Paccar – that manufacture heavy trucks exclusively (see Figure 6.5). The three companies where the largest percentage of production consists of heavy trucks are Scania, Paccar and Volvo Truck. Notably, these companies also have the highest profit margins (see Table 6.2).

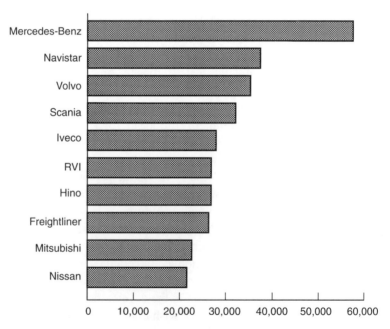

Figure 6.4 How the world's ten largest manufacturers carve up global heavy truck production.

Source: Östling (1990).

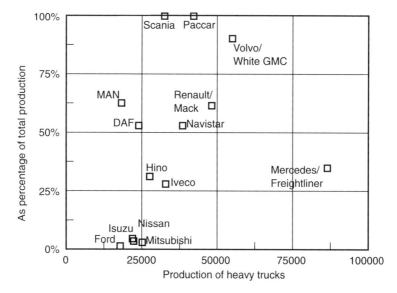

Note: The Renault Vehicles Inudstriell (RVI) Group includes RVI Europe and Mack Trucks Inc. Mercedes-Benz encompasses both Mercedes-Benz Europe and Freightliner. Volvo also includes White GMC. Source: Östling (1990).

Figure 6.5 Heavy truck production as percentage of total production.

	1986	1987	1988	1989	1990
Scania[a]	15.6	17.0	16.6	15.2	12.7
Volvo[b]	6.6	9.0	11.2	8.8	5.3
Iveco[c]	3.2	4.2	4.6	4.8	0.2
RVI[d]	−5.9	1.0	4.6	3.9	4.9
DAF[e]	1.5	1.7	2.8	3.3	0
MAN[f]	0.2	−1.5	1.2	2.3	3.0
Paccar[g]	3.0	4.6	5.6	6.9	2.5
Navistar[h]	0.1	0.9	6.0	2.0	0
Mack	−1.8	0.2	1.5	−10.6	0
Nissan Diesel	3.0	0.1	0.7	0.9	1.0

Table 6.2 Profit margins of truck manufacturers

a Profit before appropriations and taxes.
b Trucks and buses (not industrial and marine engines).
c Including forklifts, which account for less than 5 per cent of sales. Figures for 1987–89 include IVECO-Ford.
d Excluding Mack Trucks.
e Excluding Leyland Trucks.
f Fiscal years 1985/86 etc.
g The 1989 figure includes net gains on sales of Wagner Mining Division: thus not entirely comparable.
h Including diesel engine sales.

Source: Östling (1990) and Scania.

Competitors

Mercedes Benz

With a product range that spans the distance from small to large models, Mercedes-Benz is the largest single manufacturer of trucks in the world. The company also owns the American manufacturer Freightliner. Despite its size, Mercedes-Benz maintains co-operation agreements and alliances with other manufacturers. Within such arrangements, the company has co-operated with MAN and has purchased gearboxes from ZF.

Renault Vehicles Industriels Group (RVI Group)

The French truck manufacturer operates manufacturing plants in Europe and North America. During the late 1980s, RVI Group's European operations performed well. The company has equity-based co-operation agreements with America's Mack and Sweden's Volvo Truck. Given major differences between American and European truck manufacturing styles, the relationship with Mack has yielded so far insignificant returns from economies of scale. The agreement with Volvo Truck opens the way for joint basic research, component development and purchases. Aside from these areas, the two companies retain separate product identities and sales organizations.

DAF

The Netherlands-based company DAF manufactures light, medium-sized and heavy trucks plus diesel engines, cabs and front and rear axles. In 1987 DAF Trucks, Leyland Trucks and Freight Rover merged to become Leyland DAF Ltd. Low profit margins may make it difficult for DAF to meet the demand for product development in the future. Indeed, even the economic boom that crested in 1989 did not result in palpable improvements in its profit margin. DAF's share of world markets has fallen: in the heavy truck segment, the company's share totals about 5 per cent.

Volvo

In Swedish markets, Volvo Truck doubles as Scania's most eminent competitor, with the two companies each accounting for around half of the domestic heavy truck market. A little more than one third of Volvo's trucks are manufactured in the United States. Volvo Truck's large-scale operations in North America date back to the 1970s; the company's efforts only got off the ground after its purchase of the truck manufac-

turing assets of America's White Motor Corporation in 1981. In 1987 a
co-operation agreement with General Motors led to the establishment of
the Volvo GM Heavy Truck Corporation, designed to develop and manufacture products in the United States under the White GMC brand
name.

Like Scania, Volvo takes responsibility for development and design
work on vital components with the aim of manufacturing fully-integrat-
ed vehicles. Volvo differs from Scania in its lack of a modularized product range: Volvo's cab and engine ranges are more extensive.

Paccar
In the face of other manufacturers' profitability problems, Paccar
remains the most successful producer in the United States. The company manufactures heavy trucks for the American market under the brand
names Peterbilt and Kenworth. Paccar, like all American truck companies except Mack, can be characterized as an assembler of purchased
components. The buyers are used to ordering customer tailored trucks
instead of choosing one truck in the manufacturer's model range.

In 1986, adopting Scania's production philosophy, but utilizing purchased components, a three-year development effort at Peterbilt culmi-
nated with the unveiling of an entirely new product range consisting of
four truck models based, so far as was possible, on the use of uniform
components.

Will the big producers become even bigger?

The heavy truck industry has become an increasingly international business. In a reversal of historical trends in the auto industry, American
and Japanese have lagged behind European manufacturers in the
exploitation of export markets. The industry is dynamic: competing
companies work extensively on the development of major truck components. Much of this development work occurs in the form of co-operation between truck manufacturers and sub-contractors, as well as
between different manufacturers. The steadily rising costs of development have led to mergers and alliances aimed at spreading development
costs over larger production volumes. The industry suffers severely
from its sensitivity to business cycles.

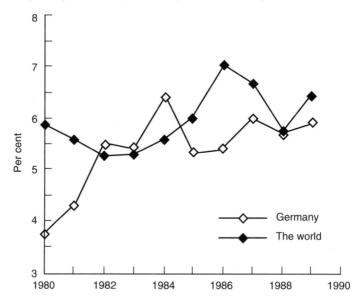

Figure 6.6 Scania's market shares in Germany and world-wide.

Source: Saab-Scania, 10-year financial summary 1989.

SCANIA

In a decline from its peak year of 1989, Scania manufactured nearly 30,000 trucks during 1990. During the 1980s, Scania maintained its share of the world market. In Germany, a country with very demanding customers, Scania managed to increase its market share (see Figure 6.6).

Scania's factories in the Netherlands, Brazil and Argentina produce nearly 60 per cent of the company's vehicles. Expansion in recent years has occurred at the plants outside Sweden (see Figure 6.7). Component manufacturing occurs mainly in Sweden, near Scania's technical development centre, while assembly occurs primarily abroad, near the company's markets.

The costs of research and development work are climbing steadily, which means that production volumes must increase. Scania's board of directors has approved a capacity increase of about 50 per cent during the next few years, which will occur at existing factories and a new assembly plant in Angers, France. This new investment entails a southward shift in the company's operational centre of gravity and leaves Scania with three large-capacity assembly plants in Europe. Scania's geographical handicap in terms of long delivery distances will thereby be reduced.

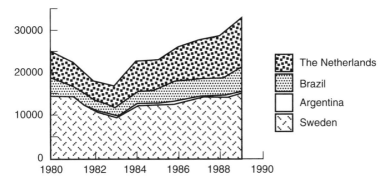

Figure 6.7 Scania's manufacturing plant expansions, 1980–1989.
Source: Saab-Scania, 10-year financial summary 1989.

Technology

High productivity at Scania stems from the company's manufacturing methodology.

- First, Scania applies a *modular component philosophy*, manufacturing central components in a small number of versions that can be readily combined in end-products tailored to customer requirements

- *Concurrent engineering.* Among other things, this means taking into account how a component can be designed to make low manufacturing cost possible

- Third, Scania has managed to maintain a very high level of *cost-consciousness*, despite high profitability

Scania itself manufactures vital components such as the engines, gearboxes and rear axle assemblies. Departing from industry norms, the company avoids purchasing major power train components from subcontractors, preferring instead to engineer its products from start to finish. Customers regard trucks as component systems; Scania is considered one of the best-optimized system producers. Increased product quality results in gains from reduced servicing and maintenance problems. Figure 6.8 shows that the annual maintenance levels for Scania trucks fell from 100 hours in 1968 to just over 20 hours in 1986.

Scania's product philosophy facilitates a continuous process of improvement. Components can be developed fairly independently of each other. Improvement therefore occurs incrementally, instead of by the kind of jumps and starts that elsewhere constitute new product gener-

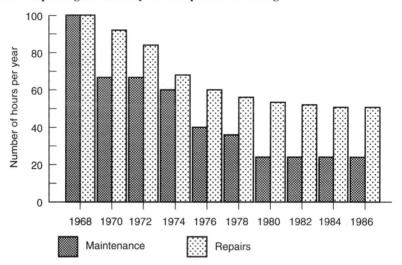

Figure 6.8 Annual maintenance levels for Scania trucks 1968–1986.

Source: Aaserud-Hermausson (1991).

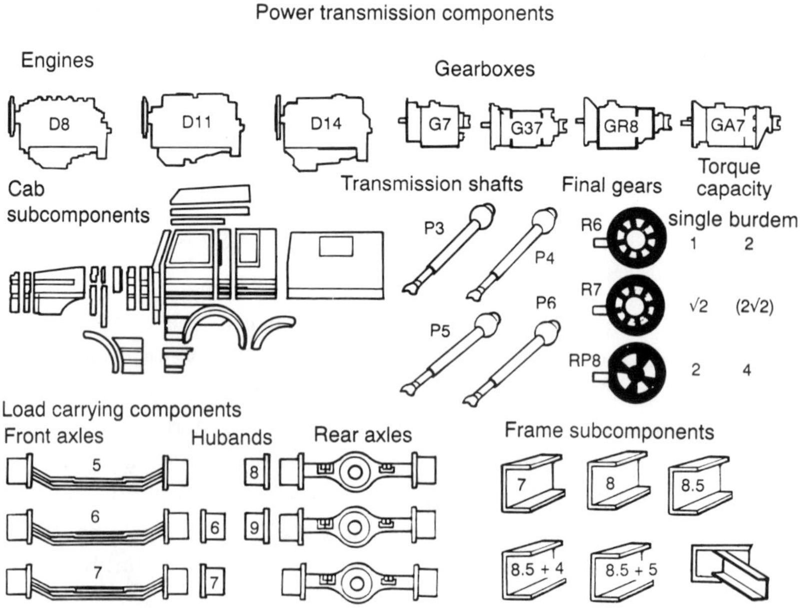

Figure 6.9 Modularized product ranges at Scania.

Source: the Saab-Scania Griffin, 1990/91.

ations. Scania's product philosophy has undoubtedly contributed to the quality reputation that enables the company to charge a price premium. At some points during the 1980s, Scania's prices stood 10 per cent higher than those of its competitors.

Scania's method of producing all major components is not widely emulated. The argument against such a strategy is that it leads to excessive development costs. The alternatives most often followed include purchasing from component suppliers with the kind of larger development resources that result from longer production runs.

Although Scania handles the development of its major components, the company also achieves economies of scale in manufacturing operations. Its modularized product range means that a smaller number of components are mass-produced. There are four main categories of components: engines, power transmission components, load carrying components and cab components. These building blocks can be combined in a number of ways, allowing Scania to satisfy the requirements of many different markets (see Figure 6.9).

The company has three basic engine models with displacements of 14, 11 and nine litres, respectively. These engines deliver varying amounts of power and torque. The highest power rating is currently 500 horsepower. Table 6.3 compares the annual engine manufacturing volumes of Scania

Manufacturer	Engine	Trucks	Buses	Other vehicles	Total
Mercedes-Benz	V8 14.6–15.0	38,500	3,500	500	42,500
Mercedes-Benz	R6 6.0	30,500	–	500	31,000
Mercedes-Benz	V6 11.0	9,000	500	500	10,000
Scandia	R6 11.0	17,500	3,500	2,000	23,000
Scania	R6 8.5	7,500	500	1,000	9,000
Scania	V8 14.1	7,500	–	1,000	8,500
Volvo	R6 9.6	14,000	4,000	1,000	19,000
Volvo	R6 12.0	12,500	–	1,500	14,000
Volvo	R6 6.7	4,500	500	5,000	10,000
Volvo	R6 5.5	8,000	–	–	8,000
RVI	R6 9.8	17,500	1,000	–	18,500
RVI	R6 5.5	10,500	–	–	10,500
MAN	R6 11.4–12.0	14,500	2,000	500	17,000
Iveco	R6 13.8	12,000	1,000	1,500	14,500
DAF	R6 11.6	11,000	1,500	1,500	14,000

Table 6.3 Annual volume for engines, 1989.

Source: Östling (1990).

and its competitors. The table indicates that Scania achieves long production runs, especially with its 11 litre engine. Table 6.3 provides no figures on batch sizes for American engine suppliers. The large U.S. manufacturers have volumes of 150,000–250,000 engines due to the fact that these engines are also used in machines and in other vehicles than trucks.

The cab range is organized in similar fashion. Scania's standard cab can be furnished with extra equipment such as sleeper facilities and wind deflectors. Interior configurations vary according to customer wishes. Economies of scale are achieved in the manufacture of cabs because all cabs contain the same basic parts. Table 6.4 shows batch sizes for selected makes. Scania's batch is 32,500 or equal to the total number of trucks it produced during 1989.

Manufacturer	Cab	Quantity
Mercedes-Benz	Forward-control	50,500
Mercedes-Benz	Normal-control	23,400
Scania	GRPT	32,500
Iveco	Forward-control	30,000
MAN	Forward-control (F90)	19,500
Volvo	Forward-control (F10/12/16)	17,500
Volvo	Low forward-control (FL7/10)	9,000
Volvo	Low forward-control (FL6)	8,000
Volvo	Normal-control	6,500
RVI	Large four-club cab (G)	11,000
RVI	Large forward-control (R)	10,000
DAF	Forward-control (not 95-series)	9,000
DAF	Forward-control (95-series)	8,500

Table 6.4 Annual volume in cab manufacture, 1989.

Source: Östling (1990).

Smaller inventories are another advantage of modularized product ranges. In general, halving the number of versions makes possible a 30 per cent reduction in inventories.

Scania's efforts at standardization have succeeded in part because its product development work has not been disrupted by alliances with other manufacturers. Collaboration with companies that do not share the same emphasis on standard modules can be difficult. Competition in time is another factor. In product development, decision-making must be rapid, and the process can be slowed if representatives from several companies expect to participate.

Scania's in-house engineering system has enabled the development department to maintain close contacts with the manufacturing plants. For many years, Scania has practiced what is now called concurrent engineering. The company has integrated product development with manufacturing. The technical director is responsible for materials as well as chassis and engines/transmissions. The executive placed in charge of engines/transmissions is then responsible for development as well as production planning and actual production.

Parallel with its line organization, a group of employees is charged with deciding product changes. Another group supervises production planning. The group that decides on product changes includes representatives from both the purchasing and marketing departments, a decision-making forum that has existed at Scania, in one form or another, for more than 40 years. The second group, which meets every month, decides on the models and items to be manufactured over the next 12 months: once again, the marketing departments enjoy strong representation in the hope of ensuring that manufacturing capacity is utilized in accordance with the wishes of the market.

The company's technical philosophy has strongly influenced its relationships with suppliers. Small components are now frequently ordered from independent suppliers; production of other more vital components – such as cabs – has been incorporated through the acquisition of subcontractors. Scania collaborates closely with its sub-contractors on product development and other matters. In the late 1970s Scania implemented a far-reaching standardization of components. These days, for example, the company uses only three types of radiator; numerous components within these units are common to all three models.

When a new main component is to be developed at Scania, sub-contractors participate in the early stages of a process that can take up to five years. Scania's system of collaboration with sub-contractors is exemplified its relationship with Blackstone, a regular sub-contractor since the 1960s. Blackstone representatives meet with Scania representatives three times a year. Zero defect deliveries are required: Blackstone's deliveries follow ISO 9000 norms. Quality control of radiators is performed entirely by Blackstone. Blackstone receives a weekly delivery plan from Scania which is definitive for the next six to eight weeks. Blackstone is affiliated with the Odette system,[5] which has helped Scania double its frequency of inventory turnover to 12 times per year.

Human Resource Management

During the 1930s, Scania's workers were the aristocrats of the Swedish engineering industry in terms of wages.[6] Few white collar workers were involved in the manufacturing process, leaving blue collar workers to enjoy far-reaching responsibility and freedom. In the late 1930s, assembly line production transformed their role and prompted reductions in the numbers of skilled workers. A period of relative calm followed until the company's introduction of Methods Time Measurement (MTM) in 1964. During the late 1960s and early 1970s, Scania led the field in the introduction of new manufacturing systems, further complicating the status of blue collar employees, but improving the lot of white collar workers.

Although Scania's current pay structure parallels those of other large industrial corporations operating in Sweden, there are now visible distinctions between wage scales at large and small companies. Small companies tend to pay their employees more, perhaps because the smaller companies recruit employees who have been trained in larger corporations. Above all, Scania offers a dominant role to engineers and technicians who now comprise 45 per cent of the white collar work force.

For at least 25 years, company policy has mandated annual reviews of personnel and personal development matters with individual employees. Although Scania was something of a pioneer in this field, relations between hourly-paid workers and management had fallen short of perfection during the 1980s. In the wake of a wave of wildcat strikes in 1990, briefs from both union organizers and company managers were sent to the Swedish Labour Court, which arbitrates disputes in the labour market.

Although senior management demonstrates a high level of familiarity with corporate aims, awareness is limited further down the scale. Some employees criticize what they perceive as a conservative and autocratic management style that results in a slow pace of change in the workplace. Not surprisingly, the company is attempting to increase the downward flow of information as a way of generating a sense of commitment and participation among employees.

Training

Scania believes that its shortage of trained workers poses a major problem. At its main Swedish plant, the company points out, employees skilled in machining operations are in short supply. Education levels among young people entering the work-force are probably insufficient: on a scale of one to five, the young people who begin their upper secondary school production technology curriculum possess average school grades of 1.5. According to Scania, employees should have a 4.5 grade point average to handle the company's complex production systems. By contrast, Scania seems satisfied with its pool of potential white collar recruits.

Internal training programmes cater for manual and professional grade workers. More than 90 per cent of those who have completed Scania's trainee programme stay in the company. At production units, skills improvement begins with a period of acclimatization. A gradual build-up of skills follows in a curriculum that mixes academic and practical studies and is linked to pay incentives. Opportunities for skills development also arise through job rotation. Absences from regular job assignments due to training total about 2.5–3 per cent, equivalent to about one working week per year.

White collar training takes the form of internal courses and job rotation. Some 50 recruits are accepted each year as trainee engineers. Perhaps half have completed upper secondary school engineering training. An average of 15 are university-level graduate engineers. The rest have college-equivalent training in economics or other subjects. This recruitment system operates completely independently of business cycles. After two years as trainees, 90-100 per cent remain with the company. After two or three more years, however, they possess a good platform from which to seek

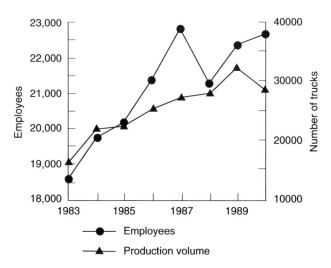

Figure 6.10 Production volume and labour levels.
Source: Scania.

new jobs. Many high-level positions are now held by former trainee engineers, creating a certain continuity in the appointment of managers.

Absenteeism and personnel turnover

The fact that no workers have been laid off at Scania since World War II undoubtedly is connected with the historic shortages of labour on the Swedish market. In 1983, when the Iraqi truck market suddenly dried up, demand fell by 3,000-4,000 units almost overnight, and up to 600 hourly-paid workers became surplus to requirements. Scania's response was novel: instead of instituting redundancies, the company invested in training to prepare the surplus workers for the next economic expansion. When it arrived, the company was able to respond with a rapid boost to production capacity (see Figure 6.10).

Absenteeism because of illness is 3.7 per cent for white collar workers and 13.4 per cent for hourly-paid workers. The latter figure includes a large proportion of workers with chronic illnesses. After a reductions in the first days' sick pay was introduced in the spring of 1991, absenteeism due to illness declined by one quarter. Annual personnel turnover runs at 8 per cent for white collar workers and 24 per cent for hourly workers.

Communication of goals and expectations

Head-to-head with a similar-sized competitor in a challenging domestic market, Sweden's two truck manufacturers find themselves in a unique competitive situation. Clearly, competitive pressures have played a major role in continuous productivity improvements at both companies. At Volvo Truck, management posts notices that compare the company's sales with Scania's during the previous week – evidence that the competitive spirit percolates down to shop-floor level.

IVECO

With 12 manufacturing units and four research centres scattered throughout Italy, France, Germany, Britain and Spain, Iveco justly describes its base of operations as Europe. The group was created in 1975 in a five-cornered merger of OM, Lancia, Fiat, Unic and Magirus-Deutz. Additional mergers boosted the company payroll by about 5,000 between 1985 and 1989 (see Figure 6.11). Unlike Scania, Iveco has grown through a conscious policy of acquisition.

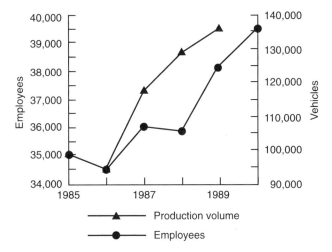

Figure 6.11 Iveco's rising production and labour figures.
Source: IVECO.

For several difficult years in the early 1980s, company earnings hovered around the break-even point. In response, Iveco managers encouraged specialization at individual production facilities and tightened the reins of co-ordination in European operations. Fixed costs in the production system were reduced. Combined with a steady rise in sales since 1984, these efforts led to a sustained revival in earnings. Nevertheless, return on total investment remains below the levels achieved at Scania.

Extensive efforts have been made to improve productivity at the various facilities added to Iveco's growing corporate network. Given an ambitious productivity management system that assigns high priority to productivity issues on a company-wide basis, Iveco may yet pose a tough challenge for industry leaders such as Mercedes-Benz, Scania and Volvo, whose advantages are not decreed by fate, and must instead be defended.

Product range and brand identity

As the product of successive mergers, Iveco has a broad product range encompassing the whole scale from light and heavy trucks. The problematic medium-sized truck sector accounts for a quarter of the production volume. As trucking companies buy vehicles designed for a specialized tasks, or for particular routes or for carriage of specific products, the truck industry's medium-size segment, traditionally devoted to all-purpose vehicles, has lost ground to an expanding market for specially-adapted heavy or light trucks. With such a large percentage of its production concentrated in the medium-size sector, Iveco has been particularly hard-hit by this transformation.

The company's history of mergers and acquisitions has bequeathed an identity problem. At Scania, Volvo and Mercedes, brand identity seems more established. By contrast, customers have approached with caution the claim that Iveco's name indicates a product that is European rather than definitively Italian. The company's reputation has suffered further from previous unfortunate component purchasing decisions. Low quality small components were at one time sourced from cheap suppliers in southern Europe, despite a relatively small price differential of about 10 per cent between such producers and more reliable suppliers located in, say, Germany, because of this IVECO had many quality problems in small components.

Manufacturing philosophy

Iveco is one of the largest diesel engine producers in the world. In a company that regards the engine as a truck's most vital component, all engines are fabricated in-house. Other segments of the power train are sourced from specialized subcontractors: rear axles from Rockwell; gearboxes from ZF or Eaton.

Iveco has begun to collaborate with suppliers to develop components that can be used in all weight segments, including driver's controls and instruments. Projects are also underway to integrate product development work with subcontractors. Elsewhere, supplier links are constantly strengthened: if the company encounters new suppliers equipped with higher product development and engineering capacity than current subcontractors, it reassesses current supplier relationships. These days Iveco looks for better, rather than cheaper, suppliers.

To streamline production at Ulm in Germany, Iveco plans to close one of its two factories there. Component manufacturing tasks previously performed at this factory will be assigned to sub-contractors, leading to lower fixed costs in terms of development work and physical assets. This will lower the crucial break-even point for truck production.

Compared to Scania, Iveco purchases relatively large proportions of components from outside sources. Within overall manufacturing costs at Iveco's plants in Ulm, materials currently account for a 78 per cent share and value-added for about 22 per cent. Roughly one-third of materials are bought from Iveco Group suppliers; the remainder arrives from outside vendors. Already limited, the percentage of value-added is becoming even smaller. Large resources are being devoted to monitoring and improving the productivity of the value-added part. The remaining 78 per cent portion of total material costs has only recently become the object of close scrutiny from the standpoint of productivity.

Cost-effective manufacturing

Apart from the TurboStar, which is made in Turin, Iveco manufactures a full range of heavy trucks at Ulm.

With so many different models on the company's production lines, assembly time varies greatly from model to model. Assembly of a heavy off-road vehicle can take three times longer than the equivalent tasks performed with a medium-sized truck. A single production run may contain several different types of vehicle: a heavy truck may be followed by a number of medium-sized models, throwing production somewhat off-balance.

Management has judged that the costs of such multiple capacity plants outweigh the benefits. Future production will concentrate exclusively on heavy trucks, as part of the overall restructuring that encourages specialized production at the group's geographically diverse European plants.

CONCLUSIONS

Heavy trucks are technically advanced, and complex to manufacture. They are generally manufactured according to customer specifications. Two driving forces lie behind the concentration that has taken place in the truck manufacturing industry during the last two decades: the steadily increasing costs of product development, and economies of scale. Our study has uncovered some key elements in Scania's and IVECO's efforts to achieve high productivity. These are the development and manufacture of long-run series of some crucial truck parts, close cooperation with suppliers of other components, and efficient assembly routines, but there are differences in other respects; Scania manufactures more key parts in-house and specializes in the heavy truck segment.

In the course of its work to merge seven independent truck manufacturers into one, IVECO has come to specialize in the manufacture of engines, and is one of the world's leading companies in this field. Other truck components are purchased from outside suppliers in accordance with increasingly efficient routines. The IVECO group was formed no more than 15 years ago, and the company is still working with the reallocation of production between different plants in order to create an efficient assembly system and establish a reputation for high quality.

The *product philosophy* that leads Scania to design and manufacture all its power train components in-house offers one profound explanation of high productivity levels. Company policy also promotes a leading role in engine, gearbox and cab innovations. A quality image allows the company to charge higher prices than its competitors.

While carrying out product differentiation, the company has managed to achieve substantial cost advantages in production. Since the 1950s, Scania's standard module concept has resulted in extensive economies of scale in production. The company's planning system is characterised by short cycles, short decision-making paths and rapid follow-up.

Corporate cost-consciousness leads to staying power in the context of recessions. The relatively small numbers of white collar workers in manufacturing and product development operations result in low fixed costs and low break-even points. In organizational terms, product development and manufacturing are integrated: even on the drawing board, preparation for manufacturing is underway.

[1]Sweden thus has high standards for truck cabs. They are supposed to withstand a force of 15 metric tons on the roof, as well as a one-ton object smashing into the front pillars from the front and into the rear pillars from behind, after which the doors are supposed to be capable of opening.
[2]Examples worth mentioning: compared to vehicles in the 1940s, today's engines are half as heavy per horsepower, consume 35 per cent less fuel and have many times longer service life, all referring to a given power rating. Maximum output has increased from around 130 hp to 500 hp.
[3]Semitrailer turntables, on the other hand, are often made at the truck plant.
[4]During the 1960s many people in Sweden favoured lowering the maximum vehicle length to 18 m. The business sector wanted an unchanged 24 m. To meet environmentalists part way, Olof Palme, then Minister of Transportation and Communications, suggested 22 m as a compromise. Representatives of the trucking industry responded that the figure then might as well be 18 m, since it must be a multiple of 6 m which was the length of a container. Faced with this, the Transportation Minister decided to leave the maximum length unchanged at 24 m.
[5]A European standard for electronic document transfer.
[6]They were even called 'The Vabis pork chops' by the local population in Södertälje. (Vabis was originally an abbreviation for 'Vagnsfabriksaktiebolaget i Södertälje,' or the Automotive Plant Company Limited of Södertälje.) Source: Giertz (1991).

7 SINGAPORE AIRLINES AND SAS

By general consensus, Singapore Airlines (SIA) leads its industry in terms of productivity. Highly profitable, boasting a modern fleet of aircraft, the airline outperforms many of its competitors when measured by the industry's own yardsticks. The acclaim of international organizations and trade press observers reinforces the conclusion. Singapore Airlines' home base also lays claim to what, in terms of international civil aviation, is one of the world's most advanced deregulatory environments. Scandinavian Airlines (SAS) is a rather different kind of organization, a three-nation consortium in which Swedish investors, public and private, own three-sevenths of the shares, with the remainder divided between Danish and Norwegian investors. As airlines, Singapore Airlines and SAS offer very similar services. Nevertheless, the two companies operate by the light of different strategies and under the influence of divergent institutional conditions.

In principle, airlines can raise productivity in three ways. First, they can increase the time that their aircraft spend in the air, thus boosting ticket revenues. (On average, airliners fly between six and 15 hours a day, with between 50 and 70 per cent of seats occupied). Second, airlines can increase the percentage of passengers who pay a premium for better service, a tactic that improves the ratio between revenues and costs. Third, airlines can produce their services internally at lower cost. Quite obviously, some of the productivity-raising tactics outlined above are mutually exclusive. What, for example, is the effect of increased flying time on levels of service? How does an airline integrate a cut-price strategy with an image of superlative comfort? Clearly, airlines attempt to find a combination of solutions that are optimal for their purposes.

In the airline industry, international comparisons of productivity based on costs are difficult. Services are not directly comparable. Figure 7.1 provides an approximate breakdown of the cost structures of Singapore Airlines and Scandinavian Airlines. Differences in the levels of fuel

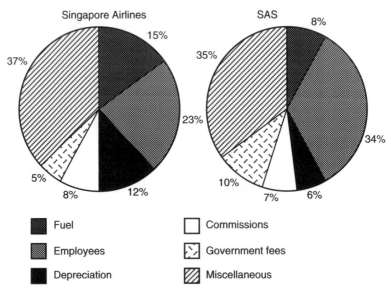

Figure 7.1   Cost structures of Singapore Airlines and SAS.

Source: Annual reports.

costs, for example, are largely explained by the fact that Singapore Airlines undertakes a larger proportion of long-haul flights. Clearly, the
length of a flight has a major effect on its cost per kilometre, as well as
on the relative significance of other cost items. But the problem runs
deeper: even if it were possible to compare airlines operating routes of
equal length, immediate statements about differences of productivity on
the basis of cost would be complicated by immense country-by-country
variations in prices of input factors. Fuel prices, for example, may vary
by as much as 50 per cent. Labour costs for pilots may vary even more.

THE AIRLINE INDUSTRY

How does a nation of 2.6 million inhabitants construct an airline as large
as SIA? The question relies on assumptions more suited to the mercan-
tilist world of 16th century France than the world of international civil
aviation defined by the 1944 Chicago Convention and the waves of
deregulation that have followed in its wake. The Chicago Convention
established the sovereign power of governments over aviation within

national air space – a provision that provided fertile ground for the subsequent growth of a regulatory jungle. The past decade has seen the postwar regulatory regime come in for some sharp questioning: some countries have started cutting through the thickets of rules. In the process of commercial civil aviation deregulation, negotiations mainly cover four areas.[1]

- Market entry: between what points, and in what ways, airlines may fly between two countries?
- Designation: how many of a country's airlines may gain access to another country's market?
- Frequency and capacity: how many seats may an airline place in service?
- Rates: airline prices must be approved by public agencies of the carriers' respective home countries. Within the International Air Transport Association (IATA), airlines get together and discuss price levels in various markets.

Partial abolition of the regulatory regime in some nations during the 1970s had major effects on American and European airlines. A wave of mergers and commercial alliances designed to restore some of the economic security provided by the old regulatory system has led to predictions of an oligopoly, in which a few airlines will operate globally, with many additional small airlines working within limited regions.

Deregulation of civil aviation has proceeded furthest in the United States, especially in that country's far-flung domestic air travel market. Elsewhere, government regulation retains a high profile. Many European-based airlines are government-owned. Instead of seeking entirely free competition, the EC would prefer some form of consensual framework for government subsidy. Even as discussions proceed, some countries are planning to privatize their airlines, following the example of British Airways, which was sold off to private interests in 1987. The company's sale was followed by a 10 per cent shrinkage in routes and a staggering 40 per cent cut in staffing levels.

Most European civil aviation routes are operated by only two competing airlines, evidence of the bilateral air service agreements that leave Europeans paying the world's highest airline ticket prices. In the mid-1980s prices for flights under 4,000 km in length were between 4 and 26 per cent higher in Europe than anywhere else in the world.

Adding their voice to the demands of customer groups, governments, multilateral organizations and certain airlines have demanded deregulation.

The many small carriers that wish to offer flights from regional centres to European capitals have already gained footholds in France, Italy and Britain, exposing the national carriers to a new source of competition. From another direction, charter airlines have taken advantage of the new seat-only ticket procedures that obviate the need to organize hotels and other ground arrangements. The major American-based carriers would also welcome a liberalization of the European regulatory regime. With a large home market base, sophisticated reservation systems and lower labour costs than many of their European-based competitors, the American carriers believe that they can compete successfully in Europe.

Stiff price competition prevails on international routes, especially in situations where new companies have gained a foothold. Routes operated by SAS between Scandinavia and New York are now losing money, with pressure from new competitors on routes between Sweden and London also slashing profits for these flights. Facing overcapacity, carriers with their own aircraft cannot cut back their seat capacity or reorganize their routes in the short term. The sale of low-price tickets does, after all, contribute something toward covering fixed costs and is thus a better alternative than unutilized seat capacity.

Excess capacity is a growing risk. In placing large orders for new aircraft, many airlines had been counting on a continued 5 to 10 per cent annual growth in passenger volume. Air travel has previously risen twice as fast as economic growth: during 1989 the number of airline passengers in the Pacific Rim rose by 14 per cent; the increase in Europe was 7 per cent; passenger numbers in the United States remained unchanged. Negative trends during 1990 and 1991 may have caused many carriers to revise their expansion plans, but given a time lag of several years from order to delivery of aircraft and heavy penalties for cancellation of aircraft purchase contracts, the situation looks bleak for many airlines.

In recent decades, rail travel has become an increasingly tough source of competition for European short-haul civil aviation operators. France provides a good example of the trend: on the 420 km Paris-Lyon route, high-speed trains have severely dented the profitability of rival air carriers. Plans exist to make Paris the hub of a European high-speed train network. Rail traffic in Germany has undergone similar developments: intriguingly, however, Lufthansa has gained control of the national high-speed train network. The aim in Germany is for the rail network to take over all routes less than 400 km or that require less than a two-and-a-half hour train journey. Rail prices are also competitive – about half the level of corresponding air fares.

Traditionally, Singapore has applied very liberal rules in terms of routes, seat capacities and prices, even allowing foreign airlines such as British Airways to operate hubs on the island. (In other words, BA can fly passengers from the south-west Pacific to Singapore, from where they can continue their journey to most major cities in Europe on BA aircraft). Why such a liberal attitude? For obvious reasons of size, the country has no domestic air traffic, and its population constitutes an insufficient base for Singapore Airlines' own international operations. The airline must therefore also carry a high proportion of foreign passengers. Under the characteristic reciprocal agreements that govern the civil aviation industry, Singapore must allow other national carriers to establish operations in Singapore if it wishes its national airline to operate routes to countries with their own national carriers.

Many airlines are drawn by Singapore's attractive geographic location, its flourishing business culture and status as a major tourist attraction. Once an airline has received Singaporean landing rights, because of the country's importance, SIA has a good chance of being granted the take-off and landing slots it wants at airports around the world. Although Copenhagen does not possess the same drawing power as Singapore,

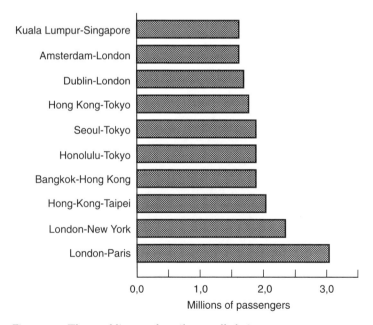

Figure 7.2 The world's most heavily-travelled air routes.

Source: Civial Aviation Statistics of the World – 1990, published by ICAO, 1991.

SAS feels that the airline has largely obtained rights to its desired routes.

The skies of South East Asia are among the busiest in the world. Measured in numbers of passengers, the Kuala Lumpur-Singapore and Hong Kong-Tokyo routes are among the most heavily travelled in the world (see Figure 7.2). The region's airlines currently report better earnings than other airlines, with higher growth in both passenger and cargo operations. Low labour outlays and high proportions of large aircraft in their fleets result in relatively low operating costs. In turn, impressive earnings figures have enabled investment in new aircraft that join some of the world's most modern and productive fleets.

Of the world's 10 largest airlines, five are American (see Figure 7.3). All major European-based airlines, with the exception of British Airways,

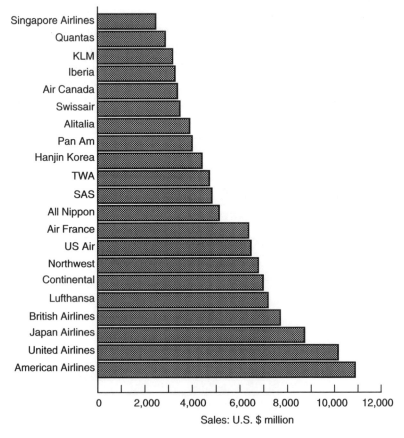

Figure 7.3 The world's largest airlines.

Source: Fortune, January 1, 1990.

are more or less government-owned. European airlines account on the average for about half of each country's civil aviation traffic with other nations. Despite challenges from new, smaller competitors, the established companies enjoy economies of scale, not least in the area of reservation systems and marketing, where costs can be spread across large numbers of passengers. Indeed, the need for reservation systems poses an important obstacle to market entry: only two systems have widespread European coverage: Amadeus and Galileo.

Economies of scale increasingly derive from the concentration of long-haul departures in a small number of airports per continent. These locations function as hubs for surrounding smaller airports (see Figure 7.4). The ability of airlines to build up a network of hubs and so-called spokes is instrumental to profitability. Revenues and costs per passenger kilometre vary greatly, depending on the length of the flight. The static nature of existing route networks also poses a major obstacle to new entrants. The availability of landing slots is limited at major airports. So far the principle has been that airlines can hold on to slots occupied during the preceding season. Scandinavian attitudes toward continued deregulation are lukewarm, primarily because of fears that existing hubs occupied by SAS may be weakened, forcing the airline to focus more resources on simply flying passengers to different hubs.[2]

SINGAPORE AIRLINES

Government is the largest single shareholder in Singapore Airlines. Accounting for about 5 per cent of Singapore's gross domestic product, the airline can be regarded as an instrument of the government's export-oriented economic policy. With their insistence that what is good for the airline is good for the country, the airline's executives maintain that the same factors are responsible for the economic success of nation and company:

- Bold investment in new equipment
- Continuous technical and service training
- Pursuit of market opportunities
- Discipline and dedication
- Consumer orientation
- Management's willingness to encourage innovative, entrepreneurial policies with sufficient research, cash and human resources

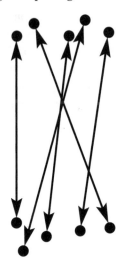 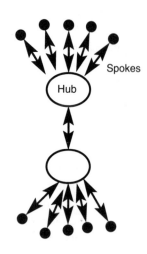

Figure 7.4 The movement to hub-and-spoke structure in the air travel sector.

Corporate philosophy and long-term goals

Many enterprises boast impressively formulated goals that have little impact on their operations. By contrast, Singapore Airlines appears to be trying to achieve its goals in ways consistent with its philosophy, and seems to have been doing so for the past two decades. Consistency and a far-sighted approach are the characteristics of a long-term strategy that focuses on planned, constant and steady expansion. Rapid expansion in good times and equally drastic contractions in bad times are seen as undesirable.

The company emphasizes the relationship between service quality, productivity, human resource practices and profitability. The company has declared its goals in written form. Employees are expected to demonstrate "innovativeness, imagination, prudent risk-taking and the entrepreneurial drive," values ideally channelled through "dedicated teamwork and the pursuit of excellence in every sphere of the Group's activity". Organizationally, democracy and decentralization are expected to reign, with delegation and training regarded as critical activities. Finally, SIA also emphasizes equality, the idea that all units in the company are important.

Strategy

In the cases studied in this book, a company's chances of achieving high productivity have largely depended on external circumstances and the strategies they have chosen. The strategies of the two airlines examined here are similar in terms of their:

- Focus on the high-price business traveller market segment

- Emphasis on quality of service as the most important means of competition

- Close co-operation and mutual ownership arrangements with outside commercial alliance partners

Differences remain. In companies closely related to its main operations, Singapore Airlines has a policy of control through majority ownership rather than by minority shareholding. By contrast, SAS resembles Air France and other airlines in its desire to create a complete "travel-related company". As a consequence of Singapore's geographic location and economic status, SIA specializes in long-distance flights between world business centres. SAS, by contrast, offers many shorter flights.

Productivity management

Singapore Airlines devotes very great care to the management of productivity, using a mix of industry- and company-specific yardsticks. Among measurements of capacity utilization, the airline uses:

- Passenger Load Factor (PLF): the revenue passenger-kilometres expres-sed as a percentage of available seat-kilometres

- Cargo Load Factor (CLF): cargo load tonne-kilometres expressed as a percentage of cargo capacity tonne-kilometres

- Overall Load Factor (OLF): the sum of the above measurements, with figures for passengers converted into tonne-kilometres

Such statistics are widely used in the industry, and even published by IATA. Many of these international yardsticks are also used internally by SIA and are displayed daily at the airline's corporate headquarters and are reported in the company's employee newsletter. Overall performance is discussed at board meetings and twice yearly at general business meetings. In its internal management training programme, company representatives discuss practical cases involving successful competitors.

Each day, SIA's aircraft spend an average of three to four hours longer in the air than SAS aircraft. Occupied seats on SAS flights average around 65 per cent of total capacity; SIA fills an average of more than 75 per cent. Passenger kilometres per airline employee are about one million per year at SAS; SIA achieves more than two million. (SAS trade union representatives maintain that the number of passengers per employee totals about 670 at SAS, whereas Singapore Airlines transports only 570 passengers per employee per year). Different route lengths again explain much of the difference.

Singapore Airlines devotes a lot of space in its annual report to information on the company's productivity. Among other things, SIA measures the load factor required to cover fixed costs and how much this load factor can decline – the load factor gap – before the company drops below the break-even point. The annual report also states revenue per load tonne-kilometre, both on an overall basis and for passenger and cargo traffic, respectively. By comparing these figures with the load factor, the company can determine whether earnings improvements are attributable to better load factors or higher prices. Value-added is also specified for operations and their various portions.

Singapore Airlines also uses productivity yardsticks to analyse resource utilization. Since the company maintains that its most important production resource is personnel, several yardsticks relate to the number of employees: revenue per employee, capacity per employee and load carried per employee. Fuel productivity is a measurement used by SIA, but not by SAS: an important figure, given the key role of fuel costs in

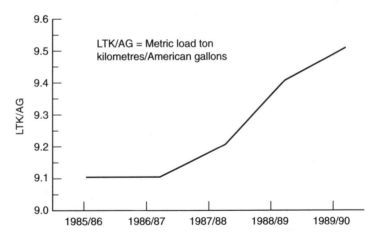

Figure 7.5 Singapore Airlines' fuel productivity.

Source: Singapore Airlines, 1989 annual report.

determining profitability (see Figure 7.5).

At Singapore Airlines' yardsticks are used as performance standards. Passenger load factor, for example, is seen as an indicator of how sales are developing in various markets. When the year-on-year load factor for several major regions dropped in September 1990, the company took rapid action, restructuring routes and changing timetables. Employees were also urged to redouble their efforts.

Service productivity

Despite their after the fact monitoring function, overall productivity yardsticks such as capacity utilization are hardly suited to daily operational management in areas such as service quality. Here SIA employs preventive monitoring, in the form of planning and budgeting systems.

Singapore Airlines has managed to maintain the highest quality of in-flight service levels. Some time ago, the company realized that its service could not be improved very much more and a three-year campaign to improve levels of ground service was instituted. For measuring quality of service in the air and on the ground, SIA uses the following and other measurements:

- Number of delays exceeding 15 minutes (primarily an indicator of ground service)
- Number of customers who have complained or expressed praise
- For in-flight service, the size of cabin crew. Singapore Airlines uses 18 people on B747–300/200s. The industry average is 16

In addition, a so-called service and performance index is based on a questionnaire listing 22 components of ground service, including effective handling of delays. After major delays, the top Singapore Airlines executive in the country where each passenger lives sends a letter of apology. First class and business class passengers even get a personal visit: the situation is explained and a representative notes the customer's views. On the ground, the airline measures speed of response to telephone calls. The aim is for 85 per cent of calls to be answered within 20 seconds. These yardsticks are monitored continuously. According to a company statement, SIA is "religious about complaints and criticism": managers read all written complaints. Serious and recurring problems are examined by a "high level review committee".

"Every complaint is investigated and a personal reply given," the statement continues. "If we have slackened in any area which has caused inconvenience to our passengers, which does sometimes happen, we will examine it for ways to improve."

The company's characteristic passion for detail is evident in the *ad hoc* task forces that analyse shortcomings in service. When the service and performance index for SIA's successful in-flight service declined in the first quarter of 1990, a task force was asked to suggest improvements in food and beverages, entertainment, information and aircraft cleanliness. Notably, a special study surveyed the needs and expectations of Japanese travellers – a customer category of growing importance.

There are trade offs between certain productivity yardsticks. High passenger volumes in the late 1980s, for example, led to high load factors but took a toll on standards of service. Given higher customer expectations and heavier traffic, certain routines proved insufficient. Ground personnel in particular found it hard to provide good service. Eager to sustain the momentum of their three-year plan for world-beating ground service, SIA headquarters advised employees, simplified procedures and cut down on paperwork in the hope that a good service culture would ultimately generate its own momentum.

At its annual business meeting for cabin crew, SIA presents a managing director's Award for Special Acts of Service, providing recognition, in the company's words, for "front-line staff who go beyond the call of duty in providing ground service". The programme to improve ground service has been implemented in three stages, each with its own slogan: "show you care", "dare to care" and "be service entrepreneurs". By the third stage, the company hopes to have fostered three values:

- Initiative: acting on service opportunities missed by others

- Perseverance: overcoming barriers when others have given up

- Creativity: forging ahead in areas that others accept as perfected

The three-year programme consists largely of employee training. The courses are also open to non-employees from airports abroad, since Singapore Airlines cannot place its own representatives everywhere. Unconcerned about training employees from other organizations, the company argues that SIA will still reap the benefits of such training.

"We must accelerate and leave the pack behind," said a SIA deputy managing director at a cabin crew annual meeting, which was reported in the company magazine. "Close attention must be paid to crew performance, so that there will not be a credibility gap between the beautiful, eye catching advertisements depicting the Singapore Girl and the actual service on board. Apart from delivering good service, attention must be paid to character moulding and mental attitude. We must be obsessed with passenger satisfaction."

Human Resource Management

The trade unions in SIA, like all Singaporean workers' organizations, are affiliated to the National Trade Union Congress, which has a close working relationship with the government. Employers, employees and the government are closely bound to one another, facilitating easier negotiation over pay and conditions. At SAS a great number of unions, partly due to the three-nation consortium, have the power to halt service production in the event of a labour dispute. The pay system at SIA is flexible: compared with SAS, basic pay levels are low, resulting in low fixed costs. A bonus wage or profit-sharing bonus is worked out according to assignments and performance. In successful years the bonus totals almost six months' wages. At 5.8 per cent per year, employee turnover at Singapore Airlines is low; absenteeism is sufficiently low for the company not to keep record of it.

SIA constantly seeks to create challenges for its employees, offering them overseas postings and planned job rotation. SAS uses a similar system, although changes in job assignments normally take place only within divisions and not between. SIA maintains that rotation creates generalists, increasing employee understanding of the company and its related operations. Training is accorded high priority in SIA, and expenditures for this purpose were equivalent to 8.5 per cent of wage costs in 1989.

Motivation of front-line personnel is a central issue. Both Scandinavian Airlines and Singapore Airlines are regarded as successful models in terms of service. The companies use different techniques to increase employee commitment and motivation.

Singapore Airlines awards monthly prizes for outstanding performance. The company's employee suggestion system is well-developed, and the best suggestions are published in the personnel magazine. Management uses this system to take soundings from the entire organization and thereby raise productivity in small but important stages. The SAS suggestion system functions less satisfactorily, but the company is trying to change this situation by other means.

Notably, at Singapore Airlines all employees are governed by the similar rules on business and free travel privileges, a policy that seems to have a favourable impact.[3]

Organizational structure

Singapore Airlines combines a relatively flat and decentralized organizational structure with strictly enforced cost controls. Depending on their magnitude, deviations from investment budgets require specific authorization from specially-appointed committees or from individual executives. Interestingly, the extensive bureaucracy invoked by such requests seems to make employees reluctant to seek additional funds for anything other than absolutely necessary investments. At service-oriented units, larger deviations from the budget are permitted if the extra costs are spent to directly increase customer satisfaction. The kind of consensual decision-making practised within Singapore Airlines compensates for lengthy consumption of time by ensuring solid support for decisions.

Decision-making on policy matters at Singapore Airlines emanates from the top. On almost all issues, management can make decisions without consulting the board. At SAS the situation is similar: both companies have similar ownership structures, in which a government holding is combined with otherwise passive private stockholders. In terms of operations, at SIA opinions tend to move upwards from the bottom of the organization, in a pattern that presupposes open channels of communication and a similarly open-minded management. At SAS, suggestions for improvement often come from top management only to be enforced within the organization. The risk of wasted ideas from employees has adverse consequences on productivity growth. The many small steps required to raise long-term productivity thus become problematic.

Value systems

The strong commitment to service and productivity at Singapore Airlines is only comprehensible in terms of the value systems that permeate a company that describes "excellence" as the habit of getting things right the first time around. There is a negative side to any such mentality; namely, fear of failure and its attendant punishments. Integrity and hard work are also highly prized.[4] Promotion on merit is another important value.

Lifetime employment, though not of the Japanese variety, is available at Singapore Airlines, where employees commonly have work histories that stretch back for 25 or even 30 years. In an informal trait common to Chinese organizations generally, company recruitment policy favours the families of employees even to the extent of special grant and scholarship schemes.

The group as a unit is so heavily emphasized in training and reward systems that one employee told an interviewer that many colleagues identify sufficiently strongly with their company to put its welfare ahead of both themselves and their families. During a recession, pilots may even change working assignments to serve temporarily as cabin crew members. Economic security and SIA's long-term growth targets are closely related to this group mentality. Harmony also appears to be highly valued: employees are encouraged to put forward ideas, but in a non-confrontational manner.

The concept of equality before the law seems to apply to all employees, including top executives who behave like ordinary white collar employees, drive ordinary cars and are, as mentioned earlier, covered by the same rules on business and complimentary travel. With the Singaporean government as a big shareholder, it comes as little surprise to find top executives espousing a civil service-style mentality in which, following the Confucian model, service and role model provision are seen as the main functions.

Ownership

When Singapore Airlines was established the national government declared that the company would operate according to strictly commercial principles. Although later partial privatization strengthened local capital markets, raised funds for the company and boosted the market orientation of managers, long-term strategy remained largely untouched. In practice, Singapore Airlines was already functioning as a private company. With its owners adopting very long-term return on investment targets, SIA works to maintain a steady rate of growth despite temporary downturns during recessions.

Technology

The average service age of aircraft in the company's fleet – 57 months (March 1991) – is far below industry averages. Newer models of aircraft deliver better fuel economy, particularly important in the context of SIA's reliance on long-haul flights. The relative newness of its fleet also enables SIA to offer passengers better service on board. A policy of continuous purchase of new aircraft also makes training a natural element of operations. Undoubtedly, passengers fixated by questions of safety are attracted to the idea of travel on relatively new aircraft. Large new aircraft are also tailored to provide the high standards of service and reliability required by the lucrative business traveller market.

Singapore Airlines tries to buy aircraft new during recessions; it sells them in used condition during economic upturns. Using aircraft mostly of one size category also allows interchangeability between routes, prompting efficient capacity utilization. Alliances with Swissair and Delta Airlines have allowed Singapore Airlines to hook up with other airlines' feeder routes, removing the need to operate them itself.

High capacity utilization is more problematic for SAS, which flies short domestic routes as well as longer European and intercontinental routes. Aircraft requirements vary according to flying distance, limiting interchangeability. Shorter flights often result in low capacity utilization, depending on high variations in load factors from hour-to-hour and day-to-day.

SAS

SAS ranks among European-based airlines operating on a global basis. Despite their smaller proportion of transatlantic routes, (see Table 7.1) airlines based in southern and northern Europe tend to be bigger in relation to their market base than their central European counterparts. In 1986 SAS came fifth in Europe on the basis of number of passengers. In terms of the number of paid passenger kilometres, however, SAS stood in eighth place, indicating that a relatively low proportion of its flights fell within the profitable long-haul category.

	All routes: Millions of passengers	Percentage of these within Europe	Percentage of these over the Atlantic
British Airways (BA)	17.7	41	11
Lufthansa (LUF)	15.2	46	11
Air France (AF)	12.0	60	7
Swissair (SWI)	6.9	66	10
KLM (KLM)	5.2	49	22
Sabena (SAB)	2.2	67	15
Iberia (IBE)	13.6	35	4
Alitalia (ALI)	8.4	42	7
Olympic Airways (OA)	6.6	18	3
Scandinavian Airlines (SAS)	11.9	46	5

Table 7.1 Passengers on European-based airlines, 1986.

Source: Association of European Airlines, quoted in Encaoua (1991).

	All routes: billions of kilometres	Percentage of these across Europe	Percentage of these over the Atlantic
British Airways (BA)	42.3	15	30
Lufthansa (LUF)	26.9	20	37
Air France (AF)	27.4	23	17
Swissair (SWI)	13.2	23	29
KLM (KLM)	19.7	9	41
Sabena (SAB)	5.6	20	36
Iberia (IBE)	18.6	29	14
Alitalia (ALI)	14.2	23	28
Olympic Airways (OA)	6.6	30	20
Scandinavian Airlines (SAS)	12.5	30	30

Table 7.2 Paid passenger kilometres on European-based airlines, 1986.

Source: Association of European Airlines, quoted in Encaoua (1991).

Table 7.1 shows numbers of passengers for each of the big European airlines. Table 7.2, by contrast, shows the size of each airline's paid passenger kilometres. The rankings of the airlines in these two tables do not necessarily coincide. The differences are explained primarily by each airline's proportion of long-haul flights. Two airlines with the same number of passengers are thus unequal in terms of paid passenger kilometres if their average flight distances are different.

Change of strategy

Since the early 1980s, SAS has self-consciously aimed at being the Businessman's Airline, investing to create very high levels of service for this customer segment.[5] Non-stop (or, at most, one stop) flights and good take-off and arrival times have contributed to the overall aim. Like Singapore Airlines, SAS has a small domestic market: a hub and spoke system centring on Copenhagen and Stockholm offers larger varieties of destinations, a strategy augmented by a policy of strategic alliances. The company's focus on business travellers has proved successful: as Table 7.3 indicates, SAS occupies first place among European-based airlines in terms of revenue per paid passenger kilometre on flights within Europe. By contrast, SAS stands at around the middle of the pack in terms of similar figures for transatlantic flights.

SAS has sought working partnerships with airlines characterized by similar corporate cultures but has not been completely successful. Employees at SAS identified readily with Swissair in this regard. On the other hand relationships with the company's American-based partner, Continental, were a different matter altogether: SAS invested great resources to raise Continental's level of service, and top managers were forced to argue the case for an alliance with Continental in the face of reluctance among their own work-force.

Expansion into closely related fields
In a move that has provoked some controversy among outside analysts, SAS recently has expanded operations to include such air travel-related service sectors as accommodation, catering, duty-free sales and charter flights.

Cost situation

In somewhat simplified terms, Scandinavian Airlines can be described as a high-revenue, high-cost airline. Among other things, employee costs are relatively high, and the ongoing process of European deregulation and the generally poor economic situation of the civil aviation industry have led the company to initiate a cost-cutting programme after sharp earnings declines in 1990 and 1991. Corporate strategy, with its emphasis on business travel and high price segments, remains unchanged.

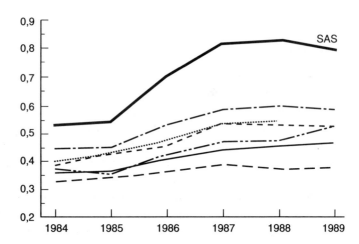

Figure 7.6 Operating expenditure for SAS and six other major European airlines. US $ per ATK*
*Available tonne kilometres

Table 7.3 shows average unit cost figures, measured in terms of cost per tonne kilometre. Table 7.4 shows the length of airlines' European and transatlantic flights. For SAS, unit cost within Europe was $1.08; the corresponding figure for transatlantic flights was only $0.40. For other airlines, costs within Europe are also two to three times higher than on transatlantic flights.

	BA	LUF	AF	SWI	KLM	SAB	IBE	ALI	OA	SAS
Unit costs[a]	91	93	92	102	99	80	62	85	40	108
Average route length[b]	868	686	760	636	616	583	1008	837	1695	621
Load factor[c]	57	54	57	53	58	52	65	55	48	54
Unit revenue[d]	177	186	176	188	164	174	111	182	84	236
Revenue per paid passenger kilometre[e]	16	19	17	20	17	18	10	18	8	20

a) Cost per available metric ton kilometres, U.S. cents
b) Kilometres
c) Paid ton kilometres as a percentage of available ton kilometres
d) Revenue per ton kilometres, U.S. cents
e) Revenue per paid passenger kilometres, U.S. cents

Source: Association of European Airlines, quoted in Encaoua (1991).

Table 7.3 Unit cost and unit revenues of European-based airlines on flights within Europe, 1986.

Even though the competition is tougher than elsewhere, European airlines remain interested in the higher load factor potential offered on transatlantic routes. For SAS, load factors in Europe average 54 per cent; the corresponding figure over the Atlantic is 68 per cent. As Table 7.4 also indicates, KLM experienced both low unit costs and low unit revenue over the Atlantic – a fact that may be related to a 1978 international air travel liberalization agreement with the United States. Since 1978, KLM has faced stiff competition on its transatlantic flights.[6]

Within Europe, Spain's Iberia boasts the lowest unit costs – at $0.62, about 40 per cent below comparable figures for SAS. Although the average length of SAS flights within Europe is fairly short, the company reports higher unit costs than airlines engaged in routes of approximately the same average length. Table 7.5 presents the cost structure of European-based airlines on flights within Europe in 1986. In analysing such cost differences, however, one needs to remember the effects of that proportion of flights run on a charter basis, flights generally marked by high load factors and relatively low costs.

	BA	LUF	AF	SWI	KLM	SAB	IBE	ALI	OA	SAS
Unit costs[a]	34	30	37	34	27	30	30	32	32	19
Average route length[b]	4394	4195	4722	4375	5827	4330	3903	4524	6401	5625
Load factor[c]	63	34	74	62	70	76	66	63	40	68
Unit revenue[d]	58	47	52	56	41	37	47	50	42	50
Revenue per paid passenger kilometre[e]	6.9	6.3	6.9	7.6	5.4	5.0	5.3	5.9	4.1	6.1

a) Cost per available metric ton kilometres, U.S. cents
b) Kilometres
c) Paid ton kilometres as a percentage of available ton kilometres
d) Revenue per ton kilometres, U.S. cents
e) Revenue per paid passenger kilometre, U.S. cents

Source: Association of European Airlines, quoted in Encaoua (1991).

Table 7.4 Unit cost and unit revenues of European-based airlines on flights over the North Atlantic, 1986.

Table 7.5 indicates that at all airlines, indirect costs exceeded direct costs. SAS had the highest indirect costs, nearly half of which were incurred in generating sales. At SAS, wage costs for flight crews – cockpit plus cabin crews – accounted for 15 per cent of total costs, the highest percentage among European-based carriers. High cost levels of this kind seem to be associated with a slow national pace of deregulation.[7]

	BA	LUF	AF	SWI	KLM	SAB	IBE	ALI	OA	SAS
Direct costs										
Cockpit crew	4.6	6.9	6.7	8.9	5.6	6.0	4.1	6.1	1.6	8.7
Fuel	6.4	8.1	10.2	7.5	6.3	8.0	9.7	7.4	6.1	9.3
Insurance	0.8	0.5	0.4	0.5	0.8	0.6	0.3	0.4	0.5	0.3
Maintenance	8.2	11.1	7.4	12.0	11.2	5.5	6.9	8.5	4.3	11.1
Depreciation	8.7	5.4	5.4	8.0	7.1	2.2	2.1	5.9	0.8	7.3
Leasing costs	0.4	2.2	4.3	0.6	3.3	0.5	–	1.8	0.5	2.6
Landing fees	8.6	7.6	7.5	8.0	9.1	4.7	4.0	4.5	1.4	10.1
En route charges	3.7	3.2	2.9	3.1	3.1	3.6	3.5	3.3	1.6	3.4
Total direct costs	41.2	44.9	44.7	48.6	46.4	31.2	30.7	37.7	16.6	52.8
Indirect costs										
Ground personnel etc.	14.9	16.2	15.2	16.9	14.5	13.1	8.2	13.7	7.3	14.6
Cabin crew	4.2	4.6	5.4	3.7	2.7	3.7	3.0	5.7	1.6	6.3
Passenger service	6.2	6.1	7.1	7.5	6.4	7.1	3.1	4.9	2.9	6.9
Sales costs	17.6	18.1	18.4	22.0	21.7	20.7	5.3	17.4	7.6	24.8
Other administration	6.3	3.6	1.4	3.1	7.1	3.9	1.6	5.2	4.2	2.8
Total indirect costs	49.7	48.1	47.5	53.3	52.4	48.6	31.3	47.0	23.6	55.3
Total	90.9	93.0	92.2	101.9	98.9	79.8	62.0	84.7	40.2	108.0

*Cost per available ton kilometres, U.S. cents

Source: Association of European Airlines, from Encaoua (1991).

Table 7.5 Breakdown of unit cost of European-based airlines on flights within Europe, 1986.

Figure 7.7 indicates that SAS costs for cabin crew members have been constantly higher than its main European competitors during much of the 1980s. SAS regulations stipulate that long-haul crews should be drawn evenly from the nationals of the three Scandinavian countries. This requirement leads to the extra cost of transporting crew members during working time to different destinations.[8]

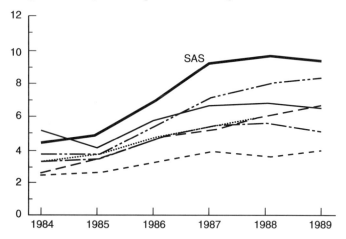

Figure 7.7 Cabin crew costs: SAS versus main European competitors.
Source: Association of European Airlines.

Direct costs at SAS – including landing fees over which the airline has little control – were also higher than among other European-based airlines. Partly due to government-imposed taxes, the Scandinavian airline's fuel costs are among Europe's highest.

Service goals and productivity management

A quality assurance programme focuses on the moment of truth that occurs when SAS employees come into contact with customers. Using two types of passenger questionnaires, performance standards that vary with passenger quality have been established within a so-called service chain of 13 different areas including waiting times and cleanliness of facilities. Unfortunately, many of the benchmarks seem to have been fixed in a somewhat arbitrary fashion, triggering discussions all the way up to the top levels of management.

Levels of service are measured at more than 1,000 locations. Measurements of qualities such as punctuality, reliability, denied boarding and the upgrading or downgrading of passengers can be taken with existing computer systems. Other measurements are taken by a variety of manual and semi-automatic systems. Everyone at SAS has access to information within the quality assurance system, which is known as QualiSAS – a factor that permits self-monitoring. Results are also disseminated via monthly reports to the relevant managers. Annual and half-yearly reports are compiled along with special reports on specific areas that require action.

Assessments of overall service quality are appended to the company's monthly financial reports, creating opportunities for the integration of quality control and financial management. In the name of avoiding so-called quality gaps, the company has defined the costs of both shortcomings and, interestingly, of instances of unnecessarily high quality.

Such calculations are difficult to make. In the case of lost telephone calls, for example, SAS asks customers who do get through by telephone what they would have done if they had not been able to do so. The proportion of those who reply that they would instead have called a travel agent or flown with a competing airline are judged to give a good idea of the true proportion of lost customers. Through its own measurements, SAS knows how often telephone calls result in completed sales. Data on the average revenue for each sales transaction are also available. Because the company also continuously estimates the percentage of lost calls, the necessary data exists to estimate the average value of a lost telephone call and the total amount of money the company loses at each sales location.

As long as shortcomings in quality exceed the cost of accepting more phone calls, increases in sales resources – new switchboard systems and new employees – are judged profitable avenues of investment. Equally, the trade-off between quality and cost can result in the closing of offices or in personnel cutbacks. The same principles are applied to as many areas of operations as possible.

Organizational structure

At Scandinavian Airlines the atmosphere is open. Although the corporate suggestion system reports an unusually small number of suggestions per employee annually, anyone can make suggestions for changes, usually by approaching individuals one step above in terms of hierarchy. Employees may also go directly to top management.

In nearly all cases, changes originate with top management before spreading through the organization. Between group companies, there are great variations in the ways in which goals and ideals are communicated to employees. Divisional managers are responsible for disseminating information. Middle managers, certainly, must be persuaded of the correctness of a given action, but in principle, decisions are questioned at all levels.

From the standpoint of customer service and efficiency, SAS has tried to delegate as much responsibility as possible. This hopefully fosters faster decisions and increased initiative. There are ample opportunities for experimentation that does not disturb general smooth functioning.

Human Resource Management

At the core of SAS corporate and personnel policy lies the desire to gain the full backing and participation of employees – "achieving success through people" – in operational matters. Employees themselves must apply for the jobs in which they are interested. Participation in the trainee programme does not constitute a guarantee of a job: trainees compete for jobs like everyone else.

Before being appointed as managers, employees go through a basic training programme. In the four-week course offered every year to 200 middle managers, goals are discussed. Depending on what definition is used, SAS spends somewhere between SEK 80 and 600 million annually on training and development, with each employee spending an average of two to four days each year in training.

Scandinavian Airlines' policy is to pay market wages but, as a popular company, it probably has attracted better than average employees. Annual personnel turnover at SAS runs at 3 per cent; absenteeism during illness is about the average for Swedish companies. Negotiations over pay and conditions are made difficult by the large number of labour unions within the company. During recessions a clear return to traditional trade union roles is discernible; reduced willingness to participate in joint development task forces generally marks the periodic return to a more traditional adversarial relationship.

Technology

During 1989 and 1990, SAS made large-scale investments in aircraft, introducing Boeing 767 long-distance aircraft to replace DC-10s on intercontinental routes. Elsewhere, DC-9s are being replaced by the MD-10. Unfortunately, excess capacity in civil aviation markets during this period has made it difficult to sell older aircraft at good prices.

CONCLUSIONS

Singapore Airlines achieves high productivity by successfully targeting high-price segments of the market and keeping its costs as low as those of competitors. The mixture of strategies that has fostered cost-effectiveness includes a focus on high load factor long-haul routes that provide economies of scale; concentration of resources on core operations;

smoothly functioning commercial alliances; and stringent cost control over fixed employee costs. At SIA, technological leadership assumes the shape of a modern aircraft fleet that offers good service, low maintenance costs and fuel consumption plus the necessity-turned-to-virtue of continuous updating of employee skills. In a relatively flat organizational structure that places a strong emphasis on productivity management, employees appear highly motivated. Operating in the context of a stable national political scene, the airline's owners have a long-term approach.

Despite its problems, SAS is one of Europe's finest airlines. The company's focus on business travellers and its creation of a hub and spoke system lie behind such success. Nevertheless, a number of productivity-promoting factors work to the advantage of SIA:

- A culture that understands the importance of constant adjustments that boost productivity

- Continuous competitive pressure that has ruled out the luxury of sole rights to certain routes

- Homogeneous operations: SIA's mainly long-haul operations have not suffered from being divided into airline operations and other activities

- Good horizontal co-ordination of operations, with a lack of the kind of divisions between separate legal entities that can pose obstacles to internal co-operation

- The same kind of far-reaching delegation of authority, but combined with tighter cost control

Scandinavian Airlines now boasts a quality control system at least as good as that of Singapore Airlines. Yet SIA is regarded as a model. Liberal crew composition rules and a more flexible wage system mean that SIA can adapt more successfully to recessionary pressures. SIA has dared to buy aircraft during recessions and has been able to sell them during boom periods. The pace and tone of Singapore Airlines' strong alliances with Swissair and Delta reflect an eagerness to learn. Most importantly, perhaps, SIA's owners declared from the start that the activities of their company should be competitive and not based on government protection or subsidies.

---

[1]Other government regulations also exist in the form of safety monitoring requirements etc. Another form of government regulation, which is a substantial cost item for European airlines in particular, is take-off and landing fees. These fees are of relatively greater importance for short flights in Europe than in intercontinental traffic. When flying in Europe, airlines must also pay

the fees to international air traffic organization Eurocontrol to be permitted to utilize airspace.

[2]Encaoua (1991), pp. 112–113.

[3]There are also many shareholders among the work-force.

[4]The following example of diligence on the job is worth mentioning. A European airline (not SAS) has a rule that regional managers work about five years at each posting, then move on. One regional manager who was approaching retirement age chose to spend his final tour of duty in Singapore. His intention was to enjoy a pleasant end to an active professional life. But when he had settled in, he discovered that his employees were arriving at the office between 6:30 and 7:00 a.m. and working until late evening. As manager, he was forced to put in the same working hours.

[5]Business travellers occupy about 55 per cent of SAS seats but contribute 65 per cent of profits. For tourists, the corresponding figures are 45 and 35 per cent.

[6]Encaoua (1991), p. 116.

[7]Encaoua (1991), p. 118.

[8]*Veckans affärer*, 1990; 43, p. 70.

8 SKF – INTERCOMPANY COMPARISON

SKF – A SWEDISH SUCCESS STORY

In 1905, Gamlestadens Fabriker, a textile company in Gothenburg, Sweden, was having serious trouble with the bearings supporting the lineshafts that transmitted power from a central steam engine to its spinning machines. A young maintenance engineer named Sven Wingquist felt that the imported bearings were of poor quality and that they could be improved. As a consequence of Wingquist's assiduous spare-time efforts to design bearings, two years later Gamlestadens Fabriker established a company called Svenska Kullagerfabriken (literally The Swedish Ball Bearing Factory) or SKF for short. The company's first products were deep-groove ball bearings (DGBBs). In its first year of operations, SKF had 15 employees and made 2,200 bearings, showing a loss of 5,372 kronor. Next, Wingquist tackled the problems caused by heavy rainfalls that led to subsidence in the foundations of the factory buildings, warping the long lineshafts of the machines. The self-aligning bearing solved this problem. This unique product became the foundation of SKF's dominant position in the bearing industry.

Rapid expansion and internationalization before *World War II*

Even during its first few years of operations, SKF expanded rapidly. By 1910 the company had a network of sales offices and agents abroad. Production soon began in France, Britain and the United States. In 1912 the first research laboratory was set up in Gothenburg, and in 1916 SKF bought a Swedish steel company, Hofors Bruk. Shortly after World War I, SKF had 12 plants, sales outlets in more than 100 countries and over 12,000 employees.

SKF continued to expand its product range, solving most friction problems where rolling bearings could be of use. By the end of the 1920s, the company was turning out more than 25 million bearings annually: of 25,000 employees, 7,500 worked in Sweden. During the expansive 1920s, beginning with a series of ten prototype cars equipped with SKF ball bearings, SKF also managed to launch the Volvo (the name came from the Latin for "I roll"). Volvo became an independent company in 1935. Despite the rapid expansion of the interwar period, demand for bearings continued to outstrip capacity and SKF experienced the most profitable period in its history.

SKF's evolution into a global industrial group

Many of SKF's European factories were bombed during World War II. During post-war reconstruction, SKF's business was influenced by changes in international business conditions. Nationalism combined with strong co-operation between groups of countries linked by commercial and ideological bonds led SKF to create a structure of centrally co-ordinated but relatively autonomous units.

Competition heated up in the bearing industry during the 1960s. SKF sought to strengthen its market position by acquisitions and a major reorganization of its European operations. The company's Global Forecasting and Supply System (GFSS) centralized the production of each type of bearing within a small number of plants. Previously, individual SKF factories had manufactured and sold many different types of bearings, mainly on local markets. Under GFSS, production is still forecasted and co-ordinated via a company office in Brussels.

Much has happened since Wingquist's first bearings left the Gothenburg factory. SKF now has plants and sales companies throughout the world and, with 95 per cent of sales and 88 per cent of employees based abroad, the company is regarded today as Sweden's most highly internationalized company. SKF's 50,000 employees produce more than 600 million bearings annually. Designs have been continuously refined; manufacturing has become much more efficient. Productivity had multiplied tenfold by the end of the 1920s; a similar hike in performance followed. Over nearly 85 years, SKF's productivity has thus increased a hundredfold.

Selection of companies for this study

SKF is the world's largest manufacturer of bearings. In many respects it sets the global standards for product and organizational performance in this field. During the past decade, SKF has shown decent earnings, despite problems in the industry as a whole. During the 1980s, however, SKF's leadership came under challenge, especially in the small DGBB segment for bearings with an outer diameter of less than 28 mm. The pattern was familiar: first, Japanese companies established a bridgehead in high volume market segments where price was an important means of competition. If these Japanese companies now move into larger, more demanding segments, can SKF respond successfully? "In marathon terms, some years ago SKF was running far ahead of us," one Japanese competitor has noted. "Now we are close enough to see its uniform number."

The original intention was to compare a Swedish unit within the SKF Group with German or Japanese competitors. However, a multinational corporation such as SKF is by no means a collection of homogeneous production units. Having learned that SKF's best-performing manufacturing unit was its factory in Fontenay, southwestern France, we decided that it might be interesting to depart from our method of comparing two separate companies and instead look at one of SKF's factories in Gothenburg, the site of Group headquarters, as a reference object. Our analysis could thereby focus more on differences in productivity that are dependent on where an operation is located.

In the SKF Group's internal ranking, the Fontenay factory has been found to be the best with regard to a number of critical yardsticks, including customer service and cost level. Its product range is subjected to heavy competition. Our point of comparison, SKF's E-factory in Gothenburg, has shown poorer performance levels in terms of scheduled deliveries and cost levels. Notably, both factories produce deep-groove ball bearings (DGBBs).

The bearing industry

Ball bearings are an integral part of most industrial machinery, as well as many household appliances. Computers employ small DGBBs (miniature bearings) to handle the friction problems of rotary motions, while large machines often contain several types of bearings. This market therefore consists of numerous variants designed to meet different requirements. The kind of bearings manufactured in Fontenay comprise more than one-third of the overall bearing market. The sales of bearings are climbing fastest in Asia, where the market's rate of growth touches 5 per cent a year – double the rate in Europe and the United States.

About 50 companies around the world manufacture bearings. Most such firms are small-scale local market suppliers or highly specialized producers focused on applications for textile industry machinery or car water pumps. Only six companies – the Big Six – have a sufficiently complete product range to sell bearings on a global basis. These companies account for more than half of the world's total bearing production (see Table 8.1). Although they do not compete with each other in all markets and do not use the same means of competition, they can be classified as a strategic group.

Manufacturer		Global market share
SKF	(Sweden)	20
FAG	(Germany)	8
NTN	(Japan)	10
NSK	(Japan)	10
KOYO	(Japan)	8
NACHI	(Japan)	4
Sum		60

Table 8.1 The Big Six and their approximate shares of the world market for bearings, in per cent.

Bearing producers can be characterized by variety of product range and production of either large or small bearings. A further basis for classification looks at regional as opposed to global sales – a factor partly related to the size of product range. Variety of product range is important: in many industrial applications, several types of bearings are required. Sales therefore frequently involve offering a number of different bearings to the same customer; one type of product can gain a market foothold with the aid of other products.

SKF has a presence in most markets and enjoys a position of strength in the production of most types of bearings. In Europe, SKF's sales are nearly double those of each of its two closest competitors, FAG and INA. SKF also enjoys a fairly good position in the United States. In Japan, which accounts for a large percentage of the fast-growing Asian market, the picture is somewhat different.

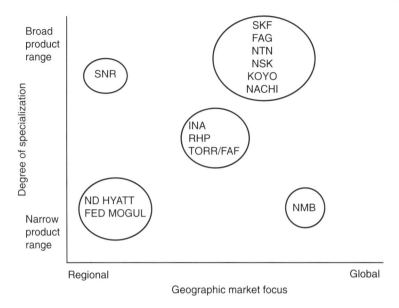

Figure 8.1 Market coverage and breadth of product range among the world's largest bearing manufacturers.

DGBBs

The product – technical development and substitutes
A deep-groove ball bearing consists of an outer ring, an inner ring, steel balls and a retainer. The product is highly standardized, with ISO standards for dimensions, clearances and vibrations frequently making bearings from different manufacturers interchangeable. Because of diverse requirements, the variations in each size and dimension series category can be large.[1]

Technical progress has placed increasingly heavy demands on deep-groove ball bearings' ability to handle higher shaft speeds and higher operating temperatures. Bearings are expected to deliver longer service life, quieter operation and scaled-down size under demanding conditions. Manufacturers must improve their product in terms of surface finish and surface roughness, tolerances and seals. Clearly, although DGBBs are relatively simple products, their manufacture requires advanced technology.

The manufacturing of DGBBs involves many rather short, high volume, production cycles. The marginal cost for producing one DGBB is very low; the set-up costs for a new batch can be high. The most important technologies are grinding, honing and hot working. In general, the companies in the industry develop grinding techniques internally. Development work in other technologies, however, does not always occur in the companies that assemble the finished bearings. Larger companies often establish links with smaller companies with skills in a specific area. SKF thus recently acquired Chicago Rawhide, the world's largest sealing systems company.

Prices, markets and customers

The market for deep-groove ball bearings can be divided into two categories, small or miniature bearings and large DGBBs. The divide between small and large bearings occurs at an outer diameter (OD) measurement of 28 mm. With small bearings, quality and price are the foremost means of competition. Because these bearings are manufactured in large quantities, production resembles a process industry in which the manufacturer calculates the marginal costs of additional production of a particular type of bearing.

Manufactured in Fontenay and at the E-factory, large DGBBs are sold mainly to companies in the automotive, electrical and machine industries. In the automotive and electrical industries, 50 buyers account for 80 per cent of the market. In the machine industry, 300 companies buy 80 per cent of all large deep-groove ball bearings. The result: demanding clients that purchase in large quantities.

Concentration of sales among fewer and larger companies probably explains the relatively low profitability of bearing manufacturers. Given that prices are mainly affected by the customer's buying volume, customers enjoy negotiating power. Customers often have several suppliers of bearings, even of the same type of bearing. This applies especially to commonly specified pieces, where more or less pronounced spot markets may arise.

The level of customer need for close co-operation with the supplier, technical support and special terms of delivery vary, depending on the industry and the customer's size. In the electrical industry, applications are usually of a relatively simple nature. Mainly bearings for rotary motions are required. It suffices for the customer to get a high-quality bearing. The application is then uncomplicated enough for the buyer's technical department to handle on its own. During the 1980s, Japanese companies managed to establish themselves in Europe as suppliers to the electrical industry in particular. Their means of competition have been relatively low prices and very high quality.

Suppliers
Steel of various kinds is the raw material. The kind of steel used is of great importance to the performance, price and quality of the final product. SKF buys half its steel from its partly-owned companies. The most commonly purchased component is steel balls. In the United States and Japan, balls are often produced by independent companies. In Europe these components are more usually manufactured by bearing makers.

Greater customer demands for flexibility are forcing producers to shorten lead times and adapt volumes and products to market requirements. Manufacturers have also increased levels of co-operation with sub-contractors in order to reduce delivery times and achieve greater flexibility and quality.

SKF and other major European-based companies are more vertically integrated than their Japanese competitors. Probably an advantage in the past, vertical integration is not too important today. In a smoothly functioning market for good components and materials, the trend is toward a higher proportion of external purchases of these items.

Competitors in the DGBB market
The strength of SKF's competitors is often concentrated in certain geographic areas or certain product sizes. Of the Big Six, two are European-based and four are Japanese-based companies. Between them, these companies account for roughly two-thirds of the world market for DGBBs.

SKF has enjoyed a dominant position, but rapid growth of Japanese markets means that relatively new companies in the DGBB field have now nearly matched SKF's capacity in this speciality. On top of Japanese domestic market expansion, Japanese companies have expanded fastest by entering the European and US markets. In the DGBB field, only SKF has succeeded in rebuffing the Japanese onslaught.

The small bearing market sector is dominated by NMB, which supplies nearly half the market and is characterized by its strategy of aggressive pricing. In the small bearing segment it is relatively difficult to compensate for high prices with other inducements. SKF's position in the small DGBB segment is therefore in jeopardy.

Japanese companies are less competitive in the large DGBB segment. The larger the bearings, the greater is the degree of custom tailored production. In this segment, customers also tend to buy additional products from the same suppliers. SKF leads in terms of product range and after-sales service. In this product segment, SKF also has more competitive prices than in small DGBBs.

SKF has 15 factories that produce DGBBs. Of these, nine are located in Europe, two in North America, two in South America and one each in South Africa and India. The largest factories in SKF's DGBB production network are two in France (of which one is Fontenay) and two in Italy. Since the 1970s SKF has sought to specialize its factories within certain product ranges, a structure that been seen as industry standard.

Focus on cost-effectiveness

During the 1960s, competition began to heat up in the bearing industry. During the 1970s and most of the 1980s, global overcapacity became marked. Despite the high levels of technical skill involved, differences in quality between companies are not immense. A reduced number of buyers possess advanced technical competence in the context of a strong negotiating position. Taken together, this has meant that SKF, and, to an even greater extent, its competitors, has experienced heavy competitive pressure during the past two decades.

The market in bearings is relatively mature. Admittedly, steady improvement comes as a result of work carried out on a more or less parallel basis among competitors in the industry. Grinding, which occurs at the end of the processing chain, has been regarded for many years as the

	Fontenay	E-factory
Deliveries, 1990 (SC[a])	100	45
Number of employees, 1990		
• Blue collar	100	25
• White collar	100	28
Factory area	100	82
Number of lines[b]	100	54
Bearing diameters (OD, mm)	28–52	52–110
Production of bearings/day	100[c]	9[d]

Index Fontenay = 100

a = Standard Cost
b = Grinding + assembly
c = October 1990
d = January 1991

Table 8.2 Data on the E-factory and Fontenay plant.

key technology. Recently, however, forming technology has grown in importance. In this area, SKF is thought to lag behind its Japanese competitors. Clearly, new technologies can develop even in mature industries: taking rapid advantage of new key technologies remains essential.

The E-factory in Gothenburg and the plant in Fontenay operate under fairly similar competitive conditions. Exposed to Japanese competitive pressures, the latter probably experiences tougher market pressures. Fontenay nevertheless reports higher profitability and a better labour market situation than the E-factory: the result is a less difficult resource situation. Both factories have to assign higher priority to cost-effectiveness than innovation because they have only limited opportunities for generating modifications that will have an impact in the form of higher prices. Innovation is more feasible in the large DGBB segment, where technical assistance and service play an important part in attracting buyers.

DIFFERENCES IN PRODUCTIVITY AT FONTENAY AND THE E-FACTORY

Fontenay is the largest of the DGBB factories in terms of employees. Its factory production is worth more than twice as much as that of the E-factory. Nevertheless, the E-factory is almost as large in area, because it also makes another type of bearing. Table 8.2 provides some data on the size and specialization of the two plants.

The Fontenay factory and the E-factory were both built in the early 1970s. Both factories were equipped with modern technology for the grinding and assembly of bearings. From the beginning, Fontenay also carried out the preceding two steps in the production process: turning and heat treating. The E-factory specialized more in final processing until 1986-87, when its operations also were broadened to include the two preceding process stages. Thus, direct comparisons are only possible for the period after the extension of manufacturing capacity at the E-factory.

The E-factory apparently has the leaner organization, with fewer hierarchical levels and production decisions decentralized to self-controlling units of between seven and ten employees. Organization at Fontenay smacks of Taylorism. Production is monitored by foremen controlling between two and four unskilled operators. The typical operator is a former or a part-time farmer. Unexpectedly, however, this traditional manufacturing format succeeds better in terms of productivity performance.

Performance levels

Profitability
SKF calculates operating earnings by subtracting costs from delivery value and dividing the result by delivery value. Delivery value consists of the quantity delivered multiplied by a standard price for each product. Using this yardstick, Fontenay shows substantially better earnings than the E-factory. Indeed, the E-factory has reported growing negative operating earnings over the past three years.

Productivity
One of the yardsticks that SKF uses to measure productivity is value-added per hour worked. Figures 8.2 and 8.3 track this yardstick in recent years at Fontenay and in the E-factory. Indexed series such as these make it possible to compare the trends in productivity between 1988 and 1990. At Fontenay, productivity has increased since 1985 by an average of nearly 9 per cent per year. At the E-factory it has declined by an average of 5 per cent per year after 1987.

Figures 8.2 and 8.3 also show changes in value-added and hours worked at the two factories. These figures help explain why productivity trends have been so much better at Fontenay. By studying the trend of value-added stated in standard prices, we can see how production volume

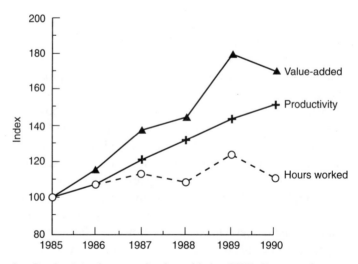

Figure 8.2 Productivity, hours and value-added at SKF's Fontenay factory.

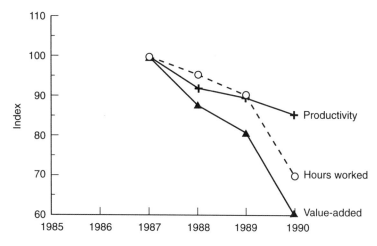

Figure 8.3 Productivity, hours and value-added at SKF's E-factory.

has changed in each factory. Fontenay expanded its operations by nearly 12 per cent annually; the E-factory, by contrast, has reduced production by more than 15 per cent annually. Finally, Figure 3 indicates that the E-factory reduced its work force more slowly than the rate of decline in production volumes. Fontenay, on the other hand, has expanded with only a minor increase in hours worked.

Increased production at Fontenay is partly explained by the fact that SKF has moved the manufacture of certain products there. The E-factory has been on the giving end of this process, suffering a reduction in volume with the removal to other plants of certain product lines.

Innovative capacity

Because the factories under study do not set their own prices, their innovative capacity does not directly affect measured productivity. Standard prices do not coincide directly with market prices. To gain some idea of innovative capacity, we studied figures that assess qualitative improvements and improved logistics. Fontenay's rejection level is somewhat lower than the E-factory's: the plant produces a larger percentage of bearings that meet stringent vibration and noise standards. It should be noted, however, that the two factories do not produce the same size of the bearings and that standards for vibration and noise are not identical for all sizes.

Data for SKF Sweden and SKF France indicate that the latter is better at handling raw material lead times. This may be explained by the French division's different product range. When it comes to the number of starts per year in a given material family, the French company also outperforms its Swedish counterpart, starting a given type of material more times per year. This, too, is partly attributable to a different product range. The existing information, however, does not indicate that flexibility affects productivity in a negative way.

Cost-effectiveness

Because we are comparing two units within a corporate group, we have concentrated on differences in cost-effectiveness. According to SKF's accounting principles, cost levels at Fontenay are about 45 per cent below those of the E-factory. This difference indicates how much less it costs to produce goods with a given delivery value at Fontenay. Yet this calculation is made using standard prices and standard costs, structured in such a way as to handicap the E-factory. If the standard figures are corrected, a more accurate difference in cost level is about 30 per cent.

To further analyse differences in cost levels, corrections can be made for any existing economies of scale. We tried to estimate economies of scale in the production of DGBBs by studying figures on volumes delivered and cost levels from six of SKF's European DGBB factories (see Figure 8.4). Their cost levels are affected by many other factors besides

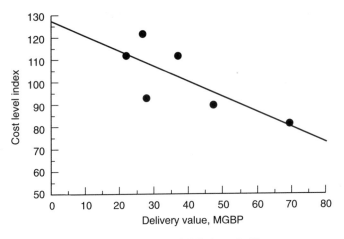

Figure 8.4 Cost and delivery value at six SKF plants in Europe.

the size (calculated in terms of delivery value) of the factories, making definite conclusions difficult. We have assumed that a reduction of about 7 per cent in costs is possible when delivery value increases by SEK 100 million. SKF has confirmed that this assumption regarding economies of scale is not unreasonable.

As stated earlier, recent years have seen an increase in volume at Fontenay and a decline at the E-factory. We therefore investigated to what extent differences in capacity utilization explain the differences in productivity at the factories. Figures from 1990 indicate that capacity utilization[2] was about 71 per cent at Fontenay, as against only about 54 per cent at the E-factory. Clearly, Fontenay covers its fixed costs better than the E-factory. We have estimated that this accounts for about 5 percentage points of the difference in cost levels.

Conclusions: productivity performance

The chart below attempts to summarize the differences in cost-effectiveness between Fontenay and the E-factory. The starting point was cost levels, which showed Fontenay coming in at 45 per cent below the E-factory. In our opinion, up to 15 percentage points of this difference can be explained by the technique for calculating standard costs. The adjusted cost level then shows Fontenay at 30 per cent below the E-factory.

If the E-factory had enjoyed the Fontenay's 71 per cent capacity utilization level during 1990, its costs would have fallen by a further 5 per cent. Next, if we compensate for economies of scale in DGBB production, a 10 per cent plus reduction results in the level of costs. On this basis, we can say that about half of the difference in cost levels between the two factories – after adjustment of standard costs – can be attributed to economies of volume and scale. Nevertheless, after these adjustments a cost difference of 15 per cent still exists in favour of the Fontenay factory.

High Swedish labour costs, including employers' social insurance contributions, are an additional factor in the explanation of cost level differences between the two factories. Labour costs for the same category of employees are 35 per cent higher at the E-factory than at Fontenay. This difference explains another 6 percentage points of the remaining difference between the overall cost levels of the two factories.[3] This implies that despite compensation for economies of volume and scale (about 15 per cent) and labour costs (about 6 per cent), the E-factory still has nearly 10 per cent higher costs than Fontenay. This residual gap indicates that the E-factory is not as cost-effective as the plant at Fontenay.

Cost-effectiveness	Difference	Remaining difference percentage points
Internal level of costs		
Fontenay		
E-factory	45	
Adjustment for standard costs		
Fontenay		
E-factory	−15	30
Capacity utilization		
Fontenay		
E-factory	−5	25
Economies of scale		
Fontenay		
E-factory	−10	15
Differences in labour costs		
Fontenay		
E-factory	−6	About 10

ORGANIZATION AND TECHNOLOGY

Institutions

Relations with employees and trade unions
To what extent can this difference be explained by the internal conditions? Both SKF Fontenay and SKF's E-factory in Gothenburg regard the
relationship between management and employees, including the organizations that represent employees, as good. French engineering-related
trade unions have often been dominated by radical factions, resulting in
frequent conflicts between labour and management.

Fontenay lacks the potential of Paris for radical trade union activities.
The perception here is that co-operation between management and labour
has steadily improved; a deep understanding of their mutual dependence
has aided this process. At SKF Gothenburg, too, trade union representatives have been pragmatic, often functioning as the driving force behind

efforts at streamlining and improvements in efficiency. Neither plant has experienced locally-inspired strikes during the past five years.

Attitudes and the social role of work

Absenteeism and personnel turnover at SKF's various factories vary greatly. Table 8.3 indicates that absenteeism and personnel turnover at the Swedish factories during 1989 was substantially higher than at the other factories. If we look only at absences due to illness, slightly different figures tell the same story (see Tables 8.3 and 8.4).

	Absenteeism	Personnel turnover
Britain	8.4	5.6
France	7.1	9.7
Italy	8.7	4.9
Spain	7.6	8.2
Sweden	29.8	23.4
Germany	9.5	8.0
United States	4.5	2.8

Table 8.3 Absenteeism and personnel turnover at selected SKF factories during 1989 (per cent).

	Absenteeism	Due to illness
E-factory	27.6	16.8
Fontenay	7.0	4.1

Table 8.4 Absenteeism due to illness at SKF Sweden and France 1989 (per cent).

At the E-factory, employees were absent for an average of 11 per cent of the time for reasons other than illness that included trade union work and training. The equivalent figure was 2.9 per cent at Fontenay. During 1989, absences due to illness were four times higher at the E-factory than at Fontenay. An upward trend in illness-related absence at SKF Sweden since 1985 contrasts with a stable situation at Fontenay. During 1990, however, absenteeism began to decline at SKF's factories in Gothenburg.

Until 1989, personnel turnover was relatively low at Fontenay and few new employees were hired during this period. In 1989, recruiting increased. When production volume then fell during late 1990, many temporary workers, known as interims, were laid off.

Unemployment in the Fontenay region is somewhat below the French average of 10 per cent. The corresponding figure for Gothenburg, Sweden, is just over 1 per cent. In Fontenay, where SKF has the region's largest industrial plant, the factory is perceived as offering high-status jobs. By contrast, factory work has low status in Sweden. Managers at Fontenay obviously feel that it is a major advantage to be located in the countryside, in a region with few competing industrial plants. In Fontenay, SKF fulfils a somewhat different role than in Gothenburg: it is worth mentioning, for example, that Fontenay employees apply for personal loans from the company on favourable terms. We were also given examples of cases where the company had helped the families of employees in distress. In Gothenburg, such matters typically are handled by the social welfare system.

Production technology

Technical characteristics

The stages of production are the same at the E-factory and at Fontenay. We have studied data on performance at both factories when it comes to turning, heat treating, grinding and assembly. Measurements showed that buffer time at Fontenay was only one-third of its equivalent at the E-factory. Although this difference does not show up directly in measures of either productivity or cost levels, it indicates that production at Fontenay is more streamlined.

Machinery and equipment are of about the same age at both plants. However, efficiency at Fontenay is more than 25 per cent higher, measured as output divided by manned capacity. The difference is partly attributable to availability and partly to the number of line change-overs. Twice as many change-overs occur at the E-factory. With stoppages of around 10 hours accompanying each line change-over, the E-factory loses a total of about 250 hours per line in change-overs, while Fontenay only loses about 130 hours per line. Still, this difference explains little of the remaining 10 per cent cost difference between these factories.

Efficiency-raising efforts

Large volume growth at Fontenay has stimulated continuous efforts to improve availability and capacity on the lines. These efforts include clearing production bottle-necks through measurements and increased utilization of machinery. Because production lines consist of machines connected in series, it is difficult to evaluate overall utilization. One simple method calculates total output as a percentage of theoretical capacity at a bottle-neck. The results show that line output is around 76 per cent of bottle-neck capacity. The corresponding figure for the E-factory was 55 per cent. At the Fontenay factory, it is estimated that calibration – the fine tuning of production – has yielded a further one per cent or so in efficiency per year.

Generally speaking, the Fontenay factory appears more driven in terms of production technology and daily efficiency-raising work. Its analyses of downtime and reductions of line change-over time are far more systematic and long-term than at the E-factory, where similar principles for measurement and control were only introduced in late 1990. A decade after Fontenay's first efforts, the E-factory has started raising efficiency on its lines in a similar fashion.

Work organization
Organization at Fontenay is more specialized and includes groups whose specific task is to raise efficiency. This is also evident from a comparison of various performance yardsticks. To the casual observer, the E-factory offers a better environment, a higher technology content, and a decentralized organizational structure that allows greater worker participation. Nevertheless, it has higher absenteeism and personnel turnover. Better social status and control at Fontenay act to lower absenteeism and turnover. Institutional factors such as differences in unemployment and medical insurance systems contribute to this situation.

The personnel situation also provides partial explanations for labour efficiency. At the E-factory, employees often lack a thorough knowledge of the process, so much so that the factory's relatively decentralized structure may lead to negative effects in the context of low competence and motivation at lower levels. For a number of years, the role of supervisors within SKF Sweden has been reduced. In Fontenay the highest level of workers, especially the so-called first man workers, are responsible for production and quality. They receive three-quarters of all training resources. They also have only a few operators working within their area of responsibility. The corresponding figure for the E-factory is between seven and ten. In addition, Fontenay devotes relatively large resources to production technicians, while the E-factory devotes all its training resources to operators. Again, this is an function of the E-factory's more decentralized structure. High personnel turnover also means that introduction of new operators takes a substantial part of the training budget.

Fontenay has allocated responsibility for improvement in clear, well-defined areas of responsibility. Results of such activities can be monitored and followed up, pointing to the importance of continuous improvement and the development of production technology know-how in the construction and efficient utilization of advanced systems. Swedish organizations, including SKF, are often very capable in the design of advanced systems. But the Fontenay factory has been able to take more efficient advantage of them.

COMMUNICATION OF GOALS AND EXPECTATIONS

Goals

In terms of the management of production goals, the Fontenay factory has worked far longer with more detailed management of efficiency and output. In particular, Fontenay monitors the key variables of productivity, output and quality on a daily, weekly and monthly basis.

These three parameters are monitored by the production manager, the two factory managers and the foremen. Foremen discuss the fulfilment of these goals with the first man workers. In principle, operators are not involved in discussions of these variables. But, with the exception of productivity, the resulting numbers are posted for each line.

The main ambition at Fontenay has been to increase availability and efficiency on the lines, in order to handle higher volumes. Goals have been defined, set and measured at the machine level since the early 1980s. As a result, detailed information has been available on bottlenecks and capacity levels in the process. Along with the fact that the number of shifts has gradually increased, this has enabled the factory to expand its production and develop good cost trends.

At the E-factory, production has traditionally been managed using performance reports, delivery figures (precision, volume/day) and, as at Fontenay, quality statistics.

Production management at the E-factory typically deploys aggregate goals such as volume per day and value-added per week. The perception at the E-factory is that these yardsticks have proved insufficient, and this is one reason why detrimental deviations have not led to corrective measures. During 1990, parameters were broken down in a more appropriate manner, as at Fontenay.

Pressure to innovate

Since 1983 Fontenay has reported a sharp increase in production volume. To cope with this, the factory has pursued efforts to maximize output in relation to capacity in the production system. Pressure to lower costs has also been somewhat heavier at Fontenay, which has manufactured bearings in the smaller size categories characterized by strong Japanese competition. Employees at Fontenay are said to be highly aware of the nature of this competition. Naturally, it is difficult to judge what role this has played in the task of improving cost-effectiveness.

Another factor that appears to have influenced productivity at the two factories is the attitude of management. At the E-factory we were told that an "indifferent" attitude both on the part of management and employees had led to neglect of productivity issues for a long period. "Management's attitude has opened the way for low productivity," we were told at the E-factory. "In the early 1970s we had sensible ratios for gauging productivity. Since then we have had a period of intellectual fuzziness in which we have lost the ability to measure and manage efficiency of production."

When it comes to customer contacts and responsiveness to the demands that customers make, the two factories are in a similar situation. Both factories sold their products mainly through group-wide units without early direct contact with the final customer, except in the case of certain high-volume orders. This has been changed in the new organization.

In summary, Fontenay has utilized more detailed parameters for production management, while the E-factory has failed to break down its goals, preferring instead to control production by using yardsticks that relate to volume and value-added rather than to efficiency and capacity utilization. This difference is partly due to differences in management philosophy. Many at SKF Sweden express dissatisfaction with the trend of management since the mid-1970s. These critics feel that SKF's Swedish operations have been characterized by loose reins rather than effective leadership and goal-oriented management. It is essential to point out, however, that such statements are broadly-framed, and that they probably reflect a diffuse dissatisfaction with the situation in the organization.

HUMAN RESOURCE MANAGEMENT

Wage and bonus systems

Wages in Fontenay are fixed. An earnings-related bonus is distributed twice a year. During 1990 all employees received a bonus payment of about £200. Notably, a length of service supplement increases their pay by 1 per cent for each year of employment. The maximum supplement for blue collar workers is 15 per cent; for white collar workers, 14 per cent; and for managers, 13 per cent.

Fontenay's 14 different wage categories are based on skills evaluation. Within each category relatively wide differentials depend on such factors as experience, formal competence and years of employment. The median wage for operators stands at index 100. For white collar workers including technicians, the figure is 131, and for managers who lead units, 171. The gap between the lowest- and highest-paid operator stands at 64 per cent. The highest-paid operators (first man workers) also earn substantially more than the lowest-paid white collar workers.

In the early 1980s SKF's wages at Fontenay were about 25 per cent below the average for the surrounding La Vendée region. Since then the gap has narrowed. In 1989 SKF stood only 1 per cent below the regional average. White collar wages have fluctuated around the regional average. At the E-factory, too, wages are fixed. Operators fall into three wage categories depending on their type of shift work. Separate wage scales exist for supervisors and white collar workers (see Table 8.5).

	Median wage index
Operator, daytime	100
Operator, 2-shift[a]	107
Operator, 5-shift[b]	131
Supervisor	111
White-collar worker	140

[a]Morning and afternoon
[b]Continuous

Table 8.5 Median wages per year at E-factory. Index = 100.

The differentials between categories are substantially narrower than at Fontenay. In addition, differentials are narrower within the wage band for operators (30 per cent as against Fontenay's 64 per cent). Operator wages at the E-factory are 50p per hour lower than those at a major car assembly plant nearby. On the other hand, the E-factory pays above the national day-time average for metalworkers. Rates for white collar workers are about 4 per cent less than the regional average.

Motivation and skills

Levels of experience among operators are higher in Fontenay than at the
E-factory, where about half of all operators have been hired within the
past five years. Corresponding figures for white collar employees
showed a more even distribution of employment duration. The number
with at least 20 years in the company was actually 10 percentage points
higher at the E-factory. Nearly three-fifths of white collar workers at the
E-factory had been employed for more than 20 years.

Personnel turnover and absenteeism figures indicate that the E-factory
has problems in terms of motivating its staff. Wage levels at both factories parallel regional averages. Compared with the E-factory, however,
the Fontenay plant makes more differentiations on the basis of skills,
type of shift and duration of employment. Along with the more evenly
distributed age range of Fontenay employees, this probably means that it
is easier for the French factory's management to motivate employees to
develop their skills, assume responsibility and remain with the company.
This may also mean that Fontenay has a higher level of skills among its
operators and supervisors: given its location, the factory is able to keep
experienced employees.

Decentralized organization at the E-factory in the context of high personnel turnover has involved direct costs and poor organizational stability with competence levels often unequal to responsibilities. In this context, supervisors play an important role as a motivating force and source
of knowledge. In Fontenay, however, supervisors enjoy even higher priority. Differences in personnel turnover undoubtedly have a number of
explanations. Apart from the question of status and employment, wage
formation at the Fontenay factory clearly aids employee retention and
skills enhancement. Individualized wage scales and rewards paid to key
employees reinforce the pattern.

CONCLUSIONS

Even with factories from the same corporate group that operate under
similar pressures, comparisons of productivity have been difficult. It can
be said, however, that productivity has climbed by nearly 9 per cent
annually in Fontenay, while it has fallen by 5 per cent each year at the E-
factory. Costs are far lower at Fontenay. A vicious circle partly explains
the E-factory's dilemma: higher cost levels have prompted removal of

some functions to other plants, and the resulting lower volumes of production lead in turn to even higher costs and new structural problems.

For a long time, SKF has attempted to increase levels of specialization at its manufacturing units, letting each focus on specific products in the attempt to achieve cost-effectiveness. Such specialization places heavy demands on the ability of these factories to vary production volumes. They must be able to adapt their capacity to needs without the luxury of switching from one product to another. Fontenay has experienced fewer problems in coping with such production volume variations. Continual increases, of course, are less of a problem than decline. Additionally, Fontenay's pool of temporary employees has acted as a buffer. The E-factory has not been able to adapt its capacity to fluctuating demand in the same way, nor has it been able to raise the working efficiency of its employees to compensate for higher wage costs.

Even if we make corrections for differences in production volume and take into account the E-factory's higher labour costs, the difference in cost levels between the two factories remains at about 10 per cent. The reasons for this residual difference can be traced at three levels. First, the E-factory operates within a much tighter labour market. Wages and status at the E-factory are clearly lower than at SKF in Fontenay, resulting in far higher personnel turnover at the E-factory. Together with the impact of high absenteeism, this has a negative effect on the plant's capacity for high productivity manufacturing. Additionally, the division of roles between the E-factory and Fontenay has not been definitive. In terms of product range, the two factories have similarities. When the problems of the E-factory began, there was a potential threat that some of its production would be moved to places like Fontenay, and to some extent this has happened. Uncertainty about the future role of the E-factory may be one explanation as to why even more vigorous measures were not taken. This does not necessarily mean that internal intervention, in the shape of better work systems and productivity management, would have been able to offset the poorer external conditions of the E-factory.

Second, when it comes to particular organizational conditions, the emphasis on productivity management was the factor that distinguished Fontenay. The factory employs more detailed yardsticks for managing production; until recently, the E-factory lacked a set of suitable goals and has used management by yardsticks related to volume and value-added rather than efficiency and capacity utilization. This difference stems partly from different management styles.

Fontenay has sought to organize its operations with output and efficiency in mind, fostering clear and well-defined areas of responsibility. In this context, we noted that Fontenay placed great emphasis on improving its existing systems. When it comes to designing advanced systems, the E-factory does not lack in competence. But it is not as good at utilizing these systems efficiently. Here, Fontenay has done better.

A third factor, finally, is the personnel situation. Decentralization leads to greater participation by employees. But this alone is not enough to achieve efficiency. It is also necessary for employees to feel motivation and commitment. The question of professional skill is important in this context, and here too, it is clear that the factory in Fontenay had an edge.

By way of summary, the Fontenay factory has managed to achieve high productivity with a more traditional and Tayloristic production format in a geographical location characterized by its surplus of available unskilled labour. The E-factory's lean production style has worked less successfully, in part because its skilled workers are in short supply. Clearly, lean production is not a general solution to productivity problems in all manufacturing industries. Rather, it is an efficient method of production only in the presence of certain prerequisites such as skilled labour and efficient sub-contractors.

[1]As an example, a No. 6203 deep-groove ball bearing alone is made in 144 versions.
[2]Staffed time out of total available time (365 × 24 hrs/year).
[3]We have also assumed that only direct and indirect labour expenses were affected. Other expenses such as services, materials and depreciation are assumed not to have been affected.

9 UNITED PAPER MILLS AND SCA

In the world's forest product industry, Finland, Sweden and Canada compete for the position of top exporting country. Finland's most successful forest product company is United Paper Mills (UPM). Svenska Cellulosa Aktiebolaget (SCA) is one of Sweden's leading companies in the same industry. UPM has coped better than most with the downturn of the early 1990s. Despite the scepticism of industry experts, during the past decade, the company made a number of technologically advanced and commercially risky investments in new paper-processing machinery. Profits have resulted, along with the lucrative capacity to manufacture high value-added products including magazine paper and newsprint.

Since the early 1960s, UPM's Swedish counterpart has shifted in the direction of large, internationally competitive production units. Once the world's largest pulp exporter, SCA has implemented forward integration into paper production and conversion that has now made it a net buyer of pulp. As a result, SCA has become Europe's largest manufacturer of corrugated board. Elsewhere, the company has diversified to become Europe's largest producer of fluff pulp-based hygiene products such as napkins and sanitary towels. During this restructuring process, SCA's profitability has held steady.

THE FOREST PRODUCT INDUSTRY

In the forest product industry,[1] greater cost-effectiveness is mainly achieved by investment in new and often bigger equipment. Productivity increases – measured in terms of man-hours per tonne produced – lower the cost of capital per tonne and frequently yield better utilization of inputs such as wood, chemicals and energy. Given the open climate of co-operation that exists on matters of technology in the Scandinavian forest product industry, the prerequisites for new investment are relatively similar and widely-understood.

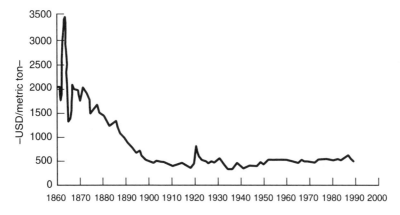

Figure 9.1 Real price of paper, 1860–1990 (US $).

Source: Jaakko Pöyry.

So far as the industry overall is concerned, statistics on the historical prices of newsprint in the United States indicate that increases in productivity and declining real prices for paper continued until the early 20th century (see Figure 9.1). Since then, real prices have remained roughly constant – a sign that the productivity of paper manufacturers has risen at approximately the same rate as the average for the whole economy.

Viewed over a shorter time-span, changes have nevertheless occurred in the industry's product mix. Boxboard, liquid-impervious paperboard for milk cartons and LWC-paper[2] are among products that have gained prominence in recent decades. Equally vital have been changes in quality. Today, newsprint meets far higher standards of printability and runnability in presses than before. Long-term productivity depends on product renewal and improvement, but new machinery typically represents a very large investment that adds a great deal of new production capacity.[3] If several competitors expand capacity simultaneously, an adverse impact on profitability may follow. Managers' tendency to approve capital expenditure during economic boom periods complicates the picture still further. By the time new capacity is added, the business cycle may have turned down. The result is a combination of scarce customers and heavy interest payments.

Key role of forest product industry

The forest product industry is a major economic force in both Finland and Sweden, where, in absolute terms, these industries are about equal in size. The pulp and paper industry's share of total industry production value in most OECD countries falls between 3 and 5 per cent. For countries with a substantial raw material base the share is between 5 and 10 per cent (New Zealand 7 per cent, Canada 8 per cent and Sweden 10 per cent). Finland's share stands at 16 per cent. Within the larger economy of these countries, forest products account for about 40 per cent of Finland's merchandise exports; the corresponding figure for Sweden stands at around 20 per cent. Finland is the world's second largest exporter of paper and its fourth largest exporter of pulp (wood fibre prepared for paper production). Sweden is the world's third largest exporter in both categories. In the world league of production output, Finland occupies seventh place, with 8.8 million metric tons, and Sweden eighth place, with 8.4 million tonnes, each corresponding to about 4 per cent of global production.

Finland's larger percentage of high value-added forest products

The production structure of the Finnish and Swedish industries differs in terms of the level of integration between pulp and paper production. In Finland, an average of 77 per cent of pulp is processed into paper. The corresponding figure for Sweden is 64 per cent.[4] Finland boasts a larger share of the market for higher value-added products such as magazine-grade and other high-quality papers. Sweden, by contrast, holds a higher market share in the pulp, sack paper, kraft linerboard and newsprint sectors (see Figures 9.2 and 9.3). However, SCA, Stora and MoDo, the three

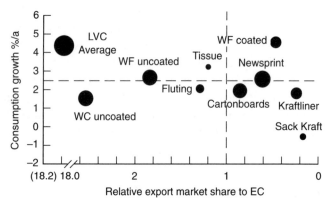

Figure 9.2 Consumption growth and relative Finnish export market share of EC.
Source: Jaakko Pöyry.

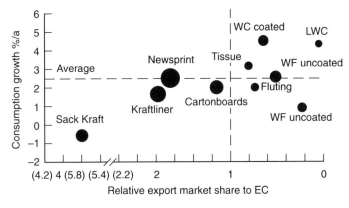

Figure 9.3 Consumption growth and relative Swedish export market share of EC.
Source: Jaakko Pöyry.

large Swedish companies, increased their capacity in different grades of printing and writing paper production with substantial acquisitions in western Europe during the late 1980s.

Fine papers account for 30 per cent of Finnish paper production, as against less than 10 per cent in Sweden. Finland's forest product companies were among early manufacturers of new product categories like LWC and SC printing papers.[5] Difficult and costly to manufacture, these products command relatively high prices. The price relationships between various printing and writing papers that contain wood are roughly as follows:

Standard newsprint	100
Improved newsprint	110
SC paper	120–140
LWC paper	150–160

Between the years 1985 and 1989, the Swedish forest product industry was more profitable than its Finnish counterpart. At most Swedish forest product companies, return on capital employed ran to around 15 per cent; the corresponding figures for the Finnish industry fluctuated between 10 and 15 per cent, testimony to a large-scale capital spending programme that may have lowered short-term profitability. During the 1985–1989 period, net investments as a percentage of sales were nearly twice as high in Finland than in Sweden.[6] As a consequence, the recession of 1991–92 has hit the Finnish forest product industry harder.

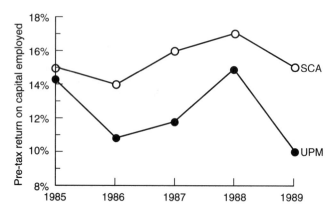

Figure 9.4 Relative profitability: SCA and UPM.
Source: Annual reports.

There are four large blocs of companies in the Finnish forest product industry: Enso, Kymmene, Metsä-Serla and Repola, which includes UPM. One of three dominant Swedish companies, SCA is about twice the size of UPM and shows somewhat higher profitability (see Figure 9.4).

The national investment climate

UPM's efforts to raise its own products' value-added is far from unique. Boosted by large investment programmes during the 1980s, several other Finnish forest product companies also shifted toward higher value-added products. Thus much of the higher investments in the Finnish paper industry were made in equipment for production of qualified printing and writing papers which are in early stages of their product life cycle. By contrast, the Swedish industry's larger companies have increased their share of the advanced printing and writing paper market mainly through acquisitions abroad. These groups of companies now have more employees abroad than in Sweden. Investment had a higher level of intensity in Finland during the 1980s. A higher share of green-field investment occurred at home.

Higher cost level and less company-owned timberland in Finland
The industry's largest cost items are wood and recycled fibre, energy, shipping and labour. For nearly all their input goods, Finnish forest product companies appear to pay at least as much as their Swedish counter-

parts. Only recycled fibre is cheaper in Finland than in Sweden. The Swedish forest product industry pays less for wood and owns a larger percentage of national timberlands than does the Finnish industry. However, the gap has diminished due to devaluations of Finnish currency. Finnish forest product companies are self-sufficient in only 10 per cent of their wood supply; SCA is about 60 per cent self-sufficient. By comparison, North American competitors often pay only half as much for their wood supplies.

	Coniferous	Deciduous	(1991)
Finland	115	108	
Sweden	100	100	
Canada East	60	48	
USA South	41	41	
New Zealand	34	36	
Brazil	25	28	

Given its nation's larger use of hydroelectric power, the Swedish forest product industry has access to cheaper energy. A skilled operator earns more in Finland, but because differentials between skilled and unskilled workers are broader than in Sweden, average wages are lower in the Finnish forest industry. Notably, the forest product industry of southern Sweden is closer to the major markets of western Europe; the Finnish industry, by contrast, is saddled with higher shipping costs. Taken as a whole, the following are approximate ratios between the costs of different production factors in Sweden and Finland, using an index of 100 for Sweden.

	Sweden	Finland	(1991)
Wood	100	112	
Recycled fibre	100	92	
Electricity	100	105	
Wages and salaries	100	95	
Shipping to customer*	100	100	

* From central Sweden
Source: Internal estimate by SCA.

Poorer prerequisites in terms of higher wood and electricity prices may partly explain why Finland's paper industry leads in terms of upgrading its product mix. The Finns have experienced stronger incentives to shift toward higher value-added product sectors in which cost disadvantages are less of a problem. Lacking their own raw material base in the form of extensive forests, they have focused their endeavour on increasing paper manufacturing expertise. Many Swedish companies, by contrast, base their operations on large forest holdings and are forced to a larger extent into optimizing the relationship between forestry and pulp and paper manufacturing.

Specialist competence in forest products
A shift to higher value-added categories of paper presupposes high levels of competence in paper coating and chemical additive processes. There are many indications that Finland has a high level of technological competence in such areas. Unlike Sweden's educational system, Finland offers a university-level engineering programme that leads to a degree in paper and pulp technology. In relative terms, Finland also spends more money on research, supporting a substantially higher proportion of full professorships in disciplines related to the forest industry.

Although SCA managers do not believe that their company has any great difficulty recruiting employees with requisite skills, the company is supporting the creation of an institute of technology to specialize in pulp and paper technology. SCA also believes that the Swedish government should invest substantially more in pulp and paper research and development at existing institutes of technology and university engineering faculties. The company believes that the number of professorships in these subjects should be sharply increased.

The industrial network
Finland boasts several large suppliers of machinery for the forest product industry, including Valmet, Strömbergs, Ahlströms and Rauma. The Finnish industry worked closely with its machinery suppliers during the major investments waves of the 1980s. In the past two decades, large-scale Swedish production of machinery for the forest product industry has declined. This decline is considered a competitive disadvantage. Both countries possess big paper and pulp industry consultancy firms.

Swedish forest product companies have sales offices in major markets and rely on agents or trading companies in smaller and more distant markets. By contrast, the Finnish forest product industry relies largely on three jointly-owned marketing organizations: Finnpap, Finnboard and Finncell, vendors of paper, paperboard and pulp, respectively. In 1990, Finnpap's ten member companies, with their 20 paper mills and 55 paper machines, delivered 76 per cent of Finland's paper exports.[7] This joint sales organization grades the products of various paper mills for quality, distributing these products to foreign customers. Finnpap thus functions as a gatekeeper, generating competition between mills that compete to gain ever more favourable positions on the organization's quality ranking lists.

According to UPM, Finnpap policy lies behind some of the company's success during the 1980s. When the company decided to invest in an on-line coating process for LWC paper, it was clearly a major advantage that Finnpap was already delivering paper to LWC customers. "It is easier to go from a total delivery capacity of 400,000 tons to 600,000 tons than to go from 0 to 200,000 tons," said one company official.

Institutional conditions
Because the Finnish forest product industry is pivotal to the national economy, it naturally enjoys an image of strength. The perception seems to be that the government supports, rather than controls, the industry. Swedish perceptions of its industry's relationship with government differs significantly, mainly because national energy and environmental policies are believed to place the pulp and paper industry at an international disadvantage.

It has often been maintained that the short-term returns demanded by institutional investors can have an adverse effect on long-term capital spending by listed companies. The major investments undertaken by the Finnish forest product industry have been both risky and long-term. Notably, large Finnish and Swedish shareholders of UPM and SCA tend to take a very long-term view of their holdings.

According to both Finnish and Swedish observers, industrial relations are more harmonious in Sweden, particularly in the case of blue collar workers. When a Finnish company raises productivity, for example, by installing a new paper machine, the wages of employees affected by this move are renegotiated. Otherwise, at least within the forest products industry itself, there are no decisive differences between the countries in terms of labour legislation.

Differences in labour legislation do, however, intervene later in a cycle of production that can stretch from forest to newsstand. A case in point is Finland's pioneering production of large-scale LWC paper which commonly is used to print brochures and catalogues. The product had a small market in Sweden, in part because of legislative constraints against the kind of round-the-clock working that is characteristic of printing plants in Finland and the Netherlands. Thus, Swedish plants were handicapped in turning out the kind of large print run publications that commonly use LWC papers. So Swedish paper mills have not had any big demand in their home market for this kind of paper.

Prices and wages have been substantially more stable in Finland. Additionally, in Sweden, uncertainties caused by high inflation and a confused energy policy have persisted. Elsewhere, while Finland follows international standards on emissions into waterways and the atmosphere, Sweden enforces stricter limits. Early in the 1980s, however, a major Swedish currency devaluation dramatically improved industrial profitability, creating high short-term profits in the wake of a long period of gloom. In the longer-term, controversy over energy policy, rapidly rising costs and high environmental standards left the industry unsure about the future competitiveness of its domestic facilities.

Conclusion: investment strategies

Higher raw material and energy costs in Finland have provided an incentive to shift production toward higher value-added products, a change that presupposes a high level of technological competence among forest product companies and their suppliers. It has also required heavy, risky capital spending. The industry's major role in the Finnish economy probably meant that companies felt they were expected to make changes and that a safety net would protect them in the case of failure. Notably, shareholders in Finnish forest product companies have engaged in long-term investment.

The Swedish forest industry's strategy of acquisition stemmed from a desire to move closer to its main markets and to increase the use of recycled fibre as a raw material for paper production. The investment climate in Sweden during the 1980s played a significant role in defining this strategy.

Devaluation boosted profitability, but combined with other uncertainties, the government's undecided attitude toward EC membership inclined the Swedish forest product industry to view acquisitions as the best strategy for development and expansion.

UNITED PAPER MILLS

In the mid-1970s, UPM was a medium-sized company with a relatively outmoded production structure. Most of its machinery was old, and its broad product range included cardboard, fine papers, sack paper and newsprint. During the 1980s, the company built no fewer than eight new paper machines, an unusually large investment for a company of this size. Mergers and acquisitions provided a further boost to capacity. In terms of profitability, the company led its domestic rivals during the 1980s. Despite its large-scale capital spending programme, debt levels remain relatively low. The transformations of the past decade have left UPM with the following position in the world market:

	Capacity, million metric tonnes	World ranking	European ranking	Per cent of market in Europe
Newsprint	1.5	5	1	20
SC printing paper	0.8	1	1	23
LWC printing paper	0.5	8	5	10

Heavy capital expenditures and technical development work

In the late 1980s, UPM's capital expenditure totalled roughly 25 per cent of its sales. This should be compared with about 14 per cent for the Finnish forest product industry as a whole. Behind the company's intensive investment programme lies a systematic strategy and a clear understanding of the requirements of profitability in the pulp and paper industry. UPM has also expanded its forestry holdings and its hydroelectric power resources. Self-sufficiency in wood supply rose from 3 to 8 per cent of UPM's total needs, and about 60 per cent of the company's electricity requirement now comes from hydroelectric power plants of which it is the sole or partial owner.

UPM specializes in low wood content paper suited to further additions of value. The company's main ambition is to be among the leading European suppliers of wood-containing writing and printing papers including newsprint, SC, LWC and MFC paper[8]. The company is trying to achieve cost superiority with modern machinery that enables it to outperform smaller firms. New production facilities for newsprint containing an admixture of recycled fibre are under construction in Britain and on the continent. Investment in production of SC and LWC papers is continuing in Finland.

UPM has a reputation as a very bold investor and technological innovator. Since the early 1970s, the company has improved its SC paper and LWC paper technologies and refined its thermomechanical pulp (TMP) process, a cost-effective method for the production of wood-containing printing papers like newsprint. In an oft-stated policy, UPM demands that machinery for new types of product should contain at least two technological innovations. "If you aim at being Number One, you end up Number One or Number Two," says one UPM manager. "If you aim at being Number Two, you end up Number Ten or last."

In its paper mills, UPM relies on machinery that offers maximum width and speed. Rather than compromise by retrofitting an existing machine that has a decent width, the company usually prefers to invest in newer – and faster – equipment. UPM managers told us that another factor behind their company's success has been working relationship with Finland's Valmet, the world's largest supplier of paper machines, and supplier of UPM's new machinery during the 1980s.

Paper machines that have become outdated over time can be used in the production of specialized types of paper. Here, too, UPM tries to specialize as much as possible. One machine previously used to produce several special categories of unbleached paper was retrofitted to produce only unbleached envelope paper. Retrofitting raised the machine's capacity from 40,000 tonnes per year to no less than 70,000 tonnes: it is now the world's largest in this niche. On the other hand, old machines are discarded if the company cannot find any suitable uses for them.

Cost-effectiveness

Paper manufacturers achieve economies of scale mainly by increasing the width and speed of their machines. A seven metre-wide machine with an average speed of 1,200 metres per minute has only 62 per cent of the production capacity typical of a nine-metre machine with a speed of 1,500 metres per minutes. The problem centres on achieving higher speeds or increased width without breaking the paper. Frequent production stops because of breaks ruin the prospect of productivity gain.

UPM's capital spending programme has seen several of its mills receive awards for high productivity. UPM also takes advantage of economies of scale by operating several machines for every type of paper, with each machine specializing in particular surface weights and qualities. Specialization reduces the need for line changes and increases machine speeds.

Innovation

An instructive example of UPM's ability to think in innovative terms is its investment in Shotton, Wales, during the early 1980s. Its purchase of a newsprint machine with an initial annual capacity of 200,000 tonnes remains the largest single new investment in the British paper industry to date.[9] At that time, the British newsprint industry was in dire straits, having suffered a decline in capacity from about 600,000 tons a year to less than 100,000 tons over the previous decade. Low capital spending had resulted in outmoded production structures; labour-management conflicts filled out a familiar picture.

UPM executives nevertheless believed that with an injection of technological expertise, it would be possible to make newsprint production competitive in Britain. A reliable supply of reasonably priced wood was readily available in South Wales. Niilo Hakkarainen, then UPM's managing director, delegated much of the day-to-day management of the group to his Executive Board and took over the Welsh newsprint project in its early stages. With UPM's chief executive on the spot, negotiations with public agencies were expedited.

UPM successfully introduced Finnish technology and working methods at the Shotton plant. Production per employee at this mill is now not much lower than at comparable units in Finland. Its profitability, on the other hand, is higher, on account of favourable wood and energy prices and low transport costs. According to UPM managers, the previously negative prospects for the British newsprint industry were attributable to inadequate equipment and a poor climate of co-operation.

The recently-announced expansion of the Jämsenkoski mill in Finland amid a general industrial climate of cutbacks, redundancies and plant shut-downs offers another case study in the rejection of conventional wisdom. The expansion involves significant investment in what will become the world's largest and most efficient SC magazine paper machine.

Productivity management

In Scandinavia, companies often exchange detailed data on cost-effectiveness with competitors regarded as among industry leaders. (In North America, anti-trust legislation seems to lead to less open relationships). With its large and efficient units, UPM boasts Europe's highest production capacity per employee in its main product categories. In terms of tonnes produced per employee, UPM's three newsprint mills rank first, second and fourth in Europe. In SC and LWC paper production, the company leads the field.

Net efficiency, or the overall utilization of available production time, is the company's central yardstick. Waste levels are another measurement. But the company does not regard what it describes as isolated yardsticks of productivity as a major concern. Instead, as managers focus on the prerequisites that tend to generate high productivity, underlying conditions are seen as more essential than statistical measurements. The company's very modern and highly productive plant structure, for example, seems to be one productivity variable that UPM bosses like to communicate to outsiders.

Communication of goals and expectations

If UPM is one of the world's leading producers of wood-containing printing paper, its customers are similarly demanding. Germany is consistently regarded as the most difficult of UPM's major markets. In SC and LWC paper, UPM's main competitors are rival German and Finnish mills. In newsprint markets, Swedish and German producers are a strong source of competition.

Commercial negotiations are handled by Finnpap, with technical customer service provided by each mill. An on-line computer link puts mills in direct contact with Finnpap's sales offices, allowing customers to obtain rapid updates on the status of production and deliveries. Good customer contacts can result from weekly or monthly deliveries to the same customers over a period of years, added to technical co-operation with leading customers. Asked whether they felt the need for outside objectivity to avoid becoming trapped within the preconceptions of an individual industrial sector, managers at UPM did not see the need because, the said, the entire company can be regarded as an outsider in its industry, at least in terms of innovation and investment.

Human Resource Management

UPM has a very low rate of personnel turnover. Each year, fewer than 1 per cent of employees quit to take other jobs. Absenteeism due to illness varies from mill to mill but averages 2-3 per cent among white collar workers and double that among blue collar workers. Recruitment appears to present no problems.[10]

An in-house training programme for technicians lasts two to three years and accepts about 70 participants annually. The company also has a large-scale graduate trainee programme. Between 3-6 per cent of the company's personnel costs are devoted to training, with each employee taking an average of two training days each year. In one programme, employees begin as operators and study toward a university-level engineering degree with company backing. UPM's organization, with 25 profit centres, seems to create a very good recruitment base for high-level white collar employees. Most members of UPM's executive board have moved up through the company in this way.

Wages and salaries at UPM are not very different from other Finnish forest product companies, but blue collar pay at UPM's biggest printing paper mills is substantially higher than the average for Finnish industry. Skilled machine operators can earn £21,000–23,000 (1991) – high by comparison with Sweden.[11] The company has no bonus system at levels below managers of profit centres. The company believes that bonus systems are costly to keep up to date and that systems to promote corporate goals are difficult to devise.

UPM's employee suggestion system annually yields about 1,000 suggestions. The employee magazine, company magazine and annual report carry many reports of employees' inventions and improvements. UPM also runs special campaigns: in 1990 the theme of the year was 'Caring for the Environment'. Courses and lectures examined global and national environmental problems, the problems of the forest product industry and the role of individuals. In what is traditionally known as White Month, 75 per cent of employees voluntarily abstain from alcoholic beverages each February.

Organizational structure and technology

High level of technological competence
The company prefers to highlight strengths that are largely related to high levels of technological competence:

- TMP skills
- Expertise in implementing major capital spending projects
- Daring and courage in approving investments and closures
- Expertise in innovations

One of UPM's declared goals is to be among the leading technological innovators in its areas of activity. In the printing paper sector, UPM believes it possesses unique know-how in TMP processes and in LWC paper production with on-line coating. The company's TMP expertise, in particular, has provided the basis for investments in its main products.

Delegation of authority

UPM's organization relies on far-reaching delegation and decentralization. The company also possesses a strong eight-person collective executive board; below this level there are 25 profit centres. Each profit centre manager reports to a member of the executive board. A system of company divisions, it is believed, would entail excessive costs, adding an extra hierarchical level between the executive board and profit centres.

Half of each profit centre's earnings are ploughed back into the profit centres, which can choose to invest in operations or to build up capital reserves. This arrangement, which UPM says is rather unique, encourages interest in earnings at all levels of the company and, it is claimed, gives employees a sense of freedom attendant on the knowledge that half of their unit's earnings are automatically credited to their profit centre.

Management culture

Executive board members come from very similar backgrounds, and almost all have 20 to 30 years of individual service. The company's strong management culture has undoubtedly been greatly influenced by Niilo Hakkarainen, UPM's managing director between 1970 and 1990. The company has had three managing directors since its foundation in 1920. With its frugality, decentralization and antipathy toward bureaucracy, UPM's management culture somewhat resembles that of IKEA – the highly successful international furniture chain founded in Sweden after World War II. "The heroes of the company are the heads of its profit centres," says one executive.

Recipe for success

We believe that the following factors explain UPM's successes.

- A decentralized working method
- Thorough planning
- Extensive experience in running new paper machine projects, all of which were completed early and under budget – unusual in the pulp and paper industry
- Boldness in large scale investment in up-to-date production units. One frequently heard comment: "Rather than compromise, we would prefer to do nothing"
- Technological boldness: the company goal of building a new paper machine at least every other year was surpassed during the 1980s. As a general rule, investment only occurs when the company's debt-to-

equity ratio is below 1.5 and when 65 per cent of finance comes from internal sources

- The great usefulness of Finnpap as a sales organization, combined with UPM's own marketing organization
- Strong executive leadership combined with decentralized working methods
- Very good working relationships with machinery suppliers, banks, universities, colleges and research institutions including the pulp and paper industry's Central Laboratory in Helsinki
- Far-sighted shareholders who understand the importance of continual investment in modern machinery and who have persuaded independent companies in the same product field to participate in mergers
- An ability to take hold of fleeting opportunities: generally speaking, UPM's executive board believes that strategic thinking must be combined with unconventional solutions. A sound scepticism toward traditional industry yardsticks permeates the company: Shotton, it is said, was an investment largely based on intuition. Attaching little importance to conventional industry forecasts, company managers are more inclined to analyse issues from their company's own position of strength
- Intelligent capital spending: mistaken investments can have serious consequences. By contrast with UPM, many Finnish companies are experiencing difficulty with new technological solutions. The success of its investments distinguishes UPM

SCA

Since the 1960s, SCA has expanded its operations by creating large and internationally competitive production plants. The company has also gradually increased the proportion of pulp processed into paper at its own mills (see Figure 9.5). An increasing share of paper is converted into corrugated board. SCA has also increased its level of self-sufficiency in wood supplies. (SCA's self-sufficiency at its forest product units in Sweden climbed from 40 per cent to 60 per cent during a period of rapidly rising production).

In the early 1970s, SCA began diversification with the acquisition of Mölnlycke, a major producer of paper pulp hygiene products. The companies' combined fibre technology know-how comprises a valuable joint research and development resource. With its large consumer product

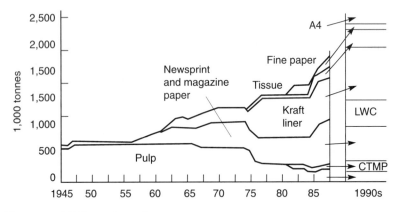

Figure 9.5 SCA's product mix: 1945–1990.
Source: SCA.

sales, SCA is more closely comparable with North American companies like Kimberly Clark than with traditional European-based forest product companies. During the 1980s, SCA further internationalized its operations, acquiring a number of companies outside its home base of operations. Foreign subsidiaries now account for about 45 per cent of production capacity and 60 per cent of the group's 37,000 employees.

SCA's operations are split among five business groups (divisions):

• Hygiene: With Mölnlycke's consumer-oriented fluff-based hygiene products, SCA competes against rivals like Procter & Gamble and Johnson & Johnson

• Packaging: production of corrugated board and container-board used in making corrugated board became the group's largest single business sector with the recent acquisition of British-based Reedpack

• Graphic Paper: newsprint, SC magazine paper, LWC paper, plus other printing and writing paper and pulp

• Forest and timber: supplies wood for the group's mills as well as the sawn timber products manufactured at four sawmills

• Energy: the group lays claim to some 30 wholly- and partly-owned hydroelectric power plants

During the 1980s, SCA improved productivity by pursuing two main strategies. The first involved increasing its cost-effectiveness by concentrating operations within large, efficient units that integrated pulp and paper production.[12] SCA's units at Obbola and Munksund in Northern Sweden are among the world's most productive mills. Second, the company has renewed its product range with forward integration, selling more packaging and consumer products. One commonly held view within the industry states that a firm must be among the three or four largest manufacturers in each of its specialities in order to be able to invest sufficiently in product development and marketing. As Table 9.1 below indicates, SCA occupies a leading position in two of the company's three main product areas: packaging and hygiene products.

Product category	Market share: %	Ranking in Europe
Packaging		
Corrugated board	8	1
Kraft liner	18	1
Test liner	8	1
Fluff-based hygiene products	15	1
Newsprint	6	6
SC paper	10	6
LWC paper	4	10

Table 9.1 SCA's market shares in Europe, by product category.

Cost-effectiveness

Most of SCA's forest product operations are based on solid expertise in fibre technology, on wood drawn from its own timberlands, and on electricity generated by its own power plants. Self-sufficient in electricity, the company sells more than 60 per cent of its generated power to outside buyers. Supplying just under two-thirds of its own wood, the company also qualifies as Europe's largest private forest owner: its holdings are equivalent in size to half of Switzerland. Nevertheless, the company has consistently tried to lower its dependence on Swedish wood, increasing the proportion of recycled fibre used at its Swedish units and acquiring mills in EC countries that use recycled fibre as a major source of raw material.

SCA's overall raw material base is now half wood fibre and half recycled fibre. Between 1975 and 1990, improvements in its production methods have lowered wood consumption per tonne of finished products

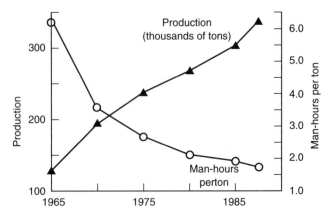

Figure 9.6 Productivity: Kraft liner production at SCA Munksund.

from 4 m³ to 3 m³ in the company's Swedish forest product operations.

SCA has also dramatically reduced energy consumption and raised productivity as measured by man-hours per tonne of manufactured goods. Investments in more energy efficient equipment and increased use of wood-based fuels saw oil consumption at SCA's domestic forest product operations fall from 250,000 m³ to 50,000 m³ during the 1980s. Production at fewer and larger units resulted in a sharp increases in production per full-time worker. Figure 6 shows productivity figures for kraft liner production and the number of man-hours per tonne of production worked at the Munksund mill in Sweden.

Productivity management

SCA managers believe that productivity is crucial to the production of container-board, the fairly standardized materials used in making corrugated board. It is very difficult to compete unless the container-board is manufactured at large, efficient mills. The company's main yardstick is capital productivity. Data on container-board production indicate that productivity, adjusted for differences in machinery, is similar at the company's various international mills.

In the graphic paper business division, which operates mills in Sweden, Austria and Britain, productivity is managed using generally accepted key ratios. Production units are compared with each other and with equivalent units owned by other forest product companies. As for productivity in terms of capacity utilization and production per metre of machine width, SCA is aware that one of its mills lags behind the world leaders. A programme has been designed to raise that mill's efficiency by 10 per cent.

Other methods are used to measure productivity, including market analyses of the quality-related parameters relevant to customers. These give some idea of each production unit's productivity in the areas of quality and sales and delivery.

Communication of goals and expectations

In the open atmosphere that prevails in the Scandinavian pulp and paper industry, continuous pressure to innovate rests on wide knowledge of competing firms' performance levels. SCA's far-flung sales network in the European market also feeds back questions raised in the on-going dialogue between mills and customers.

The targets that SCA group management establishes in partnership with its five divisions include mainly financial and market-related ratios, such as return on investment and market share. Productivity targets are established for each division or mill. Results are compiled by division, permitting internal and external comparisons.

SCA obtains an outsider's perspective on its operations through Mölnlycke, among other sources. This consumer product company works in a different environment and, as a result, has a production and organizational structure different from the pulp and paper industry. When SCA was expanding its international corrugated board operations during the 1980s, the company found it useful to apply some of the organizational and product development experience gained at Mölnlycke.

Human Resource Management

Generally speaking, the Swedish pulp and paper industry has fewer problems with absenteeism due to illness and with personnel turnover than many other industrial sectors. Supervisors and trade union representatives told us that the nature of SCA's production technology reinforces awareness of the importance attached to good team-work at all levels in a pulp and paper mill. At its Ortviken mill, SCA has made a sizable investment in leadership training, mainly at the foreman level. This has included engaging well-known athletic team leaders as lecturers. In most mill towns, the fact that most of the employees know each other makes for clear lines of social control.

The following personnel statistics from SCA's Ortviken mill indicate that absenteeism due to illness is a percentage point or so higher than at UPM. Training time totals more than three days per employee per year, again somewhat higher than at UPM.

Number of employees	1,200
Percentage of women	13
Average age	
White collar workers	42
Blue collar workers	35
Training hours per year	40,000
Absenteeism due to illness, per cent	
White collar workers	3
Blue collar workers	7.6

SCA production units in Sweden are distinguished from their counterparts elsewhere in western Europe by higher rates of blue collar absenteeism and systems that thus have to supply substitute employees. Lower maintenance staff levels are also common at SCA's mills in western Europe.

SCA offers its employees a number of general bonus systems including a profit-sharing plan run by an employee-owned foundation that has become one of the company's large shareholders. Furthermore, an SCA fund owns and manages some 100 vacation cottages for the use of employees. In relative terms, the employee suggestion programme is of about the same size as at UPM.

SCA and the labour union that organizes its blue collar workers are beginning to agree increasingly that greater wage differentiation is necessary and desirable. Compared with neighbouring industrial plants, SCA's production units pay relatively high wages that are attributable in part to the need for 24-hour operations. Working at SCA offers high status in the industry and at SCA's main mill towns. At SCA, as at UPM, it is possible to start out as a mill operator and pursue studies leading to a university-level engineering degree.

Organizational structure and technology

SCA practices far-reaching decentralization of authority to each division. Like UPM, SCA wants to maintain a relatively flat organizational hierarchy and to minimize central staff units. SCA was one of the first companies in the forest product industry to introduce a divisional structure. Essential group-wide functions include capital supply, long-term research, and human resource practices and recruitment. SCA managers believe the company achieves substantial productivity gains in research and product development because its know-how in wood fibre technology can be applied within several divisions.

Recipe for success

The following factors can be regarded as crucial within SCA's development from the beginning of the 1970s:

- Long-term perspective: SCA has developed large internationally competitive units based on several forest industry products

- Renewal through diversification and vertical integration: new products include fluff-based hygiene products and corrugated board, areas in which the company can act as a substantial supplier of intermediate products and enjoy economies of scale in research and product development

- Increased use of recycled fibre: SCA uses a high proportion of recycled fibre as raw material for paper production. SCA has wholesale trading companies for collecting waste paper in Britain and other countries

- Internationalization: during the 1980s, SCA increased its European production of mainly recycled fibre-based products

- Leadership and decentralization: after Bo Rydin became the company's president in the early 1970s, the company engaged in far-reaching decentralization and delegation

CONCLUSIONS

Our study of the pulp and paper industry has shown that productivity comparisons between companies are not uncomplicated, even in this relatively homogeneous sector. Cost-effectiveness is easiest to analyse. In this respect, both UPM and SCA are very similarly advanced. Both have focused on the creation of large, internationally competitive production units. Both have also tried to compensate for their most serious competitive disadvantage, the high price of wood, by specializing in products with a high yield per tonne of wood input such as newsprint and LWC printing paper. UPM and SCA have also invested large sums in the development and use of TMP pulp, a mechanical pulp with very high wood yield which is made from spruce, the most common tree in Scandinavia.

SCA, in particular, increased its use of recycled fibre during the 1980s by means of a far-reaching internationalization of production. Both companies have located their mills close to sources of this raw material in major European countries. Generally speaking, the increasing use of recycled fibre means that the mills in non-Scandinavian Europe are becoming more competitive than Scandinavian and transatlantic production sites.

The two companies have also achieved greater cost-effectiveness with integration of pulp and paper production. SCA has integrated forward from paper to paper products, a natural outcome given that SCA's packaging products are more well-suited to forward integration than such products as newsprint, SC paper and LWC paper. In cases where it has made sense – such as in the production of sack paper – UPM has also instigated forward integration.

The relevant differences between the companies, and perhaps between their respective national industries, lie in the areas of innovation and expansion. During the 1980s, UPM invested more than SCA in new wood-containing printing paper machinery. SCA, by contrast, invested relatively large sums in acquisitions that partly reduced its dependence on traditional forest product operations with increasing production of consumer-oriented items.

It is impossible to predict which of these two strategies will be more successful. It may well turn out that both of them will work satisfactorily. By making heavy investments in new kinds of printing paper, UPM has taken the larger risk. UPM may also benefit from greater opportunities if these products turn out to be in heavy demand. By contrast, SCA is less sensitive to business cycles because of its sizable holdings of timberland and because its product range is more diversified and integrated.

[1]When we speak of the forest product industry in this study, we are referring only to the pulp and paper industry. As more generally used, the term encompasses all trades that use wood and related products as their main raw material and thus also includes sawmills, carpentry shops and factories that manufacture fibreboard and related products.

[2]Light-weight coated paper contains wood (mechanical pulp) and is used for high-quality catalogues, brochures and the like.

[3]For example, UPM's most recent expenditure for a magazine paper machine at its Jämsänkoski mill is budgeted to cost £300 million and represents 300,000 metric tons of added capacity per year.

[4]This difference can be explained by the fact that Sweden has one big company, Södra Skogsägarna, specializing in pulp. The company is owned by private forest owners in southern Sweden.

[5]Supercalendered magazine paper, a high-gloss printing paper, is used in advertising materials and periodicals.

[6]About 14 per cent in Finland and 7 per cent in Sweden.

[7]Enso and Kymmene do not belong to these joint organizations, but instead have their own sales organizations.

[8]Machine finished coated paper.

[9]United Paper Mills' capital spending project in Shotton included two paper machines with a total capacity of about 400,000 tons a year. It was one of the largest industrial investments in Britain during the 1980s.

[10]One interesting fact in this context is that several children of UPM executives are studying pulp and paper technology at a Helsinki university.

[11]About SEK 240,000–260,000.

[12]By integrating production, the company avoids having to dry the pulp before shipping it to the paper mill.

10 YAMAZAKI, ABB ROBOTICS, MANDELLI AND SMT

MANUFACTURING OF MACHINE TOOLS – A KEY INDUSTRY

Industrial companies partly increase productivity by automation. Machine tools capable of cutting, forming or shaping metals are of crucial importance in this context. Half of total industrial production involves their use. Computer-aided technology has already led to major productivity gains and may revolutionize the future of manufacturing. Already, companies can switch production more rapidly in response to market conditions. Clearly, then, machine tool manufacturers wield great influence on the productivity of other industrial firms. Machine tool manufacturers, it can be said, form an industrial sector of strategic importance.

During the 1980s, Japan, Germany and Italy boasted the world's most successful machine tool industries, with the Italians becoming the world's third largest exporter by edging ahead of the previously so successful American industry. In this chapter, we draw on the accumulated experience of companies from these nations, comparing Japan's Yamazaki Mazak with Sweden's ABB Robotics. Another comparative effort focuses on Italy's Mandelli and SMT.

Yamazaki Mazak's internationalization of its operations has set the trend in an industry that, until relatively recently, retained a very domestic focus. The company operates five factories in Japan, and one apiece in the United States and Britain. British magazine *Management Today* has rated the latter one of Britain's best-run factories in terms of productivity, automation and quality. A study of Yamazaki Mazak's British subsidiary, we thought, may offer insights into the application of Japanese manufacturing methods in a European country.

The Yamazaki Mazak Corporation sells its products under the Mazak brand name and is the world's largest – 4,000 employees – and most profitable machine tool manufacturer. Based in Worcester, Yamazaki Mazak United Kingdom (YMUK) has 325 employees and produces nearly 90 pieces of machinery a month. Value-added per employee is about £200,000 annually. A comparable reference company in a closely-related industry, Sweden's ABB Robotics AB is one of the world's largest and most successful manufacturers of industrial robots.

As in the mobile telephone industry, we can distinguish between machine tool makers that focus mainly on the sale of machines and those that sell systems that include machines. Yamazaki Mazak supplies mainly machines but has proved successful in supplying small systems.

By contrast, many European machine tool manufacturers concentrate on large systems. We therefore also chose to study a leading system supplier: Italy's Mandelli Group, currently one of the fastest-growing and most innovative manufacturers in the business. Mandelli has about 1,600 employees and ranks second in the world in sales of Flexible Manufacturing Systems (FMS).

As a reference company for Mandelli, we have chosen Sweden's SMT Machine Company AB, another system supplier and part of a national machine tool industry, that like its American counterpart, has fallen on hard times.[1]

What is a machine tool?

Machine tools cut, form or shape metals. Milling and turning are common operations; other machines drill and grind. The application of electronics means that the definition of a machine tool now stretches from simple familiar formats to fully automated manufacturing systems and factories.

Electronics opened the way for automation of machine tool operations, increasing performance and quality. Operators can change the settings on an electronic machine more quickly, enabling the manufacture of components with different geometries. Electronic machine tools can also work in a co-ordinated fashion, with production in the first machine controlling operations in a subsequent machine.

Productivity of machine tool manufacturers

Longer production runs and greater use of automated manufacturing systems lead to greater cost-effectiveness for machine tool manufacturers. Machine tools once represented such a large capital outlay that only big companies could buy them. More advanced machine tools were therefore usually manufactured in short production runs. Lower prices for machines providing similar performance has since opened a much larger market consisting of medium-sized and small companies. Technological progress has now enabled better performance, with higher-speed spindles, higher-precision machining and multiple operation capacity often encompassing both milling and turning. A number of machine tool manufacturers, including Yamazaki Mazak, are now selling laser-equipped machines. Manufacturers are also increasing sales by supplying machines and systems that meet specific customer requirements, installing the equipment, or even delivering it on a turn-key basis.

The historical evolution of production technology[2]

Ever since the industrial revolution, machine tools have underpinned industrial expansion. Designs for early steam engines, for example, presupposed metal cutting and forming capacity. Initially, industrial firms made their own machine tools. Later, in the 1850s, the so-called American system, with its emphasis on interchangeable machine tool parts, enabled longer production runs and economies of scale on the part of machine tool manufacturers. Universal milling machines and universal grinding machines added further refinements. During the second half of the 19th century, American companies set the pace, exporting costly high-performance machine tools to Britain, Germany and France.

In the 20th century, the automotive industry replaced the ordnance industry and bicycle manufacturers as the foremost users of machine tools. Assembly line production played a major role in the further evolution of the machine tool industry. To lower manufacturing costs, in the late 1940s the Ford Motor Company introduced large-scale automation in the form of mechanical devices that moved materials between machines. Often referred to as Detroit-style (or fixed) automation, such methods called for heavy investment and very large volume production of identical components.

The most important technological developments of the past 40 years originated in the aircraft industry. In the late 1940s, the Massachusetts Institute of Technology (MIT) offered the U.S. Air Force a new idea for manufacturing aircraft components. The result was the first numerically controlled machine tool (NCMT). In the 1970s, integrated circuits and minicomputers paved the way for Computer Numerical Control (CNC). A sharp improvement in the performance-price ratio of NCMTs followed, making shorter-run manufacture possible. Figure 10.1 shows how

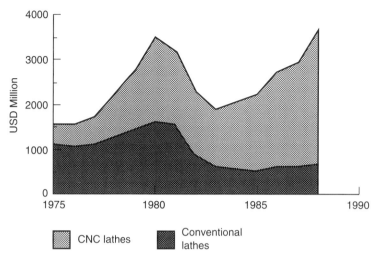

Figure 10.1 Replacement of conventional lathes by CNC lathes in OECD nations.
Source: Ehrnberg-Jacobsson (1991)

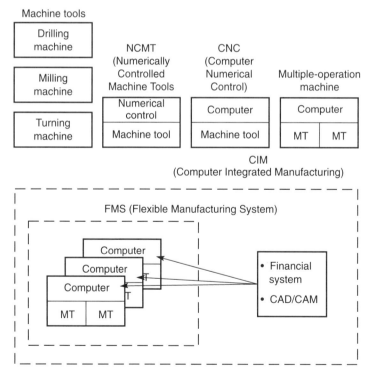

Figure 10.2 From multiple operation CNC machines to Flexible Manufacturing Systems

conventional lathes are being replaced by CNC lathes in the 24-nation OECD area.

Multiple-operation CNC machines equipped with different tools can choose tools suited for individual tasks (see Figure 10.2). Several such machines working in series forms a Flexible Manufacturing System (FMS). With the addition of data from a Computer Aided Design/Computer Aided Manufacturing (CAD/CAM) system or from a central planning system, computer integrated manufacturing (CIM) results. FMS and CIM point the way toward the fully automated factory of the future: experiments have shown that throughput times in conventional manufacturing may be more than a hundred times higher with CIM systems.

These technologies place new demands on industrial companies: accounting systems, premises and managerial skills are all affected. Studies in Italy and elsewhere also indicate that the new technology has led to major changes in work systems.[3] As certain manufacturing tasks disappear, others appear, often requiring operators equipped with a higher level of knowledge. The magnitude of these changes is set out in Table 10.1.

	Before	After
Space utilized	16,500 m²	6,600 m²
Equipment/system (number)		
• CNC machines	66	38
• Other machines	24	5
• Total	90	43
Employees per system		
• Operators	170	36
• Others	25	3
• Total	195	39
Average processing time per component		
• Machine time	35 days	3 days
• Component assembly	14 days	7 days
• Final assembly	42 days	20 days
• Total	91 days	30 days

Source: Jaikumar, R (1986)

Table 10.1 Changes in connection with the introduction of flexible automation technology: example from a Japanese factory.

Closing the circle

Manufacturing technology has thus undergone major changes in the past two decades. Table 10.2 indicates that, in many ways, today's advanced manufacturing technology once again resembles old-fashioned craft-based production, at least in terms of flexibility and size of factory. The differences lie elsewhere, with much-improved productivity and quality.

	British system	American system	Scientific management	Dynamic world	NC-era	Computer integrated manu-facturing
	1800–	1850–	1900–	1940–	1965–	1985–
Number of machines	3	50	150	150	50	30
Smallest effective size (number of employees)	40	150	300	300	100	30
Administration/ workers	0:40	20:130	60:240	100:200	50:50	20:10
Productivity increase, compared with proceeding era	4:1	3:1	3:1	3:2	3:1	3:1
Proportion of defective products	0.8	0.5	0.25	0.08	0.02	0.005
Number of product style variations	Infinite	3	10	15	100	Infinite

Source: Jaikumar, R (1988)

Table 10.2 Comparison of six historic levels manufacturing technology.

Microelectronics in machine tools have revolutionized the organization of production. Programmable automation allows machines to perform several different tasks, erasing the distinction between small-scale production equipment and mass production machine tools. Thus, computer-aided technology allows profitable short run, small factory manufacturing.

From knowledge- to science-based industry with a mass market
Technological developments create threats and opportunities for machine
tool manufacturers. The industry has evolved from a knowledge-base to
a science-base. Technological development was once a matter of imita-
tion, of learning-by-doing and of transfers of knowledge between manufacturer and customer. Today, machine tool manufacturers must perform
research in fields additional to mechanical technology: information technology, laser technology, artificial intelligence, sensors and new materials. It comes as no surprise, then, that some machine tool companies
have research and development budgets equivalent to nearly 10 per cent
of revenues.

Fewer buyers demand standard machines. Instead, they look for solutions to specific production problems. As a result, manufacturers must be
able to integrate various systems, a capability that presupposes broad
technological competence and that opens up new opportunities for ser-
vice-sector companies in the areas of applied engineering and information technology.

The technological breakthroughs represented by FMS and CIM have
only recently become widespread. FMS is moving from a niche into the
mass market. In an industry long characterized by craftsmanship,
improved lead times and production flows are becoming vital. The combination of cost-effectiveness and innovation has become critical.

Producer countries

During the 1970s, Japanese companies managed to alter the competitive
conditions prevailing in the industry.[4] With the introduction of numerically controlled machine tools, customers began buying high-quality
machines at reduced prices. Unlike European manufacturers, the Japanese also produced machines for small- and medium-sized companies.
This increased production volume, resulting in economies of scale and
substantially lower costs.

European machine tool manufacturers have concentrated more on niche
markets, offering package systems designed to customer specifications.
Here, too, Japanese competition is on the increase: modularization and
standardization of components are expected to lead to a gradual blurring
of distinctions between standard machines and custom-tailored systems.

Japan

Japan became the world's largest machine tool manufacturer early in the 1980s. Sharp increases in production followed, prompted by large-scale machine tool replacement on the part of Japanese industrial firms. Further, within the past five years, Japanese automotive companies have started implementing minor and major product changes on an annual basis. Such modifications require extensive changes in machine tool capability. Clearly, customer sophistication and 'user pull' have been strong driving forces behind expanding Japanese machine tool production capacity.

Domestic rivalry has played a significant role in developments during the 1980s. Competitors work in close geographical proximity, resulting in a high rate of knowledge transfers. Ownership of Japan's machine tool industry is unusually concentrated. Numerous mergers of small family-owned businesses in the 1960s and 1970s started a trend that has since become nationally-sanctioned. Japan's 14 largest machine tool companies now account for two-thirds of their industry's revenues. The Ministry of International Trade and Industry (MITI) participated actively in this process of concentration, specifying product standards, proposing specialization among companies and promoting exports. In a further example, MITI encouraged one company, Fanuc, to develop standardized numerical controls for various types of machines. Fanuc's efforts were then made available to other Japanese manufacturers. The company now has nearly half of the world market for such products.

Japan's labour shortage has influenced the manufacturing strategies of industrial companies. Studies indicate that Japanese manufacturers assign top priority to FMS investments; American and European industrial firms, by contrast, concentrate mainly on lead-time reduction.[5] The scarcity of human resources in Japan will probably result in continued strong demand for advanced equipment.

Italy

During the 1980s, parts of Italy's manufacturing sector experienced modernization that had a positive impact on the country's economic prospects. The domestic machine tool industry played a significant role in this transformation. After Japan and Sweden, Italy now boasts some of the world's highest relative usage of automation technology, partly because the labour troubles of the 1970s led many companies to reduce their reliance on human labour. A good investment climate and high savings ratios during the 1970s and 1980s contributed to the process.

Italy contains about 200 machine tool manufacturers, many of them family businesses. Strong domestic competition is one reason behind a marked tendency toward high levels of cost-effectiveness and innovation. Family ownership enables a long-term perspective and a greater inclination to undertake new capital spending. Two-thirds of the Italian machine tool industry is geographically concentrated around the city of Piacenza. As in the Japanese example, this fosters competition and the exchange of knowledge and information.

Domestic markets – textiles and engineering – are highly sophisticated. Ferrari was one of the first car companies in the world to use intelligent FMS. The precision required by Ferrari and other customers stimulated improvements that were later utilized in simpler machines and systems.

The Italian machine tool industry's singular organizational style favours specialization and custom manufacture. Entrepreneurship is balanced by the family loyalties that bind together individualists. Suited to custom-tailored production, this model is perhaps less suited to large production volume industries.

Sweden

Historically a net importer of machine tools, Sweden has developed a machine tool industry that has been highly successful in certain market segments. Yet despite a ready supply of highly skilled labour and a sophisticated domestic market for new production technology, the industry has remained relatively small.

Strategic groups

There is no generally accepted way of dividing machine tool manufacturers into categories. It is therefore difficult to specify both the size of the market and the market shares of individual companies. The CNC lathes and multiple-operation machines in which Yamazaki Mazak specialize comprise more than 60 per cent of the NCMT market. But manufacturers of such machines also frequently build FMS equipment.

The world's machine tool manufacturers can, however, be classified by strategic group, according to whether production is geared to machines or systems, and depending on whether their primary means of competition is price or custom-production.[6] In Figure 3 below, most of the market is located in the upper left-hand corner of the matrix. Here we find Yamazaki Mazak and the other machine manufacturers, each annually producing between 1,500 and 4,000 machines distinguished by good performance-price ratios. The lower right-hand corner contains manufacturers like

Machine suppliers	Systems suppliers	
Deckel Hitachi Seiki Makino Mori Seiki Okuma Yamazaki	?	Cost leadership
Index Max Muller Sajo Traub	Comau Huller Hille Mandelli Scharman SMT Werner & Kolb	Differentiation

Figure 10.3 World machine tool manufacturers by strategic group.

Source: Adaption of Ehrnberg-Jacobsson (1991).

Mandelli that compete mainly to sell packages to customers with special speed and precision requirements. Typically, these companies annually produce fewer than 1,000 machines. As Figure 10.3 indicates, no manufacturer can yet convincingly combine systems sales with large volume cost superiority. However, there is evidence that from different directions, Yamazaki Mazak and Mandelli are converging on this central nexus.

Even though some machine tool manufacturers produce robots, the industrial robot industry as a whole is not directly comparable with the machine tool industry. Most robot manufacturers are specialists. ABB Robotics and Japan's GMF/Fanuc, the largest of the bunch, claim respective global market shares of around 12 and 11 per cent. Both have broad product ranges and sell about 2,500 units per year. ABB Robotics has been the industry's most stable company, displaying steady growth and decent earnings during the past few years.

Competitive conditions
Generally speaking, machine tool manufacturers were once small companies with weak bargaining positions vis-a-vis customers and suppliers. Large clients virtually dictated prices. This has changed, however.[7] By the time YMUK was established, many British machine tool companies had gone bankrupt and former suppliers were eager to gain a new customer. YMUK transformed customary supplier relationships, basing them instead on purchases of no more than 20 to 40 per cent of suppliers'

production totals, in a move designed to force suppliers to seek other customers. (Similar philosophies are to be found at ABB Robotics: in this case, based on purchases of 20 per cent of each supplier's production). Both YMUK and ABB Robotics also enjoy relatively strong positions in relation to their customers, which include small- and medium-sized firms.

It is unlikely that new competitors will establish themselves in YMUK's and ABB Robotics' markets. To compete successfully, a company would need technological competence in mechanics, electronics and software – plus traditional machine-building skills. With their unlimited potential for exchange of data between design, engineering and production departments, future CIM systems will require heavy development spending, a fact that points toward the emergence of global companies with extensive research and development resources.

Both YMUK and ABB Robotics are experiencing strong competitive pressure. YMUK considers itself a European company and regards German, Japanese and Italian companies as its foremost competitors. ABB Robotics has no domestic competitor. Strong international competition from Japan is a motive force behind the success of this Swedish-based company.

Italy's Mandelli and Sweden's SMT have supplied a large share of the flexible manufacturing systems so far installed in the world. Both companies have large experience in hardware and software development on behalf of large-scale customers. Software, not least, accounts for a very large proportion of total costs.[8] Operating in an Italian market characterized by a preponderance of small and medium-sized firms, Mandelli enjoys better prospects than SMT, which typically supplies large customers equipped with strong bargaining positions.

Mandelli and SMT may soon encounter heavier competition in the systems market from Japanese companies that until now have mainly specialized in individual machines. A number of these companies increasingly supply customized FMS equipment. These Japanese companies possess solid manufacturing expertise and are steadily improving their knowledge of systems. If FMS equipment also becomes more standardized, systems expertise will be of relatively lesser importance, while machine expertise will mean more.

The main battleground in the machine tool industry will probably occur in the upper right corner of Figure 10.3. Those companies that can develop and quickly deliver a standardized FMS with good price performance ratio will win out. The strategies adopted by Yamazaki Mazak and Mandelli betray a clear awareness of this situation.

YAMAZAKI MAZAK UNITED KINGDOM (YMUK)

Internationalization of production and research and development is a relatively new phenomenon. Unusually, a desire to move production closer to customers rather than the urge to overcome trade barriers has been the main motive. Heavily committed to technology transfer, Yamazaki Mazak has pioneered this process. Its various manufacturing units are already on-line via satellite, permitting global production management.

A Japanese subsidiary company in Britain

The secret behind YMUK's success can be traced to three organizational principles:

- Use of the very latest production technology
- Harmonization of the best in Japanese and British work practices
- Well-developed working relationships with suppliers

Flexibility is the motto, common sense the method. Yamazaki Mazak wanted a factory in Europe to shorten European delivery lead times from three months to four weeks. Adding to the impetus provided by an EC investment grant, Worcester's machine tool manufacturing traditions offered availability of engineering skills and suppliers.

The new plant's work system was based on the principles of group solidarity, meaningful work assignments and the power to influence one's situation. Inaugurated in 1987, the factory was more highly automated than any other machine tool industry plant in the world. Productivity increases have followed.

The factory's machining section operates round-the-clock, seven days a week. Manned for 12 hours a day and unmanned the rest of the time, two sets of employees alternate on a four-day shift pattern. Assembly, by contrast, operates on a two-day shift pattern. Recruited after extensive testing for willingness and ability to learn and adapt, employees' average age is under 30. Only three per cent of recruits had previous experience in the machine tool industry.

Cost-effectiveness

YMUK manufactures about 90 machines per month, a large volume that offers substantial economies of scale. In general, the international literature on Japan's so-called transplants has devoted much attention to organizational issues at the expense of advances in production engineering. YMUK uses highly sophisticated production technologies. Components that need machining, for example, can be run on the same FMS line. Yamazaki Mazak maintains that its batch size is one production unit – a maximally flexible system.

The company stresses the value of continuous small improvements (*kaizen*, in the Japanese terminology). Employees are encouraged not to discuss mistakes generally, but instead to recognize their own mistakes in particular, within an overall atmosphere that stimulates improvement. It is essential to have channels through which information on improvements is disseminated. About 75 per cent of the machinery and systems used is manufactured in-house, making the factory a full-scale laboratory for machinery that will later be placed on the market.[9]

Innovation

Yamazaki Mazak has a reputation for rapid product development. Although YMUK currently has no formal in-house research development operations, continuous product development is used to customize machinery – the factory's *raison d'être*. From this year onward, a new development centre tasked with researching fields such as ultra-precision technology will make YMUK part of its parent company's global research and development network, which is expected to be in full operation by the end of 1992.

Innovations are inspired by a mentality of continuous improvement. Externally, innovation often stems from contacts with customers and, not least, from constant comparisons with the company's other operating units. Like Mandelli and ABB Robotics, Yamazaki Mazak operates a network of technical centres: 30 in Japan, 12 in the United States and eight in Europe. The small- and medium-sized companies that form the majority of YMUK's customer base discuss quality and productivity with experts based at the technical centres. After-sales service including programming instructions and operator training are part of the centres' function. A club for all users of the company's machines provides a forum for exchange of information, keeping members informed of the latest developments in manufacturing technology.

According to YMUK management, in a company where any given procedure may only have a life-span of two or three months, constant internal changes sometimes complicate the planning of major strategic shifts. On the other hand, an organization that makes continuous operational adjustments probably suffers less from strategic gaps: major strategic interventions can be minimized.

Productivity management

YMUK managers meet to discuss production data on a weekly basis. Hours per machine manufactured, rejection levels, absenteeism, overtime worked and sales figures are among the statistics used. High capacity utilization in automated systems depends on control of metal-cutting processes and prevention of downtime. YMUK keeps track of the remaining service life of the tools in each machine, enabling timely replacement and consequent increased reliability, reduced lead times and higher capacity utilization.

Another system monitors and adjusts the electricity consumption of each machine. Maximum cutting capacity is predetermined for each tool in terms of electricity consumption. When, because of deteriorating tools or more resilient working materials, the machine exceeds this level, the electrical feed rate is automatically reduced to control the risk of machine breakdowns.

Organizational structure

The just-in-time principle attempts to achieve a heavy production flow without the burden of large inventories. Traditional manufacturing systems are not well-suited to the task: Yamazaki Mazak realized early on that CIM provides a solution, with functions such as production planning, component supply, order processing and machining on FMS lines. Relatively small, the factory's production area is not cluttered with buffer stocks. An automated warehouse and automatic guided vehicles (AGVs) enable delivery of components and parts to the production lines on a just-in-time basis.

The use of CIM systems requires high standards of organization and management. YMUK has four hierarchical levels: operators, supervisors, managers and directors. Operators are classified into three categories based on experience. YMUK has two rule systems. One comprises general rules of conduct in the factory: working hours, dress, hygiene, no-smoking areas and so on. The second comprises the rules of each work team. Within this general framework, teams of employees are free to improve their own situations.

Technology

Establishing norms is an important part of YMUK's management system. Equally important are the higher standards of knowledge and motivation required by CIM. The company's highly advanced FMS utilizes rapid automatic tool changers. Sensors that monitor tool performance facilitate high-precision tasks to such a level that subsequent quality inspections become unnecessary. Downtime has been reduced, and capacity utilization runs as high as 85 per cent.

The parent company's process technology development efforts mandated the testing of three generations of the CIM system currently deployed at the British plant. In turn, current heavy investments at Yamazaki Mazak's American factory will make it the company's most sophisticated production unit. Experiences gleaned in the U.S. plant will then be applied to the company's other units.

Communication

"This plant," says one manager, "is powered not by energy but by information". Supposed to take place at the level of operations, problem-solving calls for good horizontal communications safeguarded from disruptive interventions from higher hierarchical levels. Superiors are supposed to participate in problem-solving more as facilitators than as a decision-makers. The organizational structure of the factory, with very few buffers, requires efficient information flow. The factory is so small that events are readily perceived by everyone; information spreads quickly. Operators, supervisors and managers work close to the production area. An operator who discovers that a component is missing can go directly to the responsible purchaser, who sits nearby. The managing director and other executives often spend time in the factory, and several employees told us of daily exchanges of information with management.

To facilitate decisions, operators are encouraged to make independent assessments, gathering the necessary information with which to solve problems. In a self-generating process, the means of preventing recurrence of visible problems are discussed. In each area of operations, employee responsibility for monitoring quality effectively banishes the need for a separate quality assurance department.

External flows of information assume great importance. In Britain, suppliers traditionally compete at arm's length, with the submission of tenders, from which manufacturers accept the lowest price. YMUK instead works closely with suppliers, providing them with suggestions for improvements. The company rejects price increases attributed to inflation, instead requiring suppliers to compensate for their increased costs. During the year before our interviews, calculated in terms of value, YMUK refused 1.6 per cent of purchases as poor quality – a fairly good level for the machine tool industry.

At annual meetings, the company's best suppliers are awarded prizes. At the factory's entrance, a bulletin board lists suppliers on the basis of punctuality, a system reinforced by monthly bulletins sent to suppliers that detail both punctuality and quality of deliveries. Not surprisingly, supplier punctuality has greatly improved (see Table 10.3). Notably, several of YMUK's suppliers have become more competitive as a result, with some striking up relationships with the Yamazaki Mazak factory in the United States.

1989	84
1990	87
1991	90 (goal)

Source: YMUK

Table 10.3 Punctual deliveries as a percentage of all deliveries to YMUK, 1989–91.

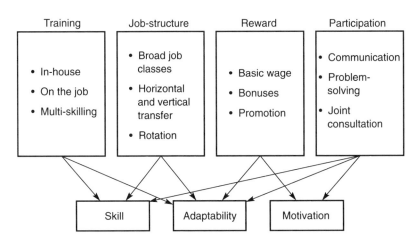

Figure 10.4 Personnel policies at YMUK.

Source: YMUK.

Human Resource Management

Personnel policies are illustrated in Figure 10.4. Increased skills, flexibility and motivation are achieved through training, job structuring, reward systems and participation in the decision-making process. Absenteeism totals 1.2 per cent. At 6 per cent, personnel turnover is considered somewhat high: clearly, say management, operators trained and educated by YMUK are being lured away by higher wage offers from rival companies.

YMUK stresses both the importance of the individual and the need for individuals to respect their work team. Wages are based on individual effort, ability and attitude.[10] Unusually for a British-based firm, equality reigns: employees all eat in the same canteen; outside the factory walls, there is a marked absence of reserved parking spaces. With the exception of late shift workers, working hours are uniform. Notably, employees do not punch in on arrival, but only when ready to begin work. At the end of the day, the same principle applies in reverse.

The relative rarity of individual job descriptions, says management, avoids the risk of the 'I'm Alright, Jack' syndrome. Employees are instead trained as members of a work team that handles all available tasks, with individual operators eventually coming to understand most of the jobs performed within any given group. As a result, temporary absences take less of a toll on production and maintenance staff can be kept to a minimum.[11] Manuals do, however, exist for different work operations. At first, they came in the form of general guidelines issued by the technical department. But operators soon wrote their own manuals, including instructions on how to perform their tasks in an optimal way. These manuals are now used for instructing new employees.

Judging from our extensive interviews, employees appeared to understand their company's overall business goals and well aware of the advantages of their own company's products. Even non-technical employees were able to describe the advantages of Mazak machine tools.

There is a clear element of competition between employees and groups of employees. Despite official comparisons of performance, co-operation seems to continue smoothly, with many workers covering for colleagues during illness. Everyone knows that his many efforts are essential to the company. Admittedly, collective bonuses dependent on monthly production goals play a large role in this context. Notably, standards of co-operation are crucial to a continuous process of employee evaluation. Unequipped with trade unions or any form of collective bargaining, employees know that loyalty to the company is noticed and rewarded. According to management, the presence of such organizational relics would imply that the company had failed to create the right environment for its employees.

The employee evaluation process
The company's employee evaluation system mandates evaluations at annual intervals after hiring. Evaluation forms vary from job to job, but, in general, employee are graded by a points system, with the total score playing a major role in the wage-setting process.

The evaluation system is also used to plan training for employees. In individual three-year rolling career plans, employees' aims and company needs are matched as closely as possible. Our interviews indicated that evaluation is perceived as fair and efficient.

Wage systems
Again unlike most British companies, YMUK pays monthly salaries, even to operators, a factor that helps to create the impression of a progressive high-status company. Differentials between supervisors and operators are about 25 per cent. Although wage differentials between operators are not made public, employees seem to feel that they know fairly well where they stand by comparison with others. Pay is regarded as a strong signal of the company's evaluation of an employee's work.

Equivalent to about 10 per cent of an operator's wage, monthly cash bonuses are paid if the company achieves production targets; since the factory opened, bonuses have been paid during all but two months. Individual employees can be denied a bonus on a demerit points system that hands down a 0.5 demerit for late arrival and double that for a day's illness (Beyond statutory sick pay, the company's portion of sick pay depends on years of employment and can be revoked on suspicion of abuse). Between 1.5 and 2.5 demerits reduce any bonus by half; above this level, the employee receives no bonus. Employees with a year's clean time-keeping and illness record receive special recognition.

Further education and careers
YMUK places great emphasis on continuing education through on-the-job training and job rotation. About one-third of operators have visited Yamazaki Mazak's Japanese factories for between three and six weeks' training. YMUK believes that sending operators, rather than executives, results in better dissemination of knowledge among the work-force. Aside from education in their job specialities, employees each receive,

on average, a week's further training every year. On Saturday mornings, special courses explain company products; participants are paid as during regular working time. Employees can apply for grants with which to purchase professional literature or participate in outside training courses.

Opportunities for internal promotion are a strong motivating factor at Japanese companies.[12] The potential for advancement is best at rapidly-growing companies with multi-level organizations. YMUK has attained optimal size: with only four hierarchical levels, employees have limited opportunities for advancement. Managers and operators alike regard this as a problem: one solution offers employees the chance to move laterally from one department to another. According to our interviewees, employees do not withhold suggestions for changes that may result in the elimination of jobs: the understanding seems to be that other assignments are available in such cases.

ABB ROBOTICS

The ABB Robotics story began in the 1970s when Asea,[13] a large Swedish-based industrial group, began the manufacture of electrical robots.[14] Asea took advantage of its expertise in electrical motors, high-precision mechanics and computer control systems to devise a new generation of products that differed from earlier hydraulic robots. Separated from Asea's core business area, ABB Robotics nevertheless devoted sufficient time and money to developing the necessary competence in technology, production and marketing that made possible a fully-fledged venture on to international markets. Today, ABB Robotics operates successfully in the face of stiff Japanese competition, setting the pace of development in the industrial robot industry.

Like other Swedish companies burdened by high labour costs, ABB Robotics found factory automation advantageous. High skill levels among blue collar workers combined well with a tradition of new working methods that had already delegated much in terms of responsibility. Traditionally, Swedish workers had not viewed automation as a threat to employment.

Asea originally lacked experience and contacts with users in its new area of production. Much effort was expended on filling these gaps in its knowledge. Today ABB probably has more experience of applied robotics than any other company in the world. Like many companies in the machine tool industry, ABB Robotics decided in the mid 1980s to concentrate on some of its best products in order to increase profitability.

The company outsources all components, preferring instead to assemble and test finished products. Increased productivity thus far is attributable to the use of fewer parts and production flows; the company is now working hard to further improve productivity by applying its own version of lean production.

Cost-effectiveness

ABB Robotics has sold and installed more than 25,000 robots since opening for business. Successful productivity schemes have included the three-year P25 programme, introduced in 1989 with the aim of reducing costs by 25 per cent. Large cost reductions have resulted from fewer components, cheaper materials and reduced development times. ABB Robotics has also started decentralization of assembly functions with new work organization principles and increased operator training.

Because ABB Robotics is an assembly plant, its purchasing department is especially vital to the productivity of the company. Purchased components account for about 60 per cent of a robot's production cost. Experiences drawn from the P25 programme have been applied to suppliers: thus, when a new supplier quoted lower prices for a control system, the original supplier returned with more competitive offer. ABB Robotics also tries to assist suppliers in raising quality by participating in their development work.

Innovation

Research and development expenditure totals 10 per cent of company revenues. The company tries to maintain high level skills in the key areas of man-machine interface and control systems. Product development is being revamped: development times for new robots have fallen from 2.5 years to just over one year. In a continuing drive to reduce component numbers, the company's latest product uses 50 per cent fewer parts than its predecessor. Defects and breakdowns, the company believes, have become correspondingly less likely.

Productivity management

The company's goal of retaining its position as the industrial robot industry's largest manufacturer is continually enunciated in internal communications. Like Yamazaki Mazak, ABB Robotics lists flexibility and reduction of lead times as guiding principles. Lead times have been reduced from four to two weeks.

Organizational structure

ABB Robotics is the only company in its industry to operate, world-wide, some 20 subsidiaries responsible for sales, installation, education, service and renovation. At these robot automation centres, basic robots are equipped with tools from local suppliers. Similar to Yamazaki Mazak's international sales network, this method brings closer contact with customers.

Asea has played a crucial role in the growth of ABB Robotics, facilitating, for example, the construction of the company's far-flung marketing organization. Its ownership by a financially stable multinational has probably had a favourable effect on long-term projects: today, the robotics subsidiary's parent company ABB Group reaps the fruits of an investment in what has become one of its most profitable units.

Organization at ABB Robotics bears comparison with YMUK. Both companies have four hierarchical levels, although ABB Robotics does draw sharper distinctions between such functions as assembling robots and control systems. Reorganization will soon divide employees into groups of between seven and ten operators who will assume total responsibility for the assembly and testing of a given robot. Supervisors will take on the new roles of recruitment, production planning and inventory maintenance, becoming heads of profit centres, and, quite possibly, in the future, paying notional 'rent' for their patches of production space.

Communication

ABB Robotics' Japanese competitors engage in constant product improvement and price trimming, leaving little room in the market for manufacturers charging higher prices or refraining from product development. All employees are aware of this fact, and it serves as a driving force behind product improvement and cost-effectiveness, leading, in particular, to ABB's own version of lean production principles.[15]

Human Resource Management

In the personnel administration field, ABB Robotics has started consultation on changes to a wage system that currently includes a piecework element and a quality bonus. In addition to current reward systems that stimulate further product development, to boost incentives and increase productivity, a new system will base wages on factors such as competence, position and team-work. Local trade union officials support the move, even though wider wage differentials among operators will be the likely result.

CONCLUSIONS: YMUK AND ABB ROBOTICS

Historically, machine tool manufacturers have combined low profitability with limited product development opportunities. They have been small companies and their customers traditionally have been the much larger corporations of, for example, the automotive industry. This situation has changed. In a rapidly expanding market, machine tools are now affordable for many small- and medium-sized companies. Some machine tool manufacturers, like Yamazaki, have themselves grown into medium-sized companies, improving their bargaining position vis-a-vis customers, and charging higher prices as a result. Better profitability has permitted more product development. Robot manufacturers are in a similar position. Fierce competition implies that only cost-effective production *enables survival*.

YMUK and ABB Robotics are high productivity companies that have improved products and processes. As speedier development work has given their new products a longer lifetime in the market, higher cost-effectiveness has enabled them to set prices sufficiently low for a growing market of small- and medium-sized companies. Yamazaki Mazak's history, in particular, resembles that of Japanese automotive manufacturers. From beginnings in a low-price market segment dominated by large production volumes, economies of scale and increased profitability allowed new product development that eventually earned the company a leading position within its industry as a whole.

Retention of a leading position is just as challenging as its achievement. By repeatedly comparing their performance with competitors and with other units in their own corporate group, both impress upon their employees the need for continuous improvement.

Elsewhere, research and development and manufacturing capacity are channelled into portions of the market where the expectation is that demand cannot be satisfied by available products. Like ABB Robotics, Yamazaki Mazak is probably moving toward the huge market potential represented by low-cost automated systems built to customer specifications. This choice of strategy is being made by management. Management skills will therefore be crucial to long-term productivity.

Finally even in a highly automated manufacturing system, people are the main factor affecting productivity. YMUK's 85 per cent capacity utilization level, for example, is attributable to the efforts of its employees. Thus, work systems at both companies regard employees as individuals with long-term commitments to their company. Skills development becomes a shared interest in the context of a smoothly functioning process of decentralization. Delegation of responsibility and authority is mingled with high levels of motivation and skill.

MANDELLI

Like Yamazaki Mazak, Mandelli is headed by three sons of the company's founder. The company sells customer-tailored machine tool systems at competitive prices to large and small clients. Realizing early on that it would have to cut prices as FMS products become standardized, Mandelli has invested heavily in manufacturing automation and research and development. The result has been a leading position in terms of FMS units sold globally. Further, Mandelli's ambitions stretch to fostering a European Silicon Valley for advanced production engineering, centred around Piacenza, the northern Italian city that is Mandelli's centre of operations and home to nearly two-thirds of the nation's machine tool manufacturers.

Innovation

In a number of respects, Mandelli has been a leading innovator. The company was first to sell machines that combined milling and turning. The Italian textile industry was among the first in the world to use FMS – supplied by Mandelli. The company's research and development costs total about 10 per cent of revenues: executives like to describe Mandelli as a company based on brain power. Notably, Mandelli developed its own control unit as early as 1980. With its emphasis on in-house development of critical components, the company's development philosophy resembles the Japanese model.

Mandelli has often accepted large, difficult assignments – such as its relationship with Ferrari – as learning experiences. Satisfying Ferrari's requirements for strict tolerances and very high precision in automotive parts has imparted accumulated experience subsequently applied to the production of simpler FMS and machine tools.

Cost-effectiveness

The European machine tool industry has so far rebuffed stiff Japanese competition by developing a competitive edge in the design of package systems. National loyalty of customers and the comparatively small volume of Japanese sales in Italy have also offered the Italians something of a breathing space. Although price, and thus cost-effectiveness, are less important to a company that sells whole systems rather than individual machines, Mandelli has been careful to control the costs of its specially tailored products.

Pressed by high labour costs, early in the 1980s Mandelli embarked on extensive automation of manufacturing operations, using its own FMS. The company is now building an automated module production facility that will be one of the largest of its kind world-wide. Of Mandelli's other three production facilities, two use some of the world's most sophisticated FMS.

Early in the 1980s, Mandelli also transformed its product development philosophy, reducing its range of models, inaugurating systems specialization, modularizing products, standardizing hardware and software and – for good measure – automating production. Mandelli began constructing systems from components that were being made in long production runs and at low cost. The result: lower costs and lower prices for advanced systems tailored to customer specifications.

Productivity management

Like successful Japanese companies, Mandelli has chosen the best suppliers and fought hard to keep them. To ensure high quality, Mandelli's certification system evaluates supplier performance every four months. Geographic proximity to suppliers probably adds another advantage, reducing the risk of faulty components from suppliers anxious to avoid losing face among in the region's tightly-knit business community.

Organizational structure

Family ownership is typical of the Italian business sector. Although Mandelli operates as a family business, its shares are quoted in the stock market – something of an anomaly in Italy. At their best, Italy's family-owned companies boast a strong and dynamic owner who keeps in close touch with his company's problems. Combined with a modern corporate management structure and far-reaching decentralization of decision-making functions, as in the case of Mandelli, paternalistic style guarantees flexibility and far-sightedness.

To an outside visitor, Mandelli's organizational system at first appears vague and unstructured, even chaotic. But the lack of organizational charts doesn't hinder pragmatism and flexibility, even in a company whose business is the assembly of complex systems comprising many components. Under such conditions, Mandelli's combination of technological competence and the 'fixer mentality' is probably unbeatable.

In the past year, Mandelli has acquired several small- and medium-sized companies. A chief technology officer – a rare appointment in most engineering companies – has been recruited to integrate these firms into the group and plan an efficient allocation of technical resources.

Mandelli tries to combine the flexibility of a small business with the cost advantages of a large company. Operations are organized around a holding company, beneath which companies now operate as independent profit centres. The intention is to eventually spin off operations without thereby terminating business relationships. For many Italian employees, such spin-offs are the stuff of dreams.

Human Resource Management

Paradoxically, Italian companies are characterized by strong group cohesiveness and individual competition. Conventional wisdom insists that Italians function badly within hierarchical organizations: they prefer, it is said, to work within known groups, preferably within the family. Under such circumstances, norms and rivalry become essential elements of personnel policy. This also applies at Mandelli. At the operator level, norms are a more important management instrument than rewards. Although trade union membership at this level is less than 60 per cent, wages are regulated by collective bargaining. Despite a two-year-old skill- and position-related wage system, differentials remain small, as does personnel turnover.

Individual competition is more common at the white collar level, where wage differentiation is also wider. Italian business executives are well paid by international standards. During the past year, systematic recruitment has garnered a group of executives who mostly have experience of working in the same industry. Experience in international business was another sought-after qualification.

Communication

Mandelli's success as an innovative company largely results from close contacts with customers. The flexibility required by Italian customers and their need to increase labour efficiency have served as significant market signals. Typically, Mandelli functions as a consultant or adviser to its customers. To provide the same services outside Italy, the company has opened service centres in Detroit, Wiesbaden, Gothenburg and Paris. Each centre has between five and 20 carefully-selected employees. The centres:

- Adapt products for easier customer use
- Produce manuals and instructions
- Provide customer training and gather information on how products are actually used by customers

Mandelli has the advantage of using its products in its own manufacturing operations. After all, machine tools exist to manufacture other machine tools. Experimentation is constant; Mandelli's facilities act as a proving ground for state-of-the-art technology.

Building machine tool systems exclusively for large customers has its problems: an unequal bargaining relationship among them. Mandelli's answer has taken the form of standardization and modularization. Expanding out of its market niche, Mandelli seeks customers in perhaps the toughest market of all, targeting its products to small- and medium-sized businesses in a head-to-head contest with Japanese competitors.

SMT

Like Mandelli, SMT builds machine tool systems. Originally known as the Swedish Machine Tool Company, SMT developed a ground-breaking CNC lathe as early as 1957. Despite other evidence of a strong innovative streak that has seen it become a market leader in certain sectors of lathe production, the company has not managed to commercialize its high level of technological competence as well as Mandelli. Indeed, the problem appears to be growing steadily. After a recent take-over, the company is now attempting to regain ground lost to competitors.

Part of the government owned defence contractor FFV[16], SMT belonged to the Volvo Group between 1942 and 1969. In 1990, SMT became a private company held by Sweden's Industor Group, a move that sparked far-reaching restructuring.

Innovation

As is often the fate of an innovator, SMT's early CNC lathe technology was imitated and modified by others. By the late 1970s, the company faced competition from German and Japanese companies offering cheaper – and occasionally better – products. A change in strategy followed, as the company began to focus instead on turn-key systems. Despite delivering 350 such systems, more than any of its competitors, the company's strategy has not met with great financial success. The company failed to establish its systems as the dominant standard.

Insufficient improvements to the machines within these systems resulted in ever-tougher competition. As a result, during the 1980s SMT spent less than Mandelli on research and development, cutting back on the number of engineers and technicians engaged in development work.

Cost-effectiveness

Unlike Mandelli, SMT does not employ cost-effective production of modularized components. Machine tool systems can easily become too advanced and expensive, offering the customer more than he actually needs. In the case of one recently delivered advanced machine tool system, for example, special features had been added that were most likely inapplicable in terms of other customers. Overall, SMT has lost customers and market share to Japanese, Italian and German companies offering products pitched at precisely the right level of cost and quality. Typically, such mistakes follow on from faulty communication with the market and within an organization.

Communication, organizational structure and personnel

SMT seems to have missed the signals that persuaded other companies to reduce their ranges, modularize and standardize their products and automate their production systems. Repeated changes of management under government ownership may be partly to blame: during this period, the goal of generating employment was accorded top priority at SMT. Training programmes were smaller than those of competing firms. Although the company embarked on several exciting new projects, investments in machinery and marketing were assigned low priority. As a result, SMT now lacks an organization beyond its domestic market equivalent to Mandelli's international service centres. The company has been unable to follow its Nordic customers abroad as they have internationalized their operations.

Because of SMT's relatively small investments in machinery, levels of automation are fairly low. Unlike Mandelli and Yamazaki Mazak, SMT does not use equipment manufactured in-house. Assembly operations are relatively unmodernized, work flow is complex, and employees boast narrowly specialized job descriptions. Assembly and testing, for example, take place in physically separated locations. Last but not least, an outdated cost accounting system has failed to foster improvements in internal productivity.

SUMMARY

The examples of Yamazaki Mazak, ABB Robotics and Mandelli demonstrate the importance of combining cost-effectiveness with a high degree of innovation. Although methods vary, depending on institutional environments, the companies have a number of features in common. Strong external competitive pressure, and management's ability to generate internal competitive pressure are among them. In addition, Yamazaki Mazak and Mandelli have successfully adapted to the structure of their respective domestic markets, taking advantage of domestic rivalry and customer sophistication in their product development and increasingly efficient manufacturing systems. Although ABB Robotics had no domestic competition, the company ventured relentlessly into the international market where it encountered stiff Japanese competition.

Behind these success stories, we find managers equipped as leaders, visionaries and communicators. The historical absence of strong, long-term ownership at SMT is probably one of the main reasons behind the company's negative development.

In Yamazaki, Mandelli and ABB Robotics one encounters that rare managerial talent of finding and creating new market segments with massive product development. Single-handedly, for example, Yamazaki has transformed the market logic that binds the entire machine tool industry.

Of great importance, internal competitive pressure – or management's method of communicating goals and expectations – assumes varying forms. Competition and comparisons, or even actual individual rivalry, are essential elements. Norms and rewards are used in varying degrees. And despite the fact that the factories at Yamazaki and Mandelli are some of the world's most automated, these companies continue to invest large amounts in training their employees. Paradoxically, as production becomes ever more automated, man appears to become ever more essential to the balance of forces inherent in efficient production systems.

Clearly, these three companies practice what they preach, making use of their latest products in their own automated manufacturing systems. These companies offer a glimpse of the factory of the future, as well as offering guidance on tackling the problems of automation in other industries.

[1]After this study was carried out SMT went into bankruptcy and has now been taken over by Várnamo Industrier.

[2]Main source: Carlsson, B., "The Development and Use of Machine Tools in Historical Perspective," in Day, R., Eliasson, G., *The Dynamics of Market Economies*, IUI and North Holland, 1986.

[3]OECD, *Managing Manpower for Advanced Manufacturing Technology*, Paris, 1991.

[4]Ehrnberg, E., Jacobsson, S., *Technological Discontinuities, Industry Structure and Firm Strategy: The Case of Machine Tools and Flexible Manufacturing System*. Chalmers University of Technology, Gothenburg, 1991.

[5]Hörte, S-Å et al, *Tillverkningsstrategier i Sverige 1982–1989*, IMIT, Gothenburg, 1991.

[6]Ehrnberg-Jacobsson (1991).

[7]There are now about 10 manufacturers of machine tools with more than 2,000 employees.

[8]For a 2–4 machine FMS, software accounts for 20–25 per cent of total costs. See Ehrnberg, E., Jacobsson, S., *op. cit.*

[9]At its Minikamo manufacturing unit in Japan, Yamazaki Mazak has even automated various types of testing procedures, which are still done manually at most other companies.

[10]At YMUK collective wage bargaining procedure does not exist. Wages from deputy managing director to switchboard operator are the subject of more or less open bargaining once a year, at which time these individual factors are taken into account.

[11]YMUK now has two employees for maintenance tasks in a factory where about 180 people work.

[12]Aoki, M, *Toward an Economic Model of the Japanese Firm*, Journal of Economic Literature, Vol. XXVIII (March 1990), pp. 1–27.

[13]Asea Brown Boveri (ABB) was established in 1988 through a merger between Sweden's Asea and Switzerland's Brown Boveri to create the world's largest electrotechnology group.

[14]"The industrial robot is an automatic position-controlled reprogrammable multi-function manipulator having several degrees of freedom, capable of handling materials, parts, tools, or specialized devices through variable programmed motions for the performance of a variety of tasks... It often has the appearance of one or several arms ending in a wrist." Economic Commissions for Europe, 1985; *Production and Use of Industrial Robots*, cited in Edquist-Jacobsson 1988, p 46.

[15]The chief executive of the ABB Group has declared that other subsidiaries with comparable technology but with less competitive pressure have not succeeded in improving productivity as much as ABB Robotics.

[16]Försvarets Fabriksverkstäder, literally the Defense Factory Workshops.

INTRODUCTION

The questions we asked in this book were:

- What can we learn from highly productive companies?
- What factors in these companies and in their surroundings create a favourable climate for sustained productivity improvements?

We did not study isolated changes, for example in connection with the restructuring of companies. Instead we looked at long-term productivity-raising programme and continuous, incremental improvements. When we began our study, we had an idea of what conditions were worth looking at. Our ambition was therefore to find concrete examples of certain conditions, and if possible to gain some idea of the weight of various factors, rather than to discover entirely new explanatory factors. Concrete examples are more persuasive than a generally formulated recommendation and are easier to use as the basis for practical follow-up. Our analyses and descriptions are based primarily on the opinions of corporate managements, although as far as possible we have tried to supplement these with information from other sources, such as competitors, labour unions and independent observers.

When we now try to generalize from our observations, we risk losing some of the effect that a concrete example provides. This is because every company is unique. It is a combination of ideas, competence, experience and equipment that has been shaped over a long period of time and that must also be viewed in relation to its surroundings.

Put simply, one of our initial theoretical assumptions was that companies that do not experience resource scarcity find it hard to be efficient. Some degree of external pressure is thus required to compel a company to be economical with resources. If resource scarcity becomes too confining, however, efficiency declines. Resources are defined mainly as the company's supply of capital, labour and input goods. We therefore had to ask the following questions:

- Does the company have a reasonable level of profitability and supply of capital?

- Does it have a qualified labour force and other necessary skills?

- Finally, is there a functioning market for suppliers of input goods?

The resource situation is very dependent on the demands of customers or competitors. The stiffer the competition, the scarcer the resources and the greater a company's efforts to improve efficiency. But other kinds of resources are also significant and can offset scarce financial resources. One such resource is the availability of a qualified labour force. The Finnish forest product industry's very scarce resource situation has been offset to some extent by Finland's high level of forest industry-related competence, manifested, for example, by the existence of a special engineering degree programme for the industry. Other relevant resources include high levels of research and education, such as Ericsson was able to utilize in developing its mobile telephone system operations.

Our second assumption was that a company that does not face new demands from customers, new threats from competitors, new technology or new input goods has no reason to adapt or be innovative. If the level of information complexity is too great, however, a company may find it hard to adapt. A high level of uncertainty or chaos in its surroundings can lead to paralysis. On the other hand, if a company's surroundings are static, there is no reason for it to change. Our hypothesis is thus that the factors behind innovation, in terms of external pressure for change, have their most favourable effect somewhere between these extremes.

Resource scarcity and new demands together constitute an external pressure for change. We began our case studies by analyzing the external pressure for change at work on each company. First, we studied the respective industries in which our companies operated. Who are their competitors, customers and suppliers? How do technological advances take place in each industry? What institutional rule systems exist? Later, we also gathered information on various conditions in the home country of each company that we studied. This included the situation in the labour market, education and research in the company's specialities and political conditions with direct implications for the companies under study.

A suitable level of external pressure for change is not enough to make a company react, act, innovate or anticipate change. If external pressure for change is really supposed to influence the company's operations, three internal company requirements must be fulfilled:

- The company must consciously interact with its surroundings
- The company must have the organizational prerequisites to adapt
- Human resources should be willing and able to help make this happen

I. EXTERNAL FACTORS

National factors

The fact that we found highly productive companies in so many countries might be interpreted as meaning that national factors are of minor importance to productivity. United Paper Mills and Yamazaki Mazak succeeded in setting up high productivity British subsidiaries despite the major problems surrounding the domestic paper and machine tool industries. These foreign subsidiaries were as productive as equivalent production units in their parent company's home country, and certainly far better than British-owned companies in the same industries. But achieving such productivity required more than mere marginal changes. It also required better management, the absence of obstructive labour unions, new work systems, access to state-of-the-art technology and a supply of qualified labour. United Paper Mills and Yamazaki Mazak also received inducements in the form of subsidies.

Although it was not the primary purpose of our case studies to examine productivity factors at the national level, we could see that the best companies often enjoyed the benefits of favourable circumstances in their home countries. Such circumstances often apply to a particular industry in a country, and not to all companies in that country.

Low personnel turnover in the best companies is probably largely a consequence of intra-company conditions, which we will discuss in greater detail below. To some extent, low personnel turnover certainly also can be explained by the fact that the best companies have a higher relative pay level and a higher relative status in their respective domestic markets. This was obvious in the SKF study, which showed that a job at the Fontenay factory is regarded in the local labour market as attractive, whereas the same is not true of a job at the Gothenburg factory. It is thus not the absolute level of pay – which was actually higher in Gothenburg

– that determines personnel turnover. Instead, how it compares to the national or local labour market is crucial. Because all companies obviously cannot pay high wages compared with other companies, one practical political conclusion is that companies that operate under international competition ought to be wage leaders.

Beyond Sweden, with its highly developed labour movement, national or local trade unions were not a considerable factor in connection with productivity. Some of these firms have no unions at all, and their attitude is that the existence of a union would be a sign that their management has not succeeded in pursuing a sufficiently good personnel policy. Behind this negative attitude toward labour unions, one can trace a desire for flexibility, especially in personnel matters – such as being able to transfer employees and change their wages – and a fear of adversarial relationships between management and employees. The best companies try to create and maintain a team spirit within the organization.

Factors at industry level

Influence of the resource situation on efficiency
One of the most interesting observations in our study was that cost-awareness is very evident in the best companies, despite the fact that most of these companies have high or very high profitability. Because we had posited a theoretical connection between a company's resource situation and its efficiency, our question was therefore why highly productive companies still have a resource scarcity, or at least behave as if they do. There are several ways to explain this on the basis of our case studies.

Some of the companies we studied perceive a potential threat that new companies will establish themselves in the same industry or will succeed in selling substitute products. This is true, for example, of the mobile telephone industry, where there is some potential competition from pagers and cordless telephones, which are becoming better and more inexpensive. In the corporate insurance field, large insurance customers may find it economically worthwhile to shoulder their own risks.

Another factor is that the best companies have strong customers or strong suppliers that have been able to hold back price increases. We have studied several industries that manufacture goods for other industries: machine tools, paper, rolling bearings, mobile telephone systems and automotive components. All these companies have other companies or institutions as their customers, which means recurrent negotiations with highly professional counterparts. A number of internal factors explain why the best companies do not feel that their resources are unlimited. One such explanation is that these companies invest a lot in fixed assets and human capital. The companies are growing relatively fast, so they make large investments that absorb much of their liquid assets and help keep their profitability figures from climbing too high. We could see this at United Paper Mills and Singapore Airlines, but also at Mandelli, Yamazaki Mazak and Scania – all companies where the accepted strategy has been to invest and expand during recessions in order to be well-placed to increase their market share during subsequent periods of economic prosperity.

This is not merely a question of investments in fixed assets. Another critical form of capital spending is a company's research and development programme. The best companies have a high level of research and development compared with their competitors. As research and development activities have become more extensive and important, companies have also begun to pay attention to the question of productivity in this area. Limiting lead times for product development and the modularization of products and computer programmes are two techniques that are used in this context.

In many situations, limited time has ended up having the same effect as limited resources. Because of the shorter lifetimes of new products, development work must take place quickly, otherwise there is not enough time for the product to earn back its development costs on the market. Demands for shorter lead times in a company also encourage more efficient solutions. We will later recapitulate some of the methods that companies use in order to create internal resource scarcity with the aid of time restrictions.

One special case is Scania, which in recent decades has paid substantial group contributions to its parent company, Saab-Scania. These contributions have been used to cover deficits or to finance operations in other parts of the Saab-Scania Group. One interesting mental experiment is to ask what would have happened if Scania had been an independent company and had been able to make use of these financial resources on its own. How great is the risk that Scania would have acquired companies or diversified its operations in ways that did not benefit its truck manufacturing operations? One of our consistent observations has been that the best companies have been fairly specialized in a field or fields that provide economies of scope in the form of shared technology. We have not found any examples of diversification or acquisition that occurred merely because a company had a good financial position. Instead, the best companies have shown strong discipline, using their financial resources only in areas that support their core operations in the long term.

We have thus found varied evidence that even the best companies operate in obviously genuine or, in some cases, perceived situations of resource scarcity. To a large extent, this is because competition is working. Their customers have a good bargaining position because of their competence and size and because of the existence of actual or potential competitors. In addition, the best companies impose a resource scarcity on themselves by means of heavy capital spending, a high level of research and development and internal demands for shorter lead times.

Information complexity and innovation
No industries and no companies live in a completely unchanging environment. Change and adaptation are continual. There are nevertheless major differences between the levels of change in different companies and industries. The mining industry and the computer manufacturing industry, for example, obviously operate under completely different conditions regarding changes in technology or product development in their industries.

One significant source of change in a company's environment is the actions of competitors. In a competitive market, moves and countermoves will occur continuously. In all the industries we studied, international companies compete with each other. Our observations do not, however, contradict the perception that domestic rivalry is of great importance. In Sweden, the competition between Volvo and Scania trucks is an outstanding example of this. This rivalry has not only involved their efforts to be the first to develop with technical innovations, but the sales departments of these two companies have also kept track of how their sales statistics compare with those of their competitors. Other cases that illustrate domestic competition can be found in the Piacenza area of Italy, where there is a concentration of machine tool manufacturers. Likewise, Yamazaki Mazak in Japan is located close to one of its main competitors and carefully monitors its moves. Although Ericsson has not had a domestic competitor, it has had a very competent negotiating counterpart: the Swedish Telecommunications Administration (Televerket), a sophisticated customer, standard-setter and business partner.

With a relatively mature product such as roller bearings, the pace of change is not so great. Customers admittedly demand increasingly high standards of performance, but during the last few decades it has been possible to meet these demands by means of gradual improvements within the framework of existing technology. There are indications that Japanese bearing producers are ahead in the development of new manufacturing technology. For SKF and other European companies in the bearing industry, there are a number of reasons why it is difficult to find out quickly what is happening at Japanese competitor companies. A more extensive intelligence network in addition to research and development activities is required if competitors are not located in close proximity.

Another reason for change is the new and higher standards demanded by customers. This is especially clear in the case of component suppliers, but it also applies to manufacturers of machine tools. As a supplier to the automotive industry, Nippondenso has constant, ongoing communications with its customers about new models and changes. Such a business relationship requires constant adaptation and change in order to meet customer demands. Customer demands are less clear in the insurance industry. In the Netherlands, independent insurance intermediaries therefore play an important role as representatives of customers. By professionally monitoring and comparing different terms and prices, these retailers provide continuous feedback to the insurance companies.

A large proportion of change is attributable to technological development work which occurs in the company, in competitor companies, as well as in the research world. Mobile telephone systems and machine tools are two cases where the companies we studied were heavily influenced by technological developments. Changes are occurring all the time in and around these companies. They consequently have to update their products, or else a competitor will come along with better technology in its product.

Technological development is vital to companies in the service sector. For example, when Singapore Airlines buys the latest aircraft model, the company not only improves its overall fuel economy, but also gains several indirect advantages. One of these is that it becomes necessary to retrain airline personnel each time a new aircraft model is purchased. As a result, employees receive meaningful training. At the same time, employees feel positive about their company's role as a leader in technology. Innovations have considerable value in such contexts, too. Singapore Airlines' new aircraft also require other organizational adjustments.

By updating its technology, the company automatically forces its existing operations to undergo certain changes and re-evaluation.

Another type of change concerns laws and standards of various kinds. These are normally very stable, as they ought to be in order to make long-term decisions possible. In recent decades, however, there have been fairly extensive changes in the rules of many industries. We were able to see this most clearly in the case of insurance and airlines. Both these industries admittedly include companies that have operated internationally, but a large proportion of the insurance and civil aviation businesses has been the preserve of companies operating in domestic markets. In the case of airlines, many air routes have been *de facto* monopolies. Competition has come from other means of transportation, but sometimes flying is the only possible means of transportation for certain travellers.

The insurance industry essentially has been characterized by oligopolies: a small number of major companies dominating each market and offering approximately the same prices and terms. Steps toward deregulation of civil aviation and insurance will create international markets. We believe our case studies have clearly demonstrated that companies which have previously operated amidst competition have an advantage over companies which have not.

Another type of regulation relates to the environment and safety. Such regulations have proliferated rapidly during the past two decades. For truck manufacturers, some of the information complexity that exists in their industry is generated by stricter official standards concerning safety, the environment and fuel consumption. In the case of Scania, we noted that Swedish standards have functioned as a driving force behind improvements. These improvements admittedly put Scania at an initial cost disadvantage, but in some cases they turned into an advantage when equivalent standards were later introduced in other countries. Other forms of regulation can halt growth, such as the strict Japanese standards on maximum lengths and widths of trucks. These standards shut out Japanese manufacturers from the heavy-duty truck segment in other countries. A standard that sets a maximum level of exhaust emissions of certain substances, on the other hand, functions as a threshold value and can be achieved through technological development work.

II. INTERNAL FACTORS

What distinguishes the best companies?

One distinguishing feature of the best companies is an awareness on the part of top management and employees of the importance of productivity. It was never necessary to explain to these companies why productivity should be an object of study. They all had a clear perception of it, even though their methods and measurements varied. In all these companies, there was also a strong will to improve productivity. This ambition was so dominant that in some cases it was almost reminiscent of a religious revival movement. Clearly, companies that have high productivity do not acquire it by chance.

In the best companies, the ambition to achieve high productivity serves as a challenge and as something positive in itself. We did not pick up any sense that the desire for high productivity was perceived as a form of pressure or as a threat. It was more like an athletic team trying to surpass its own or its competitors' previous personal best.

It is not possible to say, on the basis of our case studies, that all highly productive companies use a particular type of model or method. Instead, it is more correct to say that they strive for efficiency and innovation, but that this effort may assume many different expressions. Superficially, for example, there is a big difference between Mandelli and Yamazaki Mazak or between Ericsson and Motorola. The Japanese company (Yamazaki Mazak) and the American company (Motorola) are extroverted and clear in their attitude toward productivity. Italy's Mandelli and Sweden's Ericsson maintain a lower profile, yet still achieve excellent productivity results. It may therefore be misleading to judge from the external appearance of an organization. It is particularly difficult to compare companies that operate in different institutional and cultural settings. We have therefore been fairly cautious in our conclusions regarding differences between our best practice companies and our reference companies.

High productivity through cost-effectiveness and innovation

It is hardly surprising that the best companies are found in good segments of their respective industries, where demand is growing or where profitability is good. This is true of Scania, which has specialized in heavy-duty trucks. It is true of Singapore Airlines, which concentrates on long-haul flights. There is no simple explanation as to why these companies occupy good segments of their industries. The companies have obviously not made their selection from a proposed list of available segments. Their segmentation is partly the result of their adaptation to gradual changes. This adaptation has been facilitated by the fact that the best companies have been far ahead technologically and have had customers that have demanded high standards and have been able to anticipate future trends in their industry. To some extent, the best companies have also created good segments by means of their own development work.

Textbooks ordinarily recommend that companies should choose one of two main strategies: either be a dominant producer possessing cost superiority or a maker of exclusive or high-performance products for small customer segments that are not price-sensitive.[1] Without a clear choice between the two strategies a company runs the risk of being stuck in the middle. One interesting finding in our case studies is that within their respective business areas, the best companies try to achieve cost-effectiveness and innovation at the same time. Motorola's mobile telephones have the best performance and the lowest production costs. When new mobile telephones are being developed, performance is improved at the same time as manufacturing costs are lowered. Even in a relatively mature sector such as the paper industry, investments in new paper machines occur in such a way that manufacturing cost is lowered at the same time that the paper is of higher quality or has new characteristics. So United Paper Mills has both the lowest production costs per tonne and the highest quality paper. Because the best companies apply both strategies, talk of "stuck in the middle" should make way for "luck in the middle".

The combination of lower costs and higher performance is necessary because most of the companies we studied operate in producer goods markets in which, for example, higher paper quality may signify larger cost savings for a printing plant than a lower paper price. Trucks are another example: quality and repair requirements are just as weighty a factor as purchase price, because this price accounts for only about 10 per cent of trucking companies' costs. In the technologies used in mobile telephone manufacture, the effects occur in both dimensions. Improvements within certain technologies can thus both increase the performance of a mobile telephone terminal and lower the cost of manufacturing it.

Interaction with the surrounding world

It is not sufficient that a company be subjected to actual competition and face new demands. If resource scarcity is to result in higher efficiency, and if information complexity is to generate innovation, certain internal company conditions must be satisfied. First, employees must be aware of the resource situation and of changing demands. Depending on how the company interacts with its surroundings and how its employees make use of the information that such contacts provide, there are a number of ways to achieve this awareness.

One way of discovering customers' demands is to systematize customer contacts. All managers at Motorola make at least two customer visits a month – not only to major customers. Yamazaki Mazak's top management spends a lot of time visiting customers, hearing their opinions of the machines the company has delivered and noting any other wishes they may have. In major markets, Mandelli and Yamazaki Mazak operate service companies whose task is to maintain close contacts with customers. Motorola runs customer advisory councils that present their opinions of the company's products. Nippondenso has joint development groups with its customers. These groups become a natural forum for exchange of information. Scania conveys the demands of the market to people within the company by giving its sales department strong representation within the group that makes the decisions on product development and the group that plans the following year's production.

Monitoring the competition may assume many forms. Most companies we studied keep fairly good track of their competitors. Truck manufacturers in Sweden post their own sales statistics and those of their competitors on bulletin boards. In certain industries, such as forest products, there are excellent statistics that enable companies to compare their own performance with that of the industry as a whole. This is also true of service industries such as airlines and insurance. Some companies, such as Nippondenso, also take pains to gather their own information about the performance of competitors. Finally, it is also worth mentioning that Motorola, along with a number of other American companies, has begun to compare its own costs and lead times with companies in other industries, a practice known as benchmarking. This means that they study how a certain activity or function, for example a billing procedure, is handled by leading companies in other industries.

One way to keep up with changes and ensure that your own organization is the best in the world is to seek out customers and markets that maintain high standards and try to satisfy their needs. Motorola has established a presence in Japan, amidst stiff competition from Japanese companies. This market incursion provides valuable experience and certainly also helps make the company more alert. Scania sells trucks in Germany, where its customers demand high standards with regard to quality, delivery times and service. Conversely, Scania avoids markets where there is only pure price competition.

There are many ways of monitoring technological developments. Ericsson places great emphasis on keeping track of technology and analysing technological advances that the company can use. As mentioned, Motorola conducts its own research even in areas where the company is only a buyer of components. In the forest product industry, knowledge of technological advances is spread by suppliers of paper machines, among others. A substantial part of the innovation work undertaken at United Paper Mills thus occurs in co-operation with Valmet, a company that builds paper machines.

It is also possible to create systems inside a company that make demands similar to those of the market. One example is Motorola's rules about feedback within the company. If these rules are followed, employees will provide each other with information that can be compared with the demands of a market. There is only a difference in degree between the demands made by the people who handle a later stage of production and the demands eventually made by a customer about the finished product.

People must be able and willing to make changes and to be efficient

It has been said that productivity is no mystery. In many respects, productivity is a question of mentality. The hard thing is to persuade employees to apply norms and methods that are well known. Our finding that the best companies devote great care to personnel matters or human resources practices was therefore expected. It is not so surprising that such great importance is attached to employees in service sector companies like Singapore Airlines and Nationale-Nederlanden. It is more interesting that a company like Nippondenso, with its high degree of automation, also has the same attitude. Even Yamazaki Mazak, whose British factory is unmanned during weekends, emphasized that it is only possible to achieve capacity utilization as high as 85 per cent of possible hours if its employees are highly competent and motivated.

Rewards and motivation

A central and controversial question concerns the connection between productivity and pay systems. Is it possible to encourage employees to change and become more efficient by offering some form of performance-related pay? Especially in the best foreign companies, the pay system is an element of efforts to achieve higher productivity. Wages and salaries at the best of foreign companies are based to a greater extent on performance than is true at Swedish companies. Most of the companies we studied offered their employees a wage or salary combined with a bonus. There were major variations between systems in different companies and countries. It is therefore difficult to present any general recommendations on the basis of our examples. Some interesting observations neverthless arise.

The bonus portion of pay is so large in some companies that the pay system has served as a buffer against recession. At Singapore Airlines, for example, this accordion-like portion of labour costs is one reason why the company can continually expand its aircraft fleet. Employees can be retained and the company does not lose their skills. Nor are there any disruptive dismissals. Balanced against these advantages are the obvious disadvantages: employees may not be able to allow their own personal economic situation to function as a buffer for their employer. Their ability to do so depends, for example, on the size of their personal savings. In some countries, however, the combination of flexible wages and large private savings may mean that economic cycles are absorbed at household level in the national economy, without having to affect the number of employees in companies. Scania, the Swedish-based heavy vehicle manufacturer, was in such good financial shape that it was able to deal with the problem of large excess capacity during the early 1980s without dismissals. Its surplus employees were kept occupied with training. The company has not laid off any employees since World War II.

Another interesting finding concerned the striking of a balance between encouraging individual effort and promoting teamwork. One normally assumes that a system which rewards individual contributions does not promote co-operation, and vice versa. Yamazaki Mazak has shown, however, that it is possible to combine co-operation at the company level with competition at the individual level. Co-operation at the company level is achieved by offering a bonus that is payable if the company achieves a certain production level. This bonus is an incentive for employees to cover for each other and help out as necessary in order to achieve this overall target volume. At the same time, there is individual competition, because a person's basic salary varies depending on competence and performance. The evaluation system that the company uses in setting individual salaries also takes into account a person's contributions as a team member.

Nippondenso, Yamazaki Mazak and Singapore Airlines place particularly great emphasis on employee evaluations. One hypothesis that is not refuted by our observations is that teamwork can function smoothly if each team member's contribution can be evaluated. The employees at Yamazaki Mazak, for example, know that positive contributions to teamwork will be reported in their employee evaluation form, which is considered very fair.

Competence

As expected, the best companies emphasize the importance of training programmes. We noted the quantitative size of their training programmes, but did not find that it differs greatly from that of our reference companies. We were not able to examine the qualitative aspect. We noticed that several companies placed great emphasis on training directly related to a person's job assignment, rather than on general and outside courses. There are, however, also examples of several companies that enable their employees to continue their education, for instance by earning a university-level degree in engineering. It was also possible to see a positive feedback effect between competence and the qualification levels of employees. Given a good level of training, it is easier to recruit capable employees, who in turn demand that employers help increase employee competence. In the best companies, there were many examples of changes in work systems and the workplace environment that had been initiated and implemented by employees.

A number of studies have confirmed the existence of learning curves or unit cost declines that accompany larger volumes of production in a company. In time, machines are fine-tuned and problems are corrected. Another reason is that employees learn to use equipment better. There are fewer interruptions. Maintenance and repairs become more efficient. Given this background, it is not surprising that we found that the average period of employment in the best companies was very long. The best companies also have low absenteeism and personnel turnover levels.

The best companies try in various ways to reward people who stay in the company for a long time. Singapore Airlines, Motorola and Nippondenso are a few of the companies that offer special benefits to long-term employees. It was also remarkable that such a large percentage of the managers in the companies we studied had been recruited internally. It was common for top executives to have had a long career in the company behind them. This was true not only at Nippondenso but also at Nationale-Nederlanden, for example.

Internal labour market

Individuals often show a natural resistance to change. The best companies have managed in various ways to make change seem less dramatic by carrying out small, frequent adjustments in the organization and by maintaining a flexible internal labour market. Singapore Airlines thus lets its employees change job assignments at the same horizontal level in the organization. The traditional division between blue collar and white collar employees is becoming increasingly irrelevant in decentralized, flexible companies. Yamazaki Mazak has an organizational structure without job descriptions, which makes it natural for employees to circulate between tasks. The frequent changes in production processes or in other routines at Yamazaki Mazak do not result in reassignment problems but instead occur smoothly. There is thus no such thing as a guarantee that employees will be entitled to stay in a certain position or continue performing a certain task. Job security is nevertheless very high at the best companies. This is naturally also related to the fact that they are successful, growing companies.

Job satisfaction is the result of concurrence between the goals of the individual and the company. There is no question that employees of the best companies feel proud of their companies. Clear examples of this are Nippondenso in Japan and Singapore Airlines in Singapore, but the same thing was also very apparent at Yamazaki Mazak's factory in England. In countries such as Japan, an employee's status as a private individual is largely dependent on whether that person is employed by a successful company. But at Scania and Ericsson, too, many employees are proud of being part of a company with a good reputation for technological competence and high quality.

One interesting question is how the best companies have managed to create such a strong sense of community within their organization. One answer is that success itself is an influential component. It is more stimulating to work at a successful company than at a company with problems. The top managements of the best companies therefore try in various ways to inform their employees about the company's successes: bulletin boards, employee magazines, large information meetings all play a role. Another factor is relative wages and salaries. The pay levels of the best companies are higher than those of the surrounding labour market. The status of these companies also influences their recruitment programmes. The best companies have many applicants for each job opening. In some cases they use highly systematic procedures to select people that they expect will fit in with the style of the company. In this way, they create a virtuous circle – highly qualified employees who demand opportunities for personal development and good work systems, which in turn leads to good earnings and high wages, which then enable the company to attract even better employees.

Organizational structure and technology

Organizing a company on a functional basis has the advantage of enabling it to achieve economies of specialization. It also provides a clear division of labour. The disadvantage is that, especially in large corporations, such a structure easily becomes bureaucratic and slow-moving. In recent decades, the need to adapt products to customers' wishes has become more important. New manufacturing technology also makes it possible to increase the number of product variations without affecting the cost of manufacturing. Adaptation to customers' wishes and flexible production presuppose the ability to make decisions quickly and across functional or departmental boundaries. Our studies have shown various examples of how this can work. At Scania, for instance, product development and manufacturing decisions are made by groups composed of people from different functions and departments.

One disadvantage or risk in eliminating functional specialization is that decisions may be of poorer quality, and the work may not be performed as well. In the best companies, one way of dealing with this risk was to raise the general level of competence among operators in manufacturing operations. At Yamazaki Mazak, for example, the goal is that all operators should be capable of handling all work assignments that arise. This means there is no longer any need for a functional structure in the company's manufacturing operations.

Another way of reducing the disadvantages of a functional organization is to reduce the number of hierarchical levels. A number of the companies in our case studies used this method to speed up the decision-making process and move decisions closer to the operative level. Three comments can be made in this context. First, as just mentioned, decentralization presupposes a high degree of competence at the operative level. If the necessary competence is lacking, decentralization may lead to poorer quality, as at the Swedish SKF factory. Second, not everything can be decentralized. United Paper Mills has many independent units, but above these is a fairly large group management that is responsible for strategic matters and for cost control. Even Singapore Airlines, which is highly decentralized in many respects, has a strong management super-structure responsible for long-term objectives and cost monitoring. Motorola has combined decentralization with a contract procedure. A product development group gets a free hand as long as it stays within the bounds of certain norms, for example technical specifications, costs or development times.

A third comment on efforts to flatten organizational structures con-cerns the subsequent availability of fewer managerial positions in the company. Yamazaki Mazak is one company that foresees problems because it cannot offer enough attractive career opportunities for its very capable operators, who are also relatively young. When the factory has reached its optimal size after a few years, the relatively small number of managerial positions will have been filled for a long time into the future. Yamazaki Mazak and some of the other companies in our case studies are trying to compensate for the problem of few managerial openings by offering managers and employees new positions at the same hierarchical level of the organization.

As expected, the companies in our case studies did not use any uni-form organizational model. Their models mainly reflected the informa-tion complexity of their respective industries. Ericsson and Motorola, which operate in an extremely dynamic environment, thus have flat and informal organizational structures, while the forest product company United Paper Mills has a more hierarchical organization.

One risk run by fast-growing companies is that their expansion will lead to bureaucracy and a poorer overview. There is probably an opti-mum size for every type of factory, although it is difficult to specify this, for example, in terms of a given maximum number of employees. Nip-pondenso is aware of this problem and never lets a factory grow beyond a certain size. Instead, the company builds a completely new factory to absorb expansion and keeps its expected optimal size unchanged.

Technological factors

Many previous studies have shown that economies of scale and the economies that result from a large accumulated manufacturing volume are a major element within cost-effectiveness. This was also evident from our research. With a glint in their eye, paper industry representatives maintain that the most productive company is the one that happens to have built the most recent production plant without making any big mistakes. This is because the industry is constantly carrying out development work on paper machines, whose performance level is gradually improving. In the production of terminals for mobile telephone systems, economies of scale and experience are substantial, as our data on Motorola indicate. At the same time, development costs are climbing with each new product generation. This points toward continued concentration of this industry among a few companies around the world. Nippondenso achieves its cost-effectiveness by means of large volume and automation. A relatively small manufacturer such as Luxor does not have the necessary volume to be able to automate production to the same degree.

One reason why the best companies operate in favourable segments of their industries is that they have invested in maintaining a technological lead. These companies use new technology aggressively rather than defensively. United Paper Mills and Singapore Airlines regard new technology as an important way of gaining competitive advantages.

In several companies in our case studies, such as Ericsson and Mandelli, we found examples of how companies had managed to achieve high levels of cost-effectiveness and innovation simultaneously with modularization. The final product is viewed as a system of modules. By limiting the number of modules, it is possible to achieve economies of scale in manufacturing and also develop new products more rapidly, with fewer defects. A limited set of modules can be combined in various ways to yield a final product that suits the needs of different customers.

In their manufacturing operations, the best companies use a variety of methods that deliberately limit their time resources, thereby generating internal pressure for change. One way of generating internal pressure is to set targets for lead times. Several of the best companies use this technique. By constantly demanding shorter lead times, Yamazaki Mazak, Nippondenso and Motorola stimulate the re-evaluation of activities and previous solutions. A better solution does not last forever: at Nippondenso it may be in operation for only a month before being questioned. Another way of generating internal pressure for change is the just-in-time principle, which Nippondenso and other companies use in their manufacturing operations. According to this principle, the flow of production should be so tightly integrated that inventories and waiting times are minimized. This places heavy pressure on manufacturing departments and on suppliers to deliver their products on time and free of defects.

The best companies also demand increasingly high standards for time to market, or the time from identification of a customer need until a product is ready for delivery. Motorola, Ericsson and Nippondenso are among the companies constantly trying to shorten product development periods. Behind this ambition are higher development costs combined with shorter lifetimes for each new product generation. To meet the demands for shorter time to market, these companies try to co-ordinate product development with the development of manufacturing tools and processes (concurrent engineering). This is accomplished by letting employees from the manufacturing department become part of the team that develops the new product. This not only means that manufacturing aspects can more easily be taken into account when the product is designed, but also that the task of producing machines, tooling and developing processes can start before the new product is completely designed. Time is so precious that it often pays to build the new manufacturing system in parallel with the product development process, then make changes in the system when the product has assumed its final shape.

The introduction of time restrictions has led to dramatic improvements in productivity at some companies. This indicates that there is great potential for productivity-raising in industry by means of improved work systems. It is not self-evident that such gains can be realized: as in the case of decentralization, the various methods for limiting time resources presuppose a high level of competence at operator level. If this competence is lacking, the introduction of time restrictions may lead to chaos, which may lower productivity.

Simple measurements

The best companies establish goals that are ambitious and fairly long-term. Ambitious goals force people to do fresh thinking. Production time cannot be cut in half without questioning current work organization and product qualifications. Ambitious goals also break down inherent resistance toward far-reaching changes. But if ambitious goals are to provide an effective challenge, new solutions cannot be created from one day to the next. Goals must therefore be sufficiently long-term to ensure that short-term restrictions do not render all change impossible. At Motorola, for example, challenges in the form of ambitious goals have a positive effect on the entire organization. The company's multi-year quality improvement programme generates continuous internal pressure for change.

Another interesting observation concerns the role of goals in challenging employees. In companies with clearly articulated and ambitious goals, these goals apparently function as a stimulus and a challenge to many employees. But this is no basis for drawing the conclusion that goals should always be set very high. It is well-known that different people view goals in different ways. Some individuals are stimulated if they can barely manage to meet ambitious goals, while others prefer less ambitious demands that they can surpass by a broad margin. People of the first type probably make up most of the applicants to Yamazaki Mazak, Nippondenso and Motorola. Even before securing an interview, job applicants at Yamazaki Mazak are asked whether they would find it appealing to work with the kind of goals that the company uses.

The choice of yardsticks for productivity is important because measurement defines work – and success. The best companies devote a lot of care to monitoring operations and measuring the factors that influence productivity. One prerequisite, however, is that companies must measure variables that employees can influence. The best companies therefore do not directly measure productivity – defined as value-added divided by work input. Instead, they use yardsticks of quality that are expected to be positively correlated with productivity.

Our comparison between two factories in the SKF Group showed that the better of these factories used more detailed production management yardsticks related to efficiency and capacity utilization. The other factory instead measured compound variables such as value-added and volume produced. Although these yardsticks were relevant for the factory as a whole, they were less suitable for productivity management purposes, because operators could not see the results of a given concrete action.

Motorola tries to measure things that are possible to influence and easy to report, such as lead times and quality. If improvements are achieved in these two respects, profitability and productivity will automatically follow. Motorola's yardsticks have a number of advantages. It is easier to gain employee acceptance for the reduction of lead times than for cost-cutting. The quality goal is related to the production of components, and to such operations as billing and other administrative services. The company's targets are clear and can be understood by everyone. As a result, they function better as management tools. Employees can decide for themselves whether a given change will affect the target, and this eliminates uncertainty about how they should act. Furthermore, the same type of goal – number of errors per million activities – can be used throughout the company, in factories and offices alike. This is essential, because nowadays labour costs for white collar employees are generally much higher than direct wage costs for blue collar employees. Having the same type of goal throughout an organization also reinforces the feeling that all employee efforts in the company are important.

In order for productivity management to have its full effect, companies must follow up their measurements and let them influence employee rewards. In this respect, too, the best companies were exemplary. Motorola has a general principle that all activities in the company should result in some form of feedback within 72 hours. Singapore Airlines constantly monitors its productivity yardsticks, and when productivity declines, the company takes vigorous action aimed at eliminating the causes of the decline.

Top executives

Outstanding leaders were instrumental to the success of several of the best companies we studied. What distinguishes these leaders, first of all, is their ability to formulate visions. In some cases, these visions have not been particularly profound, but have been more in the nature of mottos – such the desire to make their company the world leader in its field. In other cases, their vision may involve a product concept; one example is Scania, where top management determined the principles of the company's product philosophy several decades ago.

Another characteristic feature of outstanding corporate leaders is their ability to motivate, or rather, to instill enthusiasm in their employees. These leaders have had a strong personal belief in their ideas. When Bob Galvin of Motorola decided to make quality-related issues such a high priority – and manifested this by leaving meetings after quality had been discussed – he was naturally taking a risk. He could not be sure at the time that his quality strategy was sustainable. United Paper Mills' managing director, Niilo Hakkarainen, was taking a similar risk when he assumed the role of project leader for the company's "hopeless" investment in Wales. By spearheading this effort, he energized his employees. If the project had failed, however, their leader would naturally not have emerged unscathed.

Top executives are especially influential when it comes to conveying the demands of the market to employees. The management of a company has the best overview of changing demands and the best grasp of resource scarcities. It is then management's responsibility to use its knowledge to formulate objectives for operations and then communicate this message to employees. In addition, through their behaviour, top executives underscore the importance of cost-consciousness. It has been our consistent impression that the managements we studied projected an image of frugality. In this way, they set a good example of thrift with the company's resources. One of our consistent observations has been that the best companies, despite their high profitability, devoted a lot of effort to the search for even minor improvements.

As mentioned earlier, to a striking degree, the top executives of the best companies were internally recruited and had spent all or most of their career in the same company. One interpretation of this fact is that a long career in a company leads to a high level of competence in the relevant field of operations and strong loyalty to the organization. These positive consequences are apparently more crucial than innovation that may be the consequence of outside recruitment of top executives. From the perspective of an individual executive in a very successful company, of course, it is also not so easy to find more attractive jobs in other companies.

III. SUMMARY

Our case studies have shown that the productivity of a company is the result of a complex interplay among many factors. The importance of some factors has been confirmed, while the importance of other factors was less expected.

- The non-Swedish companies that we studied have high status and pay levels in their local labour markets. This may be one reason behind both their lower personnel turnover and their low absenteeism.
- External pressure for change is necessary. It is generated by actual or potential competition and can be strengthened by a company's internal demands for shorter lead times and higher quality.
- Economies of scale play a crucial role in productivity in most of the cases we studied. Nothing has emerged which indicates that the importance of such economies will diminish. On the contrary, it appears as if their importance is growing, as for example, in the component supplier industry. It is possible to improve economies of scale by modularization of the product. This is also possible in such service-oriented fields as computer programming. Achieved by using the same technology in several product areas, economies of scope also generate higher productivity.

- The leading companies are technologically advanced. They are quick to take advantage of new technology, and in many cases they develop it themselves. Research and development enjoy high priority.
- Productivity in individual companies depends on whether a company is situated in an industrial segment that shows growing demand or good profitability. Segmentation is not a matter of simple choice. Positioning occurs gradually and is based on experience, because the company closely monitors developmental trends and works closely with customers and suppliers that can be regarded as pace-setters. Companies can also create good segments in their industry by means of successful product development.
- Highly productive companies are not isolated islands. They belong to networks of suppliers, customers and other institutions with long-term relationships. Productivity in a large component supplier company, for example, depends on what is happening in both earlier and later stages of production. Productivity is determined by how well the relationships in the network are maintained.
- Our case studies have also confirmed the importance of competence. The best companies carefully examine applicants for new jobs. Training programmes are a high-priority area for all categories of personnel. In the most efficient manufacturing plants, operators are trained to handle all tasks that arise.
- There is a connection between high productivity and a decentralized organizational structure with good horizontal contacts. Limited hierarchical levels and smooth co-operation across departmental boundaries characterize the best companies. This breakdown of functional boundaries is possible, among other things, because employees receive training and become competent in more fields.
- At the same time as the organizational structure of the best companies is decentralized, there is strong synthesis in the form of a vigorous group management responsible for cost control, feedback and contracts.
- The best companies pay good wages and salaries in relation to the surrounding labour market and generally offer both company-wide bonuses and performance-related individual wages.

- Top management plays a central role in the company's productivity. The best companies are associated with visionary leaders who have an image of simplicity and the ability to enthuse their employees.

- The best companies do not specialize in making either cheap products at low cost or more exclusive products at high prices. They make products that provide high performance at a competitive price.
- The best companies have employees who demonstrate great pride, solidarity and loyalty to their company. Such companies function both as a tool for raising employees' competence levels and as a social organization. Work is an important part of the lives of these employees and provides great challenges.
- The best companies are strongly aware of the importance of high productivity. Measurements and follow-ups are performed thoroughly and systematically.
- Although the best companies are highly profitable, they are fussy about small things. The attitude remains that even when an investment has been placed in service, a large proportion of the productivity gain it represents still remains to be collected.

[1]Our analysis of productivity in terms of cost-effectiveness and innovation is, of course, also an expression of this mind-set.

APPENDIX ONE
The selection of companies

The selection of companies as topics of our study began with a compilation of possible candidates. Requests for suggestions were sent to members of the Royal Swedish Engineering Academy and to Swedish scientific and technological attaches worldwide. A list of nearly 150 suggested companies resulted.

We gathered annual reports and articles covering a large percentage of the suggested companies. We also studied information on prizes and distinctions that had been awarded to companies in certain countries for their high quality or productivity. Using interviews and inquiries, we tried to ascertain the reputation of these companies in their industries. We asked about the path of their development during the 1980s. Most of the suggested companies, we concluded, appeared sufficiently interesting to be included in the study.

The final selection of companies took into account the following criteria:

- Representation from sectors of interest in a Swedish industrial policy perspective
- Given the numerous productivity studies already conducted in this sector, we ruled out car companies
- A broad range of countries
- To enable us to complete the study within a very tight time frame, we occasionally allowed our researchers' previous experience of various industries to determine the choice of company

Six of the companies that we initially contacted declined to participate. It remains our hope that our final selection, consisting of ten companies, can provide answer to the question: What can we learn from the best companies?

Implementation

We began our research effort by working out a questionnaire. As indicated in Chapter 2, its questions are mainly derived from the theory of industrial organization and from organizational theory. (The questionnaire is reproduced in Appendix II.) The case studies were then conducted simultaneously, all using the same questionnaire and interview guide. (The research associates responsible for each case study are listed in Appendix III.)

a) First the researchers gathered material about the industrial sector and country in question. This included articles, research studies and official statistics.

b) Interviews and data gathering at the companies. Interviews with technical directors, research directors, marketing managers, personnel managers and trade union representatives.

c) Additional written questions to the companies.

d) Compilation of reports, consisting of 100-250 pages per case study.

e) Analysis of the reports and compilation of the summaries found in this report. This task was done mainly by the project leader and the steering committee. To keep the presentation from being weighed down by footnotes, only a minimum of references to sources were included in this book.

f) Discussion of the summaries with contact people at the companies and trade union representatives. It should be emphasized that reference people are responsible neither for the facts nor the conclusions in the chapters.

APPENDIX TWO
Questionnaire Subject Headings

The study was made with a more detailed questionnaire in connection with a inter-view guide giving background and comments on the questions. The questions in groups 2, 3, 4 and 6 are based on Porter (1980) and (1990), where the reader will be able to find the theoretical background.

1. PRODUCTIVITY

1.1 Performance
1.1.1 Profitability
1.1.2 Value added per employee
1.1.3 Market share
1.1.4 Turnover
1.1.5 Price recovery
1.1.6 Capacity utilization
1.1.7 Number of working hours per year
1.1.8 Rewards and prizes

1.2 What internal measures are used for controlling productivity?

2. INDUSTRY STRUCTURE

2.1 Entry barriers
2.1.1 Economies of scale
2.1.2 Proprietary product differences
2.1.3 Brand identity
2.1.4 Capital requirements
2.1.5 Access to distribution
2.1.6 Absolute cost advantage
2.1.6.1 Proprietary learning curve
2.1.6.2 Access to necessary inputs
2.1.7 Government policy
2.1.8 Expected retaliation

2.2 Rivalry determinants
2.2.1 Industry growth
2.2.2 Fixed cost/value added
2.2.3 Intermittent overcapacity
2.2.4 Product differences
2.2.5 Brand identity
2.2.6 Switching costs
2.2.7 Concentration and balance
2.2.8 Information complexity
2.2.9 Diversity of competitors

2.2.10 Corporate stakes
2.2.11 Exit barriers

2.3 Buyers
2.3.1 Bargaining leverage
2.3.1.1 Buyer concentration vs. firm concentration
2.3.1.2 Buyer volume
2.3.1.3 Buyer switching costs
2.3.1.4 Buyer information
2.3.1.5 Ability to backward integrate
2.3.1.6 Substitute products
2.3.1.7 To what extent does the product influence the quality of the end product?

2.3.2 Price sensitivity
2.3.2.1 Price/total purchases
2.3.2.2 Product differences
2.3.2.3 Brand identity
2.3.2.4 Impact on quality/performance
2.3.2.5 Buyers' profits
2.3.2.6 Buyers' incentives to bargain

2.4 Substitutes
2.4.1 Relative price performance of substitutes
2.4.2 Switching costs
2.4.3 Buyers' propensity to substitute

2.5 Suppliers
2.5.1 Differentiation of inputs
2.5.2 Switching costs of suppliers
2.5.3 Presence of substitute products
2.5.4 Importance of volume to supplier
2.5.5 Cost relative to total purchases in the industry
2.5.6 Impact of inputs on costs or differentiation
2.5.7 Threat of forward integration relative to threat of backward integration by firms in the industry

2.6 Strategic positioning within the industry
2.6.1 What is the strategic position of the company concerning cost efficiency and differentiation?
2.6.2 Which companies are the main competitors within this strategic position? (home and international markets)
2.6.3 Market share of the company and its main competitors in the home market and in the international market
2.6.4 Profitability of the strategic position relative to the industry

2.7 Home country
2.7.1 Factor conditions (five-ten years ago)
2.7.1.1 Human resources
2.7.1.2 Infrastructure
2.7.1.3 Knowledge resources

5. ORGANIZATIONAL CAPITAL

5.1 Organization
5.1.1 Number of hierarchy levels: the organizational chart
5.1.2 Integration and differentiation mechanisms
5.1.3 Team work: boundaries of specialization between activities and departments
5.1.4 Resources and time devoted to experimental work
5.1.5 Organization of research and development departments

5.2 Institutions
5.2.1 Labour relations, trade unions
5.2.2 Social control
5.2.3 The social importance of work
5.2.4 Attitudes to work

5.3 Technology
5.3.1 Integration of design and manufacturing: how are product design and investments in new machinery integrated or planned?
5.3.2 Renewing of machinery and plant: average age of machinery

5.4 Owners
5.4.1 Who are the three biggest owners and what share of capital or votes do they have?
5.4.2 Who are members of the board of directors? Do the owners appoint all members of the board? Do the members of the board suggest strategic actions or do they merely discuss issues put forward by the CEO?

5.5 Management
5.5.1 Management style

6. COMMUNICATION OF GOALS AND EXPECTATIONS

6.1 Goals
6.1.1 Goal formulation
6.1.2 Sub goals
6.1.3 Do you use competitors' performance levels as bench-marks?

6.2 Control
6.2.1 Feed back
6.2.2 What kind of quality control do you have?

6.3 Outsider perspective
6.3.1 Do you buy industry studies from research institutes, etc?
6.3.2 Is anyone in top management recruited from outside your own company?

6.4 Exposure for market demands
6.4.1 Who are the most demanding and sophisticated customers in your industry? Which customers are hardest to satisfy? Do you sell to them? Do you try to establish relations with them? How?
6.4.2 Are your customers international companies?
6.4.3 Which are the most demanding channels of distribution? Do you use them?

6.4.4 Do you have internal standards for products or services that exceed the standards of the market?

6.4.5 Which are the most advanced and most internationally active suppliers to your industry? Do you buy from them?

6.5. Perceiving industry change

6.5.1 Which customers and which distribution channels have the most anticipatory demands? Have you contact with them?

6.5.2 Which new customers and which new distribution channels have appeared during the past five years? Have you investigated them or got information about them?

6.5.3 Which new competitors have appeared during the 80's? Have you studied them?

6.5.4 Which country has the most demanding standards or the most demanding customers? Are you established there?

6.5.5 Which are the most important trends concerning the factor costs? How do you get information about such trends and how do you use the information?

6.5.6 What kind of contacts or relations do you have with research institutes and important business and technological schools?

6.6. Interchange within the national cluster

6.6.1 What relations do you have with your suppliers concerning co-operation or exchange of information?

6.6.2 What relations do you have with your distribution channels concerning co-operation or exchange of information?

6.6.3 What relations do you have with your customers concerning co-operation or exchange of information?

6.6.4 What relations do you have with companies in related industries concerning co-operation or exchange of information?

6.6.5 How close to your main customers, suppliers and competitors are you located?

7. HUMAN RESOURCE MANAGEMENT

7.1 Vocational training

7.1.1 Costs for vocational training as a percentage of labour costs

7.1.2 Percentage of employees participating in training during a year.

7.1.3 How is training organized?

7.2 Reward systems

7.2.1 Wages and bonuses: how are the wages determined? How large is the bonus share? How large is the spread between the highest and the lowest wages within different departments of the company? What factors influence the spread?

7.2.2 Do you have some kind of profit-sharing scheme? How is it defined?

7.2.3 What kind of rewards or reinforcement do you have? Diplomas, company magazines, etc.

7.2.4 What kind of reprimands are used? What could trigger such a reprimand?

7.2.5 The wages of your company relative to other companies? How high are the wages of your company compared to other companies within the industry? Compared to the general level in your country?

7.2.6 Can you easily recruit personnel to your company ?

7.3 Various methods for upgrading the competence of the employees. Study trips, job rotation, careers and so on.

7.4 Motivation and competence

7.4.1 How many employees quit per year?

7.4.2 Are there any kind of communications or common activities between management and employees?

APPENDIX THREE
Research Associates

Ericsson/Motorola

Mr Christer Oskarsson, Lic. of Engineering, M.Sc., MBA
Mr Niklas Sjöberg, M.Sc.
Department of Industrial Management and Economics
Chalmers University of Technology
Gothenburg, Sweden

Nationale Nederlanden/Skandia

Mr Thomas Åstebro, M.Sc
Institute for Management of Innovation and Technology (IMIT)
Gothenburg, Sweden

Nippondenso/Luxor

Mr Henrik Brandes, M.Sc.
Center for Management and Industry Studies
Linköping University
Linköping, Sweden

Johan Lilliecreutz, M.Sc.
Department of Management and Economics
Linköping University
Linköping, Sweden

Scania/Iveco

Mr Carl-Henrik Nilsson, M.Sc.
Mr Jörgen Dernroth, M.Sc.
Department of Industrial Management
Lund University
Lund, Sweden

Singapore Airlines/SAS

Mr Mats Johansson, M.Sc.
Center for Management and Industry Studies
Linköping University
Linköping, Sweden

Dr Hans Jansson
Department of Business Administration
Lund University
Lund, Sweden

SKF

Dr Per Lindberg
Department of Industrial Management and Economics
Chalmers University of Technology
Gothenburg, Sweden

United Paper Mills/SCA

Mr Alarik Arthur, MBA
RCM Consulting AB
Norrköping
Sweden

Yamazaki/ABB Robotics
Mandelli/SMT

Mr Gerth Andersson, M.Sc.
(Royal Swedish Academy of Engineering Sciences: IVA)
Swedish Institute for Quality
Gothenburg, Sweden

Mr Enrico Deiaco, M.A.
Royal Swedish Academy of Engineering Sciences (IVA)
Stockholm, Sweden

APPENDIX FOUR
Steering Committee

Doctor of Technology, Mr Björn Svedberg
Chairman
Telefon AB LM Ericsson
Stockholm, Sweden

Professor Hans Ahlmann
Department of Industrial Management
Lund University
Lund, Sweden

Professor Sven-Erik Andersson
Managing Director
The Swedish Institute of Production Engineering Research (IVF)
Gothenburg, Sweden

Mr Gunnar L. Johansson
Chairman of the Board
Federation of Swedish Industries
Stockholm, Sweden

Mr Leif Johansson
President
AB Electrolux
Stockholm, Sweden

Mr Curt G. Olsson
Chairman
Skandinaviska Enskilda Banken
Stockholm, Sweden

Dr Lars Wohlin
Managing Director
The Urban Mortgage Bank of Sweden
Stockholm, Sweden

Dr Carl Johan Åberg
Managing Director
The National Swedish Pension Fund
First, Second and Third Fund Boards
Stockholm, Sweden

APPENDIX FIVE
Companies selected for the study

Company	*Country*
ABB Strömberg Oy	Finland
AGA	Sweden
Ahlström, A. Ltd	Finland
Alfa Laval Thermal AB	Sweden
Andersen Corp. Bayport,	U.S.A.
Apple	U.S.A.
Ascom-Hasler AG	Switzerland
Atlet AB	Sweden
Audi AG	Germany
B.T.	United Kingdom
Banco Popular Espanol	Spain
Berardi Rino	Italy
Black & Decker	United Kingdom
BM	U.S.A.
Boliden Mineral AB	Sweden
Brüel & Kjaer	Denmark
BT Products	Sweden
Canson et Montgolfier	France
Chips & Technologies, Inc	U.S.A.
Daifuku	Japan
Dairiki Iron Works	Japan
Danfoss A/S	Denamrk
Danieli & Co	Italy
Diab-Barracuda	Sweden
Domilens	France
Dow Chemical Co.	U.S.A.
Dowty Fuel Systems & Dowty Seals	United Kindgom
Electrolux Motor	Sweden
Ericsson Radio Systems	Sweden
Fanuc Ltd	Japan
Farley Engineering	Australia
Farm Frites	U.S.A.
Ford Motor Co	U.S.A.
Forsmark Nuclear Power Station	Sweden
Frito-Lay/Pepsico, Inc.	U.S.A.
Fuji-Xerox	Japan
G.E.C.	United Kingdom
Genentech	U.S.A.

Gist-Brocades NV	The Netherlands
Glaxo	United Kingdom
Globe Metallurgical Inc.	U.S.A.
Gunma NEC Corporation	Japan
Hager & Elsässer	Germany
Haindl Papier, Schongau Mill	Germany
Hamamatsu Photonics K.K.	Japan
Herman Miller, Zeeland MI	U.S.A.
Hewlett-Packard	Singapore
Honda	Japan
Honda	U.S.A.
Horiuchi Machinery	Japan
Håg A/S, Oslo, Röros	Norway
IBM	U.S.A.
IBM Germany, GmbH, Stuttgart	Germany
IBM Svenska AB, Järfälla Factory	Sweden
IBM	United Kingdom
IBM, Havant	United Kingdom
Intel Corporation	U.S.A.
J.C.B. Excavators	United Kingdom
Jumberca, S.A.	Spain
Kao Corp.	Japan
Kaukas	Finland
Kellog M.W. & Co.	U.S.A.
Kett Electric Laboratory	Japan
Kimberly-Clark Corp.	U.S.A.
Kone Corporation	Finland
Konica	Japan
Korsnäs AB	Sweden
Kymi-Kytnmene Oy	Finland
L'Air Liquide	France
Lamb-Litton	U.S.A.
Lauxide Corp.	U.S.A.
LKAB	Sweden
Lorentzon & Wettre	Sweden
Lucas	United Kingdom
Mandelli spa	Italy
Marysville Automobile Plant	U.S.A.
Maxxam Inc	U.S.A.
McDonalds	U.S.A.
McDonnell Douglas	United Kingdom
Merieux, laboratories	France
Microsoft	U.S.A.
Mitsubishi	Japan
Mitsubishi Aluminium Fuji Plant	Japan
Motorola Communications & Electronics, Inc.	U.S.A.

Murata Machinery	Japan
Nationale Nederlanden	The Netherlands
NEC Corporation	Japan
Nederlandse Philips Bedrijven BV	The Netherlands
Neles Oy	Finland
Neste Polyeten AB	Sweden
New Nippon Steel Co. Ltd	Japan
Nippondenso Co.	Japan
Nissan Motor Co.	Japan
Nissan	U.S.A.
Nordstrom	U.S.A.
North Pacific Paper Corp.	U.S.A.
NUCLEUS	Australia
Nucor Corporation	U.S.A.
Omron	Japan
Outokumpu Steel	Finland
Pechiney	France
Pedigree Petfoods/Mars Ltd.	United Kingdom
Perstorp Golv AB	Sweden
Automobiles Peugeot	France
PLM	Sweden
Polygram	France
Robert Bosch GmbH	Germany
Rolls-Royce	United Kingdom
Saab-Scania AB, Scania Division	Sweden
Saab-Valmet Oy AB	Finland
SAMEFA	Sweden
Sandvik	Sweden
Seegate Technology	U.S.A.
Seiko Instruments	Japan
Singapore Airlines	Singapore
Skaltek AB	Sweden
Skanska	Sweden
SKF	Sweden
SMH Société Suisse de Midroelectronique et d'Horlogerie	Switzerland
Sociedad Cooperativa Limitada Grupo Fagor	Spain
Société d'Exploitation des Celluloses d'Alizay	France
Société Francaise Hoechst	France
Sony Corp	Japan
Spectral	France
Stanford University.	U.S.A.
Sun Microsystems Inc.	U.S.A.
Svenska Handelsbanken	Sweden

Sweden Postal Group, Postal Giro Production Facilities, Mail sorting centres	Sweden
Södra Skogsägarna	Sweden
Tandem Computers	U.S.A.
TDK	Japan
Tetrapac	Sweden
Thann et Mulhouse	France
Tonsjö AB	Sweden
Toshiba Corp.	Japan
Toyota Motor Co, Ltd.	Japan
Tulip Slagterierne	Denmark
Udhe GmbH	Germany
Unilever	United Kingdom
United Paper Mills	Finland
Vicat S.A.	France
Viggo AB	Sweden
Wal-Mart	U.S.A.
Waste Management Inc.	U.S.A.
Westfalia Separator AG	Germany
Westinghouse Electric – College Station	U.S.A.
Wärtsilä Diesel International, Ltd	Findland
Xerox	U.S.A.
Yamazaki	Japan
Yamazaki Mazak UK Ltd	United Kingdom

BIBLIOGRAPHY

Aaserud, J., Hermansson, S., *Fordonsteknisk utveckling*, 1991

Aoiki, "Toward an Economic Model of the Japanese Firm", *Journal of Economic Literature*, Vol. XXVIII (March 1990), pp. 1-27

Armitage, H.M., Atkinson, A. A., "The Choice of Productivity Measures in Organizations" in Kaplan (1990)

Carlsson, B., "The Development and Use of Machine Tools in Historical Perspective" in Day, R., Eliasson, G, *The Dynamics of Market Economies*, IUI and North Holland, 1986

Cecchini, P., *The European Challenge 1992*, Gower Aldershot, 1988.

Croon, I., *MoDo Business Report*, MoDo, 1991

Dagens Industri May 2, 1991 s. 16

Dagens Nyheter July 23, 1991

de Wit & Vrancken, *Mimeo*, Nationale Nederlanden, Haag, 1990

Dr Toshiro Kunihiro (NEC) Paper presented at the 7th World Productivity Congress, Kuala Lumpur, 1990

EC Commission, *The Trauma of the Single Market*, 1988

The Economist, February 24, 1990

Edquist, C., Jacobsson, S., *Flexible Automation: The Global Diffusion of New Technology in the Engineering Industry*, Basil Blackwell, Oxford, 1988

Ehrnberg, E., Jacobsson, S., "*Technological Discontinuities, Industry, Structure and Firm Strategy: The Case of Machine Tools and Flexible Manufacturing System*", Chalmers tekniska högskola, 1991

EMC World Cellular Report, no 10, April 1990

Encaoua, D., "Liberalizing European Airlines", *International Journal of Industrial Organization*, North-Holland. 9: 1991

Falk, J., Sjöberg, N., *En industri och teknikanalys av mobil-telefonbranschen*, examensarbete vid Institutionen för industriell organisation och ekonomi, Chalmers tekniska högskola.

Fortune, January 1, 1990

Försäkringsinspektionen: Enskilda Försäkringsföretag, 1987-90

Försäkringstidningen, 1, 1990

Giertz, E., *Människor i Scania under 100 år - Industri, arbetsliv och samhälle i förändring*, 1991

Goodman, R.L., Insurance: "Bold leaps in a game of inches", *The McKinsey Quarterly*, 1990:4

Hörte, S-Å m fl, *Tillverkningsstrategier i Sverige 1982-89*, IMIT, Göteborg, 1991

International Civil Aviation Organization, *Civil Aviation Statistics of the World*, Montreal, 1986

Iveco-Magirus AG Konzerngeschäftsbericht Iveco BV, 1987 Och 1989

Jaikumar, R., "Postindustrial Manufacturing", *Harvard Business Review*, November-December 1986, pp. 69-76

Jaikumar, R., "From Filing and Fitting to Flexible Manufacturing: A Study in the Evolution of Process Control", Harvard Business School, working paper, February 1988

Kaplan, R. S., 1990, *Measures for Manufacturing Excellence*, Harvard Business School Series in Accounting and Control, Harvard Business School Press, Boston

Lawrence, P.R., Dyer, D., *Renewing American Industry*, The Free Press, Macmillan, New York, 1983

OECD, *Managing Manpower for Advanced Manufacturing Technology*, Paris, 1991

Porter, M.E., *Competitive Strategy, Technique for Analyzing Industries and Competitors*, The Free Press, New York, 1980

Porter, M.E., *The Competitive Advantages of Nations*, The Free Press, New York, 1990

Saab-Scania, *10-year financial summary*, 1989

The Saab-Scania Griffin, 90/91

Scania World Bulletin #5, 1990

SIND, *Leverantörer till fordonsindustrin*, Allmänna förlaget, Stockholm, 1990

Singapore Airlines, *Annual Reports*, 1989-90

Susaki, K., 1987, *The Manufacturing Challenge*, The Free Press, New York

Svenska Dagbladet, July 1, 1991

Trygg Hansas bolagsjämförelser, Trygg Hansa, Stockholm, 1985-90

Veckans Affärer 1991:10 s. 45

Veckans affärer 1990:43 s. 70

VPP Magazine, Amsterdam, nr 2, 1988

Östling, L., *Scania: Structural Changes in the Heavy Truck Industry*, European Trucks Outlook Conference, December 18, 1990

INDEX